Gender Equity or Bust!

Gender Equity or Bust!

On the Road to Campus Leadership with *Women in Higher Education*®

Mary Dee Wenniger, Mary Helen Conroy

Foreword by Lesley A. Diehl

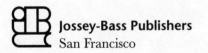
Jossey-Bass Publishers
San Francisco

Jossey-Bass books and products are available through most bookstores. To contact Jossey-Bass directly, call (888) 378-2537, fax to (800) 605-2665, or visit our website at www.josseybass.com.

Substantial discounts on bulk quantities of Jossey-Bass books are available to corporations, professional associations, and other organizations. For details and discount information, contact the special sales department at Jossey-Bass.

 Manufactured in the United States of America on Lyons Falls Turin Book. This paper is acid-free and 100 percent totally chlorine-free.

FIRST EDITION
PB Printing 10 9 8 7 6 5 4 3 2 1

THE JOSSEY-BASS

HIGHER AND ADULT EDUCATION SERIES

CONTENTS

To the lives and spirits of Liz Farrington and Carolyn Desjardins, whose contributions to the creation and success of *Women in Higher Education* are incalculable.—*M.D.W.*

To the awesome loving women and understanding men who have led me to today, and to the incredible sons who share my life, Michael and Paul.—*M.H.C.*

FOREWORD, OR FROM THE GRIME OF THE GOLD MINE TO YOUR HOME AS CLASSROOM

Like the gold rush, and subsequently the land, timber, and other rushes in California, gender equity is that elusive prize for which many women in higher education have dedicated a good portion of their time and talents. Just as many gold rushers were ill prepared for the difficulty of the journey to the gold fields and ill equipped both in skills and knowledge about the job of panning and mining gold, women have struggled toward gender equity without a road map, naive about what would be required of them both individually and as a group to attain this goal. Often they were overwhelmed and exhausted by a system that appeared uninterested in hearing their concerns or in entertaining their ideas for change.

Women Have a Dialogue

But women do talk to each other, and that's a good thing. It's hard to imagine gold miners, most of whom were men, talking as much as do the women with whom I've spent the last three decades in institutions of higher learning. When I think back on the really rough times in academe, I'm struck by how differently many women and men I've worked with have approached crisis and change. Men often have weathered the crises by toughing them out. Their reward for using this strategy has been to be labeled good soldiers. Some of these good soldiers have risen in the ranks to be vice presidents, deans, and presidents.

On the other hand, women have talked with one another about the times, but particularly about issues and the strategies that could be used to effect change. Some of these approaches have proved successful. We have more women presidents in higher education than ever. Whatever strategies women have used to move into higher education in greater numbers—more women students, more women professors, more women administrators—the struggle has been demanding and often frustrating. And we have yet to mine the gold we rushed to find, that is, true gender equity. For although women make up more than 50 percent of college students today, we do not have nor do we foresee in the near future fully established benchmarks of gender equity—a representative number of women in higher levels of administration or as full professors with tenure; a college community free from the threat of sexual harassment or rape; women's studies integrated into the curriculum; and equal access to education for women, minorities, and the poor, to name just a few.

What we do have, however, is the continued dialogue between women about how to effect change. Some of this dialogue has appeared in the form of scholarship in women's studies and even in the traditional disciplines. Some of us have researched these areas and written about our findings. And some of our scholarship has been rewarded through grants, promotions, and pay increases. More often than not, however, work on women's issues in higher education has not received the recognition it has deserved for several reasons. Much of the scholarly work has appeared in journals read only by those in our own discipline and only by those sympathetic to our point of view. Therefore, the strategies for change that might have emerged from our dialogues have failed to hit the mainstream of higher education.

A second and equally important reason for our words falling on deaf ears is that women's lives are too busy, too crammed with both professional and personal issues for many of us to read outside of our areas of training or to read lengthy and intellectual articles and find the application for the specifics of our own lives. We've often felt isolated, and this isolation has furthered our sense of despair. We've been encouraged to believe either that change is monumental and we have missed it, or that it has not occurred at all.

The Dialogue Is in Print and on the Web

So along came the *Women in Higher Education* newsletter in 1992, and suddenly we had a road map for our trek toward gender equity. Each month we waited eagerly for the issue so that we could read the words of other women in similar circumstances. Women talked turkey about what was bothering them, how they dealt with various situations that arose, and how successful they were at handling these situations. The articles spoke of success and failure; sometimes they reinterpreted failure as success.

Women redefined the educational enterprise and their role in it. We came to understand that women's contributions in higher education were significant because we spoke our own words, chose our own vocabulary, and reconfigured the landscape of our work experiences. Because this landscape was constantly shifting, a shift that women have experienced continually and adjusted to daily, women understood that their words and the words of others would be recycled through the good and bad times along the pathway of gender issues. So as women spoke with one another, their words became timeless as well as timely. *Women in Higher Education* chronicled this journey and taught us that our individual stories were important.

Gender Equity or Bust! captures this changing and cyclical landscape by organizing some of the best voices of the newsletter's monthly issues into driving lessons by and for women. From where we have been to where we are going and how to get there, this book provides wit, humor, serious intention, and sharp insight into the continuing presence and contributions of women in higher education. We will not go away, and we will not be silent.

Journalism, Not Jargon

The honesty of the contributors does not hide behind a scholarly facade but is as up-front as sharing the stall in a one-person women's bathroom. In this case it's not necessary to rifle through your old issues of *Women in Higher Education* to find support for your leadership style or see yourself in the classroom with others who use your unorthodox approach toward learning communities. Do you feel different from other women who talk collaboration while you're excited by competition? You're in this book. The chapters underline what we all know about women. We find support, empowerment, and strength in other women, but most of all, these chapters confirm women as individuals. And this is a celebration of what comes from affirming individualism through group endeavor.

You can replace your monthly issues of *Women in Higher Education* in the magazine rack in your bathroom with this single volume. You'll create a warm and intimate learning experience for all who thumb through the volume and hit upon an article that speaks to them. Men are not exempt from this influence. Actually, they may be more willing to pick up the book in the privacy of your bathroom than they would in a more public forum such as your living room or off your desk at the office. It's pure luxury to have so much wisdom in one place, kind of like taking a bubble bath where each bubble is the voice of a woman imparting her experience directly to you.

Too bad those gold miners weren't more loquacious. They might have found panning for gold a lot more rewarding if they had had others guiding their efforts. The road to gender equity may be difficult and exhausting, and the goal constantly shifting in its composition, but at least we have one another on the road and in the fields sharing the dirt, dust, and, finally, the gold. The quest for gender equity is not one that ends in any one location. Rather, it's a search in which changing an institution's character is the goal. These articles make it clear that women have already begun this process. The process is called education, and gender equity is the assertion that education is for all of us.

LESLEY A. DIEHL, PH.D.
Emerita professor of English
State University of New York, College at Oneonta
Retired college and university administrator
Writer and clay artist/potter

PREFACE

In the year 2001, we are witnessing a major disconnection among shareholders in the higher education system in the United States. Leaders of the academy struggle to face the challenges of sea changes in technology, student demographics, sources of funding, globalization, partnerships with other sectors, the political environment, and other factors. Without enlightened leadership, the engine that's driving higher education can easily run out of fuel, stray off the road, or become so outdated and irrelevant that the whole postsecondary enterprise is endangered.

Women, who have historically been excluded from higher education and then marginalized when finally admitted into it, can provide creative solutions and new hope for an endangered system. But chipping away at the bedrock of patriarchy in higher education can be a lonely, frustrating, seemingly hopeless task to the women who would give their energies and their professional lives to the process.

Women leaders are different, their styles and values being so distinct from those of men that often they are not even on the same wavelength. While men would focus on the result and believe that the end justifies the means, women savor the process of being inclusive and collaborative so that all stakeholders believe their voices are heard in the process of making decisions and policy.

Launched in January 1992, the *Women in Higher Education* newsletter is dedicated to the proposition that higher education is too important, too valuable, and too fragile to be dominated by one sex, especially because the majority of its stakeholders now are of the other sex. Its mission is to enlighten, encourage, empower, and enrage women on campus to change the values and styles in academia to those that recognize the importance of a diversity of perspectives and skills. In such a climate, women and men can work together to shape the academy into one that serves all people, not just middle-aged white males.

Over the years, the newsletter has become an advocate and a chronicle, a teacher and a learner serving more than twelve thousand readers, both in a printed version and on the Web. A subscriber calls it "a practitioner's news journal" because articles contain practical tips as well as theoretical frameworks, individual as well as systemic solutions. Others have called it "the *Saturday Night Live* of higher education" and "the closest thing to a mentor I have." Comparing articles from 1992 to those of 2000, a reader will find the general topics remain the same, but the solutions are more subtle, individualized, and enlightened.

Selecting which articles to reprint from the more than one thousand included in the ninety-six monthly issues was the toughest challenge. Of course, the newsletter editor insisted on certain favorites, and the authors negotiated over others; the resulting book preserves the rich variety of viewpoints and topics represented in the issues.

Translating what appeared in the newsletter to a book format was an inexact process. Strong differences in tone and style between individual articles will become evident to readers. Some articles are based on scholarly papers, some on journalistic interviews, and some on professional opinions or personal recollections. Similarly, specific sections of the newsletter produce unique articles. For example, those articles appearing as a "Profile" of a successful woman leader on campus are based on an interview with her. The "In Her Own Words" section includes more personal opinions, and the author is listed first. The editor's monthly "Last Laugh" column reflects her somewhat twisted view of national and campus situations; it usually ends with the words "last laugh" in the final sentence.

Together we approach the subject like a cruise across the country, behind the wheel of a fast car, perhaps the editor's red convertible, which delivers readers to their destination through sunshine and snow, despite the inevitable roadblocks and detours along the way. We sought to cover a wide range of issues from both practical and theoretical perspectives, conveying the wit and humor of those who have succeeded and some who have failed in their trials.

Chapter One deals with the realities of life on the road for campus women, including the history, today's demographics and challenges, and the ways that women can be an integral part of leading the changes in the academy that will help it meet the challenges of a new century.

In Chapter Two, we examine why women can be better campus leaders, review some personal stories of success and failure, and consider the unique problems of women who are in double or triple jeopardy because of their ethnicity, sexual orientation, or faith.

In Chapter Three, we discuss specific leadership skills that women need in order to survive and thrive on campus. Sections include general leadership strategies for women, tips on how women can recognize and develop the specific leadership skills they need, and information on what new administrative leaders need to know to be successful.

Chapter Four deals with learning to read a career map so that women can plot where they've been, see where the roads go, and take charge of their lives as they proceed on their career paths.

In Chapter Five, we help readers anticipate and overcome the inevitable road-blocks and road rage that challenge their progression in the academy. Some are external, but some are internal, as women make professional and personal choices that must reflect their own values and priorities.

Chapter Six deals with sex on the road, recognizing that a career path that is equal for women and men is not necessarily equitable. Differences in biology are a fact, and so are the resulting issues of sexual harassment as it affects students, faculty, and administrators.

In Chapter Seven, we honor the driver within, knowing that leadership is much more than a set of specific skills. We acknowledge that who leaders are at their core is what it's all about and affirm the importance of a leader discovering and embracing her authentic self.

Chapter Eight concludes the book by asking the inevitable question "Are we there yet?" Some say, "We've come a long way, babe," but some point to the re-maining long path before us. Articles include strategies for success, the various fronts on which women on campus are solving the problems associated with gen-der inequities on campus, and the ways that women are contributing to assure that higher education remains viable for our children's children's children.

None of these articles could have been written had women not been su-perlatively endowed with their single most useful attribute: willingness to share their information, power, stories, and strategies with others around the world. Many of the articles were written by experts in their areas; others were written by freelance writers, based on presentations at conferences and interviews with the presenters. The articles are reprinted from the pages of *Women in Higher Education* virtually as is, so readers can note the historic progression as well as the develop-ment of the issues. Many of the authors and presenters have since moved on to other jobs, but we have preserved their titles as they were at the articles' original publication to provide an accurate context for them.

For their pioneering efforts to bring women to the table of leadership, we thank women like Johnnetta Cole, Carolyn Desjardins, Carol Gilligan, Christine Grant, Cynthia Secor, Donna Shavlik, Judith Sturnick, Sheila Tobias, and hun-dreds of others upon whose foundation this book and women's careers on cam-pus are constructed.

Thanks to their efforts, *leadership* today is no longer a gender-specific term.

For granting permission to reprint their articles, we offer sincere thanks to all the authors: Martha Burns, C. Ann Carver, Donna Clevinger, Melanie Conklin, Sarah Gibbard Cook, Lesley A. Diehl, Janice M. Edwards, Runae Edwards-Wilson, Sandra Featherman, Barbara Gellman-Danley, Suzanne Forsyth, Doris Green, Diane Grypp, Virginia Lopez Hansen, Linda Hartsock, Jennifer Hirsch, Sheila Huff, Dianne Jenkins, Bernita Krumm, Claudia Limbert, Geneva Lopez,

Adena Williams Loston, Judy Mantle, Patricia Matthews, Linda McCallister, Thomas McDaniel, Anne Mulder, Mary Ann O'Donnell, Karina Persson, Miriam Shillingsburg, Sharon Siverts, Mary Soroko, Marlene I. Strathe, Barbara Tedrow, Judith Van Baron, Emily R. Ward, and Caroline Westerhof.

For selflessly presenting and sharing their insights with the world at conferences, in both the *Women in Higher Education* newsletter and here, a huge thank-you goes to Veronica Alexander, Kathleen Rex Anderson, Kelli J. Armstrong, Jacquelyn M. Belcher, Laurel G. Bellows, Marcia Boyles, Margarett Campbell, Noreen Carrocci, C. Ann Carver, Stephanie Clemons, Josephine Davis, Florence Deacon, Barbara Deck, Carolyn Desjardins, Eric Dey, Suzanne Forsyth, Verna Fowler, Ann H. Franke, Jane Gallop, Ophelia Garcia, Barbara Gellman-Danley, Eugenia Proctor Gerdes, Louise Goueffic, Carol Hurd Green, Sally Z. Hare, Cynthia Harrison, Cynthia Haston, Audrey D. Hawkins, Ellen Heffernan, Sharlene Hesse-Biber, Leslie Heywood, Linda Hill, Joan Hrubetz, Sheila Huff, Marianne M. Jennings, Kate Johnson, Theo Kalikow, Janet Kerner, Daryl Koehn, Jessica Korn, Lana Hartman Landon, Martha Kaniston Laurence, Georgia Lesh-Laurie, Brigid McGrath Massie, Patricia Ann Matthews, Suzanna McCorkle, Marie V. McDemmond, Patricia Ann McGuire, Caryn Medved, Betsy Metzger, Betsy Morgan, Lucy Morros, Caryn McTighe Musil, Pat O'Connor, Jane Ollenburger, Anita M. Pampusch, Maria Perez, Barbara Baxter Pillinger, Janine Pretty On Top, Maureen Quinn, Joel Read, Charles Reed, Lawrence J. Rifkind, Lisa A. Rossbacher, Linda Sax, Donna Schmitt, Lois S. Self, Marilyn Sheerer, Sanford C. Shugart, Margaret Stetz, Judith Sturnick, Barbara Taliaferro, Jill Tarule, Kathy Vargas, Tanya Ward, Brenda A. Wirkus, Janet Wright, and Marie Wunsch.

MARY DEE WENNIGER
MARY HELEN CONROY
January 2001

BILL OF RIGHTS FOR WOMEN IN HIGHER EDUCATION

1. We have the right to be taught as we want to learn, respecting that there are multiple, valid paths to wisdom—not only the classical, hierarchical, step-by-step method—in both careers and classes on campus.

2. We have the right to have our opinions and our life experiences valued and respected.

3. We have the right to enjoy classes and jobs free of sexism and gender discrimination.

4. We have the right to enjoy classes and jobs free of sexual harassment.

5. We have the right to expect opportunities to be unrestricted by our gender in all things on campus, including but not limited to administration, admissions, financial aid, health services, degree requirements, funding, career advice and job placements, tenure, promotion, salary, decision making, research, teaching in the classroom and elsewhere, and sports participation and administration.

6. We have the right to place a value on family and personal life without deprecating our commitment to our careers.

7. We have the right to support those actions that reflect our values and reject those actions that contradict them.

8. We have the right to conduct research in a manner harmonious with both the discipline and subjects, rejecting arbitrary standards that undervalue qualitative and participative studies.

9. We have the right to value cooperation and collaboration to the same extent that we value individual competition and aggression.

10. We have the right to be judged by equitable standards that favor neither gender.

Women in Higher Education
March 1993

ROAD MAP TO ASSOCIATIONS AND CODE ABBREVIATIONS

AACU   American Association of Colleges and Universities
AAHE   American Association for Higher Education
AAUP   American Association of University Professors
AAUW   American Association of University Women
AAWCC   American Association for Women in Community Colleges
ACE   American Council on Education
CIC   Council of Independent Colleges
CUNY   City University of New York
CUNA   Credit Union National Association
EEOC   Equal Employment Opportunities Commission
GLBT   Gay-Lesbian-Bisexual-Transgendered
HBCU   Historically Black Colleges and Universities
HERS   Higher Education Resource Services
NASPA   National Association of Student Personnel Administrators
NAWCHE   National Association for Women in Catholic Higher Education
NAWE   National Association for Women in Education (emerita)
NILD   National Association for Leadership Development
OSCLG   Organization for the Study of Communication, Language and Gender
SUNY   State College of New York
WWHEL   Wisconsin Women in Higher Education Leadership

THE EDITORS

Mary Dee Wenniger

As founder of the international newsletter *Women in Higher Education* in 1992, editor Mary Dee Wenniger approaches her assignment as a journalist rather than a scholar. Unlike her male professors at the University of Wisconsin-Madison, where she earned her B.A. and M.A. degrees in journalism in the 1960s, she believes there is no such thing as objectivity in journalism and has created this activist publication that makes no such pretense.

Her true credentials are surviving being fired from three professional positions in fifteen years in the academic, business, and nonprofit sectors of the workplace, attesting to the widespread failure in all three sectors to accept a woman with brains and an attitude.

First to fire her was the University of Wisconsin-Madison's Management Institute, where she was director of advertising and promotion in the early 1970s. She was the only female in the department who was not a secretary or administrative assistant. In 1994, the university agreed to settle a sex bias lawsuit brought by former Management Institute professor Gloria Hay for $235,000, the largest University of Wisconsin settlement for bias ever at that time.

Next to fire her was Magna Publications in Madison, Wisconsin, where she was director of marketing and then publisher of the academic group of newsletters. There her idea to create a *Women in Higher Education* newsletter was vetoed by the president, who declared he could see no compelling need or profitable market for the publication.

Finally the Credit Union National Association (CUNA), where she was on the editorial services staff, fired her after just thirteen weeks on the job. During this time she laid the plans to completely revamp one legal publication and to save almost $50,000 a year in postage for the association's nine periodicals, both of which plans were soon implemented. When she was fired on her forty-seventh birthday, her boss said, "Mary Dee, you just don't fit into the culture here, and in some ways that's a tribute to you."

A month later, she was researching and testing the market for the *Women in Higher Education* newsletter, and five months later she mailed the first issue to two hundred paid subscribers.

The venture was made possible by a small inheritance from a great-aunt, Mary "Mae" Walters of Waukesha, Wisconsin, an independent woman and milliner in the 1940s who divorced her husband because he was a "dandy." The inheritance came through her mother, Mae W. Wenniger, who was named after her great-aunt Mae. Only recently did Mary Dee realize that she, too, had been named after her great-aunt, whose real name was Mary.

In editing *Women in Higher Education* for nine years, Mary Dee has learned that her previous "failures" in the workplace have actually been the failures of male leaders in all three sectors to recognize and value the alternative viewpoint she presents and to espouse the doctrines of fair play and diversity.

She is the single parent of a year 2000 graduate of Smith College; both the child and the college have provided inspiration and direct material for the publication.

Mary Helen Conroy

A lifetime of experiences has led Mary Helen to *Women in Higher Education*. Raised by a widowed mother, this eldest of three daughters lived in a home where being female was always honored. The singular gender of her home made all things possible. Education was valued; both parents were teachers; and college was not only a dream but an expectation. Mary Helen received her B.A. degree in liberal arts and began immediately to fulfill her dream of being a professional librarian by receiving her M.A.L.S. from Rosary College in Illinois. She had started her career at the age of ten volunteering and became the administrative librarian ten years later.

Librarianship consumed the first twenty years of her career. As a public library administrator, she led three Chicago suburb libraries through the growth periods of new buildings and computers. She became a professional building consultant for libraries, aiding over twenty libraries to see their dreams of a new library become a reality.

Moving to Madison, Wisconsin, in 1991, she decided that people retire after twenty years of service and that she would use her talent of sharing information in other ways. She returned to school, the University of Wisconsin-Madison, to work on her doctorate in adult education. It was during a class on women in higher education that she met the editor of the *Women in Higher Education* newsletter. This meeting opened a new world of possibilities for her, including working on the newsletter. As an independent contractor, she directs the Career Connection section of the newsletter, bringing position announcements to women each month in the print issue and through the Web site. Each ad means that there can be more editorial in an issue, a mission she enjoys. The newsletter editor often describes Mary Helen as a "recovering librarian and not doing it well," "alpha geek," or "high priestess" depending what needs to be done.

Her adult education background presented opportunities for teaching at the Wisconsin campuses of Cardinal Stritch University. She has recently been promoted to associate adjunct professor and teaches self-management courses within the accelerated business management program as well as serving as the Wisconsin region's librarian. Empowering adult students so they know they can succeed in the classroom is her mission.

Mary Helen's passion for learning and risk taking into new avenues has provided a role model for her two sons, Michael and Paul, who both attend the colleges of their choice this year. These two fine young men, whom she will always love, but also likes, are the real joy of her life.

Gender Equity or Bust!

CHAPTER ONE

CURRENT ROAD CONDITIONS FOR WOMEN DRIVERS

As we begin our joyriding journey toward gender equity on college and university campuses, let's look at the history and then assess the current road conditions for women at the wheel. Over the years, American women have come a long way both as passengers and drivers of higher education.

History of Women Students in U.S. Higher Education

Once we admit that higher education was based on the Germanic model and invented by and for men, it's easy to understand why the present American system remains so narrow and dated, and thus increasingly unsuccessful and irrelevant, and why women must lead the way in retooling it for the new century.

Traditional higher education was designed in the horse-and-buggy era to serve the young, rich, white, able-bodied sons of aristocrats: the leisure class. Its culture was patriarchal, competitive, and linear, and its approved teaching method was Socratic. Students lived at their schools; corporal punishment was acceptable discipline; and creativity was actively discouraged, as all were expected to fit one mold of the serious scholar. No wonder it doesn't work in the era of superhighways.

According to the Women's College Coalition in Washington, D.C., four societal trends in the mid- to late nineteenth century increased the demand for higher education for women:

- The growing public school system needed more teachers, and female teachers were considered better and cheaper to hire.
- Writers produced more literature for women, which they could read at night thanks to the newfangled gas and oil lamps.
- The industrial revolution brought domestic labor-saving devices like matches, cookstoves, and sewing machines, giving women more leisure from household drudgery.
- The Civil War increased contacts with the outside world. Women's activism as abolitionists and volunteers behind the lines allowed them to make contributions that history recorded.

The first U.S. college chartered to confer degrees to girls in 1836 was Georgia Female College, today Wesleyan College in Macon, Georgia. It is considered the oldest women's college.

Exclusively women's colleges offered a respite from some of the patriarchal aspects of higher education. Often started as teachers' colleges and sources of religious and health education, women's colleges continued to grow until, at the height of their popularity in 1960, they numbered 296. By 1999, all but 73 had closed, merged, or become coeducational. Of the elite Seven Sisters colleges sometimes called the Women's Ivy League, only 5 remain single sex today: Barnard, Bryn Mawr, Mount Holyoke, Smith, and Wellesley.

Women Gaining Admission to Colleges with Males

Founded in 1636, Harvard University is the oldest and most prestigious U.S. university. Because Harvard steadfastly refused to admit women, in 1879 a group of very refined women, who certainly didn't want to harm Harvard in any way, founded Radcliffe College to provide women with a Harvard education. To reach the seats in a heavily curtained back room where Harvard professors taught them, the female students had to climb through windows. Harvard began admitting women in 1943 and fully included them by 1965; Radcliffe College itself merged into Harvard in 1999. Its only remnant is the Radcliffe Institute for Advanced Research, which doesn't even have the words *gender* or *women* in its name!

In 1933, Oberlin College in Ohio became the first formerly male college in the United States to officially admit women. The last known bastions of male exclusivity are four private colleges whose combined enrollment is less than five thousand students: Deep Springs College in California, Hampden-Sydney College and Morehouse College in Virginia, and Wabash College in Indiana.

In the mid-1990s, two public military colleges spent about $5 million each to continue their 150-year-old policies of excluding women as cadets: The Citadel in South Carolina and the Virginia Military Institute. In 1996, the Supreme Court told the Virginia Military Institute that it must admit women. After a federal appeals court order, The Citadel had reluctantly admitted Shannon Faulkner as a cadet in 1995, but she was drummed out of the corps within six days. Finally in fall 1996, The Citadel admitted four women as cadets amid much planning and fanfare. Two quit after a semester and sued for illegal hazing, and the other two graduated in 1999 and 2000, respectively.

Women in Higher Education

In the last thirty years, women students have become the statistical majority on many college campuses, but they still do not have the rights they deserve. The cultural tradition of male dominance still prevails in academic leadership, teaching, curricula, and standards for promotion and tenure. Here's a snapshot of today's women on campus.

Women as Students

The percentage of students who are women has been steadily increasing since the 1970s. Female students were 55.6 percent of all undergraduates in 1999, a change that affects social patterns, gender equity in athletics, and virtually all other aspects of campus life. In fact, in 1999, higher education leaders actually held a conference to address the change in their market's gender, asking where the boys had gone, why, and what to do about it.

In graduation rates as well, women are steadily gaining, now surpassing men in earning bachelor's and master's degrees. Historically, women earned 19 percent of all bachelor's degrees in 1900, 40 percent in 1930, 43 percent in 1970, 55 percent in 1994, and 57 percent in 1999. Of master's degrees awarded in 1999, women earned 52 percent. Among doctoral degrees earned by U.S. citizens in 1999, women earned almost half, 48 percent compared to men's 52 percent. Unless the trend reverses, soon U.S. women will earn more doctorates than U.S. men.

The demographics of today's students continue to favor women. College and university students are more likely than in an earlier era to be older (age twenty-five and up), attend part-time, live off campus, and have other responsibilities like a job and a family. Older females are most apt to return to the classroom when their relationships end due to death or divorce, believing it's their turn to do something for themselves.

With the increasing feminization of the student market, those campus leaders involved in marketing—admissions, student services, public relations departments, development—have been adapting their strategies and their product to appeal to the new demographics. Because these are the same offices on campus most likely to be led and staffed by women, it's working.

Research indicates that, in the classroom, female students prefer a style of learning that includes discussion, favors an inclusive process, and values experiential learning. This preference still meets resistance by traditional academic leaders who favor the lecture and "the sage on the stage" over the "guide on the side."

Women as Administrators

The number of women in administration has been increasing steadily since 1970, fueled by the women's movement, affirmative action, feminists, women's strong work ethic and abilities, and the goddess herself.

Five percent of all presidents of colleges and universities in 1975 were women, according to the American Council on Education's Office of Women in Higher Education. The percentage had increased to 12 percent by 1992, 16.5 percent by 1995, and 19.3 percent by 1998. The largest percentage of women presidents lead private two-year colleges, 27 percent. Next comes private four-year colleges at 15 percent and public universities at 14 percent. Women are most likely to head smaller schools: 71 percent lead schools with three thousand or fewer students. There is also a trend toward more women being hired to lead public schools; the percentage of presidents of state schools who are women increased from 11 percent of presidents in 1975 to 36 percent in 1984 and 48 percent in 1995. Women are now being tapped to lead community colleges, which traditionally emphasize teaching over research; those troubled schools considered at risk that are more likely to take a chance on a woman; and colleges that require interim presidents, where a free trial period allows both sides to test the fit. According to *The Third Sex* by Patricia McBroom, women leaders have become like Amazons: they dress and act like males and do not marry or bear children. Women presidents seem to fit the mold: the American Council on Education's 1991 data indicate that only 53 percent of female college presidents were married, compared with 91 percent of male presidents.

In other top administrative jobs, women are increasing in the ranks of provosts, vice presidents, and deans. Women are an estimated one-third of department chairs. Unfortunately, women are also increasing in dead-end administrative jobs, such as directors of programs and affirmative action offices, where their skills have a minimal chance to affect policy and they have virtually no chance for advancement.

Women as Faculty

Despite recent gains, the gender of the faculty in higher education has remained predominantly male, as have the standards by which faculty are judged for hiring, salary, and promotion. From 1925 to 2000, the percentage of full-time faculty that is female has increased just 5 percent, from 19 percent to 24 percent. Many women now in their fifties recall having never had a female teacher in college.

In gaining tenure, women are making slow progress. In 1989, 22 percent of tenured faculty were female. By 1998, that percentage had increased to 26 percent. The percentage of faculty on the tenure track who are female increased over those years from 38 percent to 45 percent.

Women hold 39 percent of all faculty positions, but women are more apt than men to fill part-time and adjunct positions. Part-time positions held by both men and women have increased to more than 40 percent of faculty; they are more likely to teach in private four-year schools or in two-year public community colleges, whose faculty averaged 65.5 percent part-timers in 1999. There has been a similar increase of those women full-time faculty not on the tenure track, from 45.5 percent to 50.1 percent.

According to an AAUW report, 48 percent of female faculty were tenured in 1999, compared to 72 percent of male faculty. The rate of tenuring women has not increased as fast as the rate of tenuring men. Over the last twenty years, there has been an increase of 1.5 percent in the rate of women gaining tenure, compared to an 8 percent increase for men.

In salaries, women faculty are paid less. According to the AAUW, women college professors earn 77 percent of what male college professors earn. Part of this discrepancy is due to women being concentrated in the lower-paying social sciences (nursing, education, and teaching), whereas men are in the higher-paying hard sciences (engineering, computers, and math). But part is also due to gender bias; studies repeatedly show that schools discriminate against women, as the 1999 MIT salary and resources survey proved.

U.S. Colleges Are Still Dominated by the Male Tradition, But We've Come a Long Way

Women faculty are increasing at all ranks across the country. Although they tend to earn less and work for smaller and less prestigious schools, women are on the increase in teaching roles. And more women are joining the tenure track, having increased from 34 percent of those on the track in 1983 to 42 percent in 1991.

But women are still less likely than males to gain tenure, especially in male-dominated departments, because the real rules are unwritten and the good old boys are reluctant to let women join their game.

Meanwhile, many schools are reducing the number of new hires who are on the tenure track, instead offering yearly contracts and hiring adjunct professors, of which the clear majority are women, to teach a few courses. At Harvard University in 1997, only 13 percent of tenured faculty were women. A 1993 report indicated that the rate of women gaining tenure over the previous ten years had increased only 0.4 percent per year, and the general climate for women at Harvard was still unequal and sometimes hostile.

Women faculty continue to get unequal pay for equal work. According to the 1999–2000 salary survey of the American Association of University Professors, there are significant pay discrepancies based on gender. At schools that grant doctorates, male full professors earn 9.8 percent more than women, controlling for time at that rank. At private schools, male full professors earn about 14 percent more than females. At public schools, the gender–pay gap increased from 10.5 percent in 1982 to 13 percent in 1998.

Women in Collegiate Athletics as Students, Coaches, and Administrators

Athletics is considered a fertile ground for developing leaders, and women are having mixed success in becoming equal partners. Since the passage of Title IX of the 1972 Educational Amendments, the federal law requiring gender equity in educational programs in schools receiving federal funds, things have changed dramatically for women in athletics. At some schools, women are beginning to get a fair shake, thanks to investigations by the federal Department of Education's Office for Civil Rights, individual lawsuits against schools that perpetuate bias against women, and concerned individuals in leadership positions who know it's the right thing to do. Some schools take the law more seriously than others. The following figures come from *Women in Intercollegiate Sport*, a longitudinal study and twenty-three-year update (1977–2000), by R. Vivian Acosta and Linda Carpenter, emerita professors at Brooklyn College, New York.

• *More women are collegiate athletes.* Since 1972, the number of young women participating in college varsity sports has more than tripled. The average number of women's teams at NCAA schools has increased from 2.00 to 8.14, although the NCAA reported in 2000 that women still are only 39 percent of all intercollegiate athletes.

• *Fewer women coach women's teams.* In 1972, 90 percent of head coaches of women's teams were women, virtually all of them working for pocket change or as volunteers. That percentage has declined steadily as pay for coaches of women's teams has risen dramatically and the typical male athletic director hires coaches who look like him. In 2000, only 45.6 percent of women's teams had female head coaches, the lowest number ever. Men have been hired for 80 percent of the new coaching jobs in women's athletics. Unfortunately, the number of women hired as head coaches for men's teams has remained at about 2 percent for the last three decades.

   • *Fewer women are athletics administrators.* In 1972, women directed more than 90 percent of women's athletics programs; in 2000, it was only 17.4 percent. In 23 percent of the NCAA women's programs, there is not one woman administrator to look out for the interests of women athletes or serve as a role model to them. In fact, there are more female college presidents in schools with Division I-A programs (with football) than there are female athletics directors there. Of the 418 new jobs added in athletics administration between the years 1998 and 2000, only 10 percent went to women.

Why Are Women Undervalued?

Born of a patriarchal tradition, higher education continues to marginalize women at every turn as students, administrators, faculty, and athletics leaders. Whether the bias is conscious or unconscious, women are being penalized consistently for their gender. The culprits are tradition, the good old boys' network, glass ceilings, tokenism, and a society that teaches men to disrespect women and women to settle for second best. The goal of this book is to help women reach gender equity in colleges and universities, plain and simple. Subsequent pages will help readers do just that, with practical solutions to challenges and the theoretical bases to explain them.

CHAPTER TWO

IN THE DRIVER'S SEAT:
WOMEN AS LEADERS

W e've come a long way since women were rarely seen behind the wheel of a
car. Now we have our own careers and our own money, and we can buy
the car of our choice to reflect our personalities and our lifestyles. As the late National Institute for Leadership Development (NILD) leader Carolyn Desjardins
once said, women's lives have changed to the point that we may have an M.B.A.,
an IRA, and a Ph.D., and believe that Kooking and Keesing are cities in China.

Likewise, in the last thirty years women have been taking over the controls in
higher education. On campus, as elsewhere, women previously were assumed
to have no leadership skills at all because leaders were defined as having attributes that are traditionally masculine: aggression, independence, linear and logical thinking, and an approach that is devoid of emotion.

An 800-page classic book on management published in 1971 claimed to assemble all the published evidence on leadership. Its few references to women were
all negative because women just didn't fit the classic white Western male style of
leadership now called the command-and-control mold: women were accused of
being less aggressive, more dependent, and more emotional than males. Further,
women were excitable in minor crises, illogical, home-oriented, unskilled at business, sneaky, and unfamiliar with the ways of the world. To which most of today's
female leaders would reply "Amen" or maybe "Ah, men. They just don't understand."

Today's characterization of women's leadership is that it comes from a completely different viewpoint, emphasizing cooperation and collaboration over hierarchy and order. The process is as important as the product, and feelings and perceptions are as important as facts. The best leaders are team players, who care about others rather than about just the bottom line. This is good because there are far fewer bottom lines in academe than in business, although that too is changing as business and education become more entwined, forming strategic partnerships and applying business concepts to higher education.

In these articles, you'll see why women make great leaders, hear some stories of success and some of failure, and learn some of the special problems of two-fers, minority women in double jeopardy.

SECTION 1: WHY WOMEN ARE BETTER LEADERS

Why Do Schools Choose Women as Leaders? Why Not?

February 1996

In the last twenty years, the number of women presidents of colleges and universities has more than tripled, from 148 in 1976 to 453 in 1996. Women now make up 16 percent of all top leaders in U.S. higher education institutions. And the number of women in the pipeline, as senior leaders, their assistants, and associates, has also risen dramatically. It is these women who are poised to take the reins in the next millennium.

Talking to the women themselves and to observers both in out of the academy reveals varied explanations for the phenomenon. Some are cynical; some are lighthearted; some reflect documented and continuing trends in society. And some reflect the stereotypes women strive to overcome. Just as many of you must excel at dancing between the land mines, you'll have to admit that there's a little bit of truth and a little bit of irony to each reason. And lest you think they apply only to top leaders, most are just as relevant for all women leaders on campus.

Practical Pat's Top Ten Reasons Women Are Skilled Campus Leaders

10. Adept at dealing with petulant children, who sometimes bear a striking resemblance to difficult faculty members.
9. Practiced at solving disputes between warring factions, such as cliques, gangs, and families.
8. Practiced at stretching budgets.
7. Willing to consider alternate solutions to problematic situations.
6. Use intuition and a form of higher consciousness to ferret out the real issues

and solutions. And are wise enough to keep quiet about the source of their inspiration.

5. Experienced at being the go-between, such as between faculty and trustees, to reach agreement.
4. Adept at balancing multiple responsibilities, juggling many things at once.
3. Can always hold a bake sale if the alumni don't come through.
2. Less likely to be married if a top administrator and thus not as diverted from important school business by family responsibilities.
1. Didn't want the job but got bullied into taking it.

Cynical Sydney's Top Ten Reasons Why Women Are Hired as Campus Leaders

10. Consider their selection as a duty and an honor, whereas men see it as a stepping-stone to even higher places.
9. Willing to grin and bear it and tolerate adverse situations.
8. Chosen as compromise solutions to other, more polarized candidates.
7. More likely to roll up their sleeves and work, rather than bask in the position and the power.
6. Haven't a clear picture of their own identities or goals, so can be recruited to do just about anything with enough sweet talk.
5. Don't demand or negotiate high salaries because they haven't a clear picture of their own true market value.
4. Willing to trade other job factors (flexibility, family life, friendly situation, and fit) rather than demanding a higher salary.
3. More likely to negotiate their areas of responsibility and authority rather than salary and benefits.
2. Naive enough to be the sacrificial lamb, having been talked into taking a job that they weren't ready for, were set up to fail, and when they failed, used as an excuse to never again consider hiring a woman.
1. Nobody else would take the job.

Candid Chris's Top Ten Reasons Why Women Succeed as Campus Leaders

10. Tend to be holistic and strategic thinkers, who view problems as multifaceted and requiring a sequence of solutions rather than a simple sweeping, and often simplistic, directed change in policy or procedure.
9. Likely to work *with* people rather than expecting people to work *for* them.
8. Do not fear saying "I don't know" and seeking expert, professional information.
7. Understand that the key resources required to change an institution are more likely to be human resources rather than fiscal or material ones.

6. Have risen to where they are in higher education despite the system, have already confronted many barriers, and are surprised by few obstacles placed in their way.

5. Skilled at using the subtle art of manipulation intuitively, due to their cultural socialization, to get others to buy into and adopt their ideas, making them their own.

4. More likely to see their selection as a special opportunity to make a difference, so they invest virtually all their time, intellectual capabilities, and energy to accomplish their goals. In short, they work harder, longer, and more productively.

3. Likely to take advantage of increased opportunities in higher education, training programs, associations, networks, mentors, and role models for women in higher education leadership.

2. More likely to try to achieve their goals by facilitating change rather than imposing it through policy or personnel changes. Although the premise of how this may be done is rarely substantiated in practice, search committees like the sound of this approach.

1. In this era of top leaders working seven days a week, sixteen hours a day, nobody else will stay on the job.

Mary Dee Wenniger. (For their contributions, thanks also to Carolyn Desjardins, Martha Burns, Linda Hartsock, Carolyn Westerhof, and several women choosing to remain anonymous.)

Ten Attributes Making Women Great Leaders and Educators

April 1998
Judith Van Baron
Vice President for External Affairs, Savannah College of Art and Design, Georgia

Recent articles list women's deficiencies, offering solutions to help women compensate by emulating men. Critics tell women their voices are too high and their stature is too short. They listen too well and are too easily interrupted. They ask too many questions and issue too few declarative and imperative sentences. And they fidget too much. Many women listen, undervaluing those positive attributes that actually tilt the playing field in their favor. As a vice president at the Savannah College of Art and Design, I've found that President Richard Rowan and Provost Paula Rowan value women and equity: the board of trustees is 50 percent women, and top leadership is 80 percent women. I believe ten major attributes contribute to women's success on campus.

The Catcher in the Rye

Because women have learned to recognize danger to themselves, they're well equipped to recognize danger to others, especially those younger, gentler, or more innocent. Unlike deer frozen in the headlights of oncoming destruction, women act if a threat arises, catching children before they run headlong over a precipice.

Thanksgiving Dinner

Especially working together, women always manage to get everything ready for "Thanksgiving dinner" at the right time. On campus, this ability translates to women being well organized, having superb timing, seeing the big picture and caring about those they serve.

Liberty and Justice for All

Just as mothers love all their children equally, I've found women administrators seek success for all their employees, and women educators seek success for all their students. In student-centered education, equity is key.

Pygmalions Persist

Women are the makers, the shapers, the recipients, becoming both the sculptor and the sculpture. Malleability is not a weakness; flexibility is a strength. Not fitting the mold is a sign of creativity and imagination. Not living up to a long-established ideal can be seen as avant-garde, progressive, growth-producing, and strengthening. Working with young people on campus, women are adept at helping them find their own way rather than forcing them down a well-trod path.

Narcissism at Work

Critics fault women for being too introspective, too analytic about relationships and what they mean, too vain and self-conscious. Some even complain about women fidgeting in meetings.

Movements considered fidgets as a woman sits down at a meeting are a means of gathering data about the space and its inhabitants. If a man moves his antennae four times and a woman moves hers nine times, who learns more?

Being self-conscious can mean you see not only your own image but others around you. Schools must look within and gather much data to make adjustments.

Quilt Makers and Basket Weavers

Women didn't invent the great monuments of civilization, but they may have made everything else, especially those things requiring attention to detail, subtle as well as obvious teamwork, and an understanding of the underlying patterns and intricacies of life. Working with thousands of students means working with the details of thousands of lives. Women have a profound talent for making order out of the most confounding intricacies of apparent chaos, moving well from the pieces to the whole, creating quilts from scraps and baskets from plants.

Whodunit?

Women are told they ask a lot of questions, raising their voices at the end of sentences in query. Perhaps they're seeking information, having been at it long before society recognized the incredible power of information and named a highway after it. Other animals do the same, using all their senses to know their environment. Called "sniffing the wind," "pricking the ears," or "narrowing the eyes" in animals, it's very valuable on campus.

What's in a Name?

Historically, women have managed to do without adding extra identities to their names such as Jr., Sr., I, or II. Their sense of self-identity serves them well as leaders and instills self-confidence, and they see themselves as individuals rather than inheritors of another's privilege, fillers of another's shoes. Often lacking a trailblazer, they have become bold, brave, inventive, and able to make a difference in their own name.

The Mothers of Invention

Necessity forces women to find solutions when resources are scarce. Whether it's greasing the pan or untangling the snarl, mentoring the student or the faculty member, women are skilled at finding answers. As higher education seeks solutions to new challenges, women can play a vital role as finders and problem solvers.

The Unbroken Circle

Life is a continuum—if not linear, at least holistic. In symbols and icons, women are often described as that perfection of continuums, the circle, represented as the egg, the centered being, the cradle of new life. Their contributions bring to education a strong, productive approach. Random experiments are infantile gestures without a centered focus to keep the continuum strong and priorities recognizable.

Women's Ways of Leading: A New Style for a New Era

November 1995

Despite some major obstacles to assuming leadership roles, women are about to enter their third stage of leadership styles, according to Donna Schmitt, professor of educational leadership in the department of leadership and counseling at Eastern Michigan University. She spoke at the fourth annual University of Vermont conference on gender issues in higher education in October 1995.

In the first stage dating back to the 1970s, women were encouraged to imitate men's style of hierarchical leadership, learning management skills based on establishing clear lines of authority. Theorists encouraged them to discard feminine behaviors. Instead, they were to work for the good of the organization, to establish team approaches taken from the world of sports, and to create utilitarian friendships and temporary allegiances based on political realities. Management bibles for women, like *The Managerial Woman* by Hennig and Jardim (1976) and *Games Mother Never Taught You: Corporate Gamesmanship for Women* by Betty Harragan (1977), taught women to act like male leaders so they would win acceptance among the males.

But Women Are Not Men

In the second stage evolving in the mid-1980s, women started to feel uncomfortable with this top-down style of management that had them acting against their socialized natures. Books published in the 1980s, like *In a Different Voice* by Carol Gilligan (1982), *Women's Ways of Knowing* by Belenky and others (1986), and *You Just Don't Understand* by Deborah Tannen (1990), discuss the implications of the differences between women and men, including expectations and roles as leaders. Today's organizations have started to value the different styles that women bring to leadership. Their strategies such as inclusion, webbing, cooperation, and quality control at lower levels of organization have become popular, even among male leaders.

In the third stage that Schmitt says is about ready to emerge, the questions have changed. Women in the first stage asked, "How can I change to fit in?" and those in the second asked, "How can I as a woman fit in?" Today's generation asks, "How do I match my talents and abilities as a woman leader to the needs of the organization, for the benefit of all?"

Downsizing, diversity, and dollars have forced new looks at leadership. Organizations now ask, "What style can we use that works best for us?" and "How can we find a fit between what this organization needs and what skills leaders have?" Schmitt says that, rather than rely on either women's or men's styles, organizations need the diversity that various people and various approaches provide. Recognizing and capitalizing on diverse talents, organizations promote leaders who offer creative ways of handling new tasks and a new workforce. She noted that of the more than three hundred public schools recently recognized as especially strong in innovation, 70 percent were headed by women.

Socialization Sabotages Women Leaders

It's no wonder most women aren't "natural leaders," says Schmitt, because their lifelong socialization process rewards them for behaviors that just don't work for most leaders. And unless women make a conscious effort to overcome the early lessons and take charge of their own lives, their efforts to move into top levels of management will be frustrated.

Although many women today accumulate the knowledge base of skills and talents to succeed, some continue to lack the "knowing base," which Schmitt calls "internal self-esteem and self-confidence," from the book *Paths to Power*, by Natasha Josefowitz. "Women are raised to be responsive, to wait for someone to tell them what to do," Schmitt says. By definition, leaders need to take risks and have confidence in their ability to accomplish their goals. "Unless you personally feel empowered, you'll never be able as a leader to move someone else to a goal," Schmitt says.

A major difference between how the socialization process differs between women and men is that men say to themselves, "I am, therefore I do," whereas women say, "I do, therefore I am." At this point in the presentation, audience member Jill Tarule, dean of the school of education at the University of Vermont, recalled the axiom "Mother loves you for who you *are*, while father loves you for what you *do*."

Leadership Course Effective

To help women overcome social culturalization, Schmitt has taught the women in leadership course at Eastern Michigan University since 1979. Started under a somewhat reluctant department head, it has been oversubscribed since day one. In it, she emphasizes the sociological and psychological aspects of women's development and socialization, and their effect on how women act as leaders.

In 1991, she surveyed about three hundred women who had taken the course to assess its impact on their thinking and development. With an 80 percent response rate, the survey found that most found the course "probably the most meaningful class they had taken as an undergraduate" in helping them become aware of and confront the juxtaposition between gender and leadership expectations.

Schmitt found that respondents clearly valued the course far more for its personal development objectives, not any "abstract and relatively sterile theories and concepts studied in a way that has little personal significance for the women students." Although her findings were similar for all women students with all levels of experience, they were especially strong for mature women over age thirty-one.

To emphasize the value of long-range planning, students in the class completed five-year career plans. The exercise caused great agony as they tried to make the "perfect" plan, one they could follow to the letter for five years. Finally, they understood that it was *their plan*, written in pencil, which they could revise at will.

Across all ages (twenty-one to fifty-seven) and years of experience (zero to thirty-six, averaging ten or more), they found these concepts of the class especially useful: learning to cope with multiple role demands, while recognizing that some workplace demands are unrealistic; developing self-assertiveness attributes; presenting a self-confident image to yourself; and presenting a self-confident image to others.

Having reexamined her priorities, Schmitt recently left administration to concentrate on teaching.

Mary Dee Wenniger

Three General Patterns Typify Women's Leadership Styles

August 1999
Barbara Tedrow
Academic administrator, Delta College, Michigan
The gathering of women had just finished an incredible discussion of women's leadership. One group concluded that "when women become administrators, they act like men . . . leadership is about getting the job done." A second group disagreed but remained silent. They didn't want to create a scene or challenge the higher-ranking women. They reasoned that these opinionated women would be retiring soon, so a confrontation would just cause trouble. "Someday this will all change. We just don't know when." A third group eventually challenged the statement, explaining that the first group's attitude might ultimately hurt women aspiring to administrative positions. The three groups of women's responses provide a glimpse into three general patterns of leadership uncovered through a qualitative study of community college women administrators.

Women Leaders: A New Genre

The ambiguity associated with women's leadership is understandable because it is a relatively new concept in higher education. It has become a point of interest in educational research as the number of women in senior-level positions has grown in the 1980s and 1990s. The American Council on Education reported that the number of female CEOs in higher education increased from 5 percent in 1975 to 16 percent in 1995, and may now have reached 20 percent.

Additionally, many researchers have suggested that women's ways of knowing, which include reflective educational processes, consensus building, and valuing differences, might better advance needed educational reforms than traditional leadership frameworks have. What is women's leadership, how do women construct a leadership identity, and how do women advance change? As part of my research for a 1998 Ph.D. at Michigan State University, I asked thirty senior women administrators from thirteen different community colleges these and other questions about their approach to leadership.

I found the women formed their leadership identity largely as a response to traditional organizational expectations and norms grounded in the experiences of men. Women built leadership identities by making choices such as adapting to, reconciling with, or resisting the expectations inherent in such traditional structures. Of the thirty women I interviewed, nine were adapters, thirteen were reconcilers, and eight were resisters.

Adapters: Fitting into the Big Shoes

One group of women chose to fit in or adapt to a traditional instrumental structure. As adapters, they became protégées of men or women who modeled masculine behaviors. This meant they relied on direct language patterns, objectivity, distance from colleagues, and competitive strategies to maintain control and achieve goals. Because questioning the structure was not part of their view of leadership, the women generally denied or minimized gender issues. They saw themselves as behaving in gender-neutral ways.

But adapting had a cost to them. It placed them in a double bind; as outsiders successfully accommodating institutional expectations, they were isolated because neither the women nor the men they worked with really accepted them. Most were enjoying their jobs but knew their tenure in them was limited.

Reconcilers: Keeping Your Place

Reconcilers used both instrumental and relational styles but in a compartmentalized fashion. Reconcilers learned to be mindfully aware of delivering the appropriate response. Success was measured in terms of a woman's ability to be non-threatening by avoiding conflict and acting as a bridge between warring groups.

Reconciliation as a response had a cost. These women were the most conflicted because they lived a complicated dual existence as they faced a never-ending series of challenges such as constructing a complex language and responses to ensure their survival. The women were often perceived as unpredictable and insincere. Most were place-bound. Though generally accomplished and capable, reconcilers tended to be cast into specific roles and were usually not considered for higher positions. By taking personal responsibility to maintain peaceful relations, the reconcilers sustained the hierarchical structure by saving it from having to respond to new influences.

Resisters: Breaking Through, Taking the Risk

Women who used resistance wanted to be themselves and tended to integrate relational and instrumental behaviors. These women understood and recognized dominant organizational patterns as male oriented and challenged them whenever possible. But more importantly, the women advanced change by infusing relational ways of knowing into change processes using an educational approach and coalitions. In the process, these women helped their schools value difference, share authority, create more inclusive forms of decision making, and foster both individual and community potential. The cost of their strategy was that although the women felt they made a difference, they were often overcommitted.

What Their Responses Mean

Each of the thirty women used adaptation, reconciliation, and resistance patterns of leadership to some extent. To what degree each woman preferred one response over another depended on the institutional culture, the situation, and the woman's awareness of how the structure shaped her responses. Yet at the most basic level, these are reactive strategies—the women were reacting to a male-dominated organizational context. Being reactive puts a greater psychological burden on women compared to their male counterparts. The negative consequence is that women spend a good deal of time and energy simply trying to survive, when they should be thriving.

The ultimate concern raised by this study is this: How can community colleges create organizational environments in which women's ways of leading are fully embraced? The results of this study suggest that increasing the number of women in senior positions will not necessarily enhance the potential of women's administrative leadership. Schools must also create a safe environment where relational and instrumental styles can thrive together. To do this, community college leaders must be willing to critically examine the college's culture. The results of the study suggest these paths:

- *Develop professional development education programs designed to take into account both institutional and individual assumptions about gender.* In particular, administrators, faculty, and staff need to deconstruct how traditional organizations and their own personal assumptions have framed women's working lives through a masculine instrumental model.
- *Learn from organizations where relational and instrumental leadership styles are successfully included.* By moving away from a cookie-cutter model of administrative leadership, relational constructs can be better understood and successfully integrated into organizational life.
- *Work in coalitions to challenge the negative assumptions about women and their abilities.* Together, women can form a critical mass of diverse voices and model a variety of effective leadership styles.
- *Encourage women to develop and use resistance leadership styles by seeking out and promoting relational women leaders, giving them critical responsibility, visibility, and recognition for their efforts.* Relational women leaders have the right inclination, and they need support in their efforts to change the traditional hierarchical leadership style on campus.

Community colleges' engagement in critical reflection and dialogue about issues of inclusion and gender can expand the opportunities for women at all levels. With the present-day environmental demands for greater cultural awareness and diversity, women are critical resources in moving community colleges toward truly becoming the people's college.

SECTION TWO: WIN SOME, LOSE SOME

"Smooth Waters Never Make a Skillful Sailor"

April 1999
Interviewing for the presidency of Norfolk State University, Virginia, in 1997, Marie V. McDemmond was quoted in a local newspaper as having noticed some "red flags" in the university's finances. As vice president of finance at Florida Atlantic University and former head of administration and finance at the University of Massachusetts, she saw signs that hinted all was not well. Even after she asked a series of pointed questions about finances, including funding for the

new thirty thousand–seat athletic facility, Norfolk officials assured her that all was just fine, thank you. Soon after becoming president in July 1997, McDemmond and the acting vice president, who had been budget director, rolled up their sleeves and analyzed all budget accounts. By December, they discovered that the college had a severe budget crisis. In fact, there wasn't enough money to make it through the academic year.

The Bearer of Bad News

McDemmond immediately chose the first open faculty forum in spring 1998 to announce the financial crisis. "I presented it clearly, explaining how the deficit came about and the things we'd have to do to get past it," she recalled. The deficit in the state and auxiliary funds, which had been covered for years by funds from other accounts that were now diminishing, required harsh measures. McDemmond laid off 116 of the 1,040 employees, raised out-of-state tuition, and secured a loan of $6.5 million from the state legislature. In addition, she reduced costs by merging nine schools to five and tightened belts in the classrooms.

In a clear case of killing the messenger, external critics began a letter-writing campaign against President McDemmond. Right after the June layoffs, they blasted her for spending $204,000 to renovate the president's house, although the funds were spent before she discovered the budget crisis and before she even moved to campus. And clearly, she says, some did not want a woman at the helm. McDemmond, age fifty-three, is the first black woman to lead a four-year college in Virginia; with 7,700 students, Norfolk is the fifth largest historically black university in the country and the largest headed by a female. Her predecessor, who had headed Norfolk for twenty-two years, was said to have favored another finalist for the presidency, one who had been his vice president and executive assistant.

If that weren't enough, McDemmond was going through a lengthy divorce at the same time. Some detractors actually went to her ex-husband for ammunition in their campaign against her. "I really didn't let it bother me," says Marie McDemmond. "I knew if I sat there thinking about it, it would be very difficult for me to have the strength and energy and courage to go forward. And I knew there were things that had to be done really fast."

Navigating Choppy Waters

How did McDemmond respond to the attacks and allegations? She didn't respond directly. But she did answer any and all questions about what needed to be done at the university. In addition to raising the issue in the open faculty meeting, she continued public meetings, including town meetings with the campus communities and students. She opened office hours several times a month for students to make ten-minute appointments, which usually booked her from 8 A.M. to 8 P.M. "I answer any questions, explain where we are and where we want to go," she says.

In fact, one reason McDemmond chose the financial side of higher education was her belief that a woman's management style was more open, which she found especially lacking in financial management. "I wanted to find a way to have the financial side of the house really understood by people," she says. "A really critical piece that was missing—and still is frequently missing—is having the fiscal people be much more open about the finances of the institution."

A recognized national authority on financial management, McDemmond has been a leader in the Higher Education Resource Services (HERS) institutes for women administrators for nearly twenty years. She teaches budget and finance at both Wellesley and Bryn Mawr, HERS institutes including the politics surrounding the budgeting procedure, where she emphasizes the importance of making money matters understandable to leaders as well as followers.

McDemmond reveals her feminine side by calling the different accounts *pocketbooks*. There are different kinds of money in different pocketbooks: student fees, grants, alumni contributions, donations, and many other categories. She stresses that in many cases the spending from these different pocketbooks is restricted to certain types of expenditures. At Norfolk, the severe shortage in the auxiliary funds generated by student fees had been covered by a university center account. But operating deficits in both athletics and housing were getting worse, and "that small positive balance overall wasn't going to last very long with all those negatives," she knew.

One of her key goals as president was to double Norfolk's 22 percent graduation rate in three years, which she is working on. Although critics charge her with focusing more on finances than on academics, she knows academics cannot be successful without sound financial backing: "You can't do *anything* without the financial wherewithal," she explains.

Armed with Her Wit

The Norfolk situation isn't the first time McDemmond has faced a challenge to her authority and decisions. Almost twenty years ago, she stood in front of a public meeting of the council of deans, seven months pregnant; a dean told her he wasn't going to submit a budget to her. Being both African American and female, she wasn't sure which attribute caused him to challenge her authority, but she used a weapon she'd found effective many times before: humor. She told him, "Honey, if you don't submit your budget request to me, then I'll submit one for you, and you may not like it."

As a president, she finds humor may be a less appropriate response; instead she often finds herself just trying not to be too serious and avoiding the negative.

For example, immediately after she revealed the financial crisis, her predecessor called a news conference to blame it on McDemmond's policies. According to Associated Press news stories, he blamed the shortfall on her stricter tuition payment rules and restrictions on fans at the new stadium, which overran construction costs by $2 million under his watch. When the press asked McDemmond to respond, she took the high ground: "I want to move on and solve the problems at hand."

Those around her seem convinced she can do just that. Shortly after she announced the financial crisis, a *U-Mass Magazine* feature on McDemmond quoted a Norfolk faculty member: "I think we've all had some concerns about the finances of the university. It was absolutely marvelous to have her up there to tell us. We are better prepared to deal with what is coming." Another said: "We're in for a stormy voyage, but we have one hell of a captain."

Just Another Challenge

McDemmond is no stranger to adversity. Her mother died of toxemia just days after she was born, and her father was accidentally shot in his New Orleans restaurant when she was a young girl. Raised by relatives, she went into education, teaching social studies in middle school. She came from a long line of schoolteachers and as she puts it, "As a little black girl in the South growing up in the 1950s, there weren't that many options open to me." Her two sons chose higher education as well; the thirty-two-year-old attends Norfolk, and the eighteen-year-old will attend MIT next fall.

Despite the challenges at Norfolk that have inspired her to lead an informal HERS session on strategies for survival as a top administrator, Marie McDemmond is upbeat. She has the support of the Norfolk faculty and is using the skills developed at Florida Atlantic University, where in her eight years enrollment doubled to twenty-one thousand students, and three additional campuses opened. In summarizing her past twenty-one months at Norfolk University, McDemmond continues the nautical analogy: "Smooth waters never make a skillful sailor."

Melanie Conklin

"I Truly Love to Transform the Community. It's the Great Beauty of Being a Community College President"

January 1993

Anne Mulder has the uncanny ability to make money appear. President of Lake Michigan College since 1985, she has led the school to its first ten-year accreditation, the largest grant a Michigan community college has ever received from the state ($5.2 million), and establishment of a grants office which boosted giving by 200 percent. "One of my favorite things is raising money," she says. "Some people get a high from downhill skiing. I get a high from $1 million grants." She learned how to raise funds as a volunteer working part-time when her daughters were young. "My life's been more evolutionary than revolutionary," she notes.

Steady Progress

After earning a doctorate in education in 1983 from the University of Michigan, she took stock, realizing that she had been at Grand Rapids Junior College for twenty-five years while her children had grown and were on their own. Having steadily made her way from assistant dean of continuing education and director of community services to dean of academic service, she felt ready for a change. Then a friend said, "Don't you know you're ready to be president?"

Mulder knew her friend was right. She felt well grounded in development, academic services, and teaching. Her small inner voice of self-doubt disappeared after she examined how college presidents were performing and realized she could do as well or better. On her first try, she landed a presidency.

"Don't turn down any opportunity to grow," says Mulder, adding that some of her best skills were learned through volunteering. Mulder also points out that judging yourself by others' timetables for progress is useless. "It's how you have done what you have done where you are," Mulder emphasizes. "You're talking to a woman who was a single parent and raised two kids. Don't be afraid if you've had interrupted professional lives. Don't forget how great you were" in the work you did during that time, says Mulder, "because all is applicable to later management."

People Come First

Mulder's leadership style puts people first. "I choose never to use or abuse people, and I never want to be abused," she says. In fact, she feels a humane workplace is so essential that she sends every new college employee, from custodian to vice president, a set of twenty-four management assumptions based on her experiences (see pp. 26–27).

Her open-door policy sees students dropping in as often as faculty. "I have the ear that's open. I can't solve all their problems, but I will tell them how to work the system," she says. Mulder, who enjoys contact with students, is currently teaching a class in governance and management through Nova University. "Teaching is very integral to my life," says Mulder. "I get very excited about new ways of applying knowledge and transferring it into communities.

"I truly love to transform the community. It's the great beauty of being a community college president," she says. Whether it's helping immigrants learn important English skills to match their professional ones, or workforce retraining toward a company's total quality management goals, Lake Michigan College is "vital to the survival of our area."

Take Time to Live

As much as she loves what she does, Mulder says her job is "very isolating by its nature." Perfectionism and lack of a private life add to the strain. Her antidote is to "strive for balance." How does she beat the stress? "Exercise," replies Mulder without pause. "My health has become more important to my physical and emotional self."

The second key is friends, both in and out of the office. "Reaching out for support and giving others that permission" is very important, notes Mulder. "Women work doubly hard, and sometimes we fail to reach out to each other." Finally, a sense of humor is a requirement. "I am able to laugh at myself," she says. "Friends say I have demystified the presidency."

Women's Ways of Leading

Mulder notes that women wrote the book on inclusive leadership before any of those actual books on it appeared. "Women have to understand that their way of leading may be very different from that of their male counterparts, and that's OK," says Mulder. "I personally think it's better than OK." "Women make a better workplace, a more centered environment," she says. "Then we can heal the great gulf between men and women, creating a sense of wellness."

Asked whether her college is sensitive toward working mothers, she quipped, "The joke is, if you want to get pregnant, go to my office to work. I have seven thousand grandchildren." The school is working with a local agency to set up a child care program.

Mentors, Networks, Sponsors

Mulder says she has had wonderful female and male mentors. In fact, the first thing she did when considering applying for a presidency was talk with several women college presidents she knew. They advised her about fine-tuning her résumé and checking out the community surrounding the school. Now she returns the favor.

At an annual weeklong workshop for women who want to be college presidents, Mulder speaks about attaining a presidency. The advice holds for women with other job aspirations too. "Be honest with and about yourself," she says. Know what sacrifices you are willing to make, for instance, in relocating.

Many participants have later become college presidents. "You can almost always pick out those who are going to make it" because they have the confidence it takes. "If you're afraid of rejection, you're not going to be able to achieve." Mulder points out that having a sponsor is just as important as having a network and a mentor. "You need sponsors to help you get there, people who have clout." Having joined their ranks, she says, "I can open up doors now."

Mulder's Management Assumptions

My working relationship with administrators, faculty, and noncontractual personnel is based on these assumptions:

1. All of us have the same ultimate objective: that is, to provide the best possible educational opportunities for the student. The manner in which we go about achieving this objective may be different. The most important consideration is that results are achieved.
2. Everyone is to be trusted.
3. Equity and fairness are basic to good morale.
4. Freedom is essential to all of us.
5. Cooperative behaviors are encouraged; competitive behaviors are minimized.
6. Everyone has a desire to achieve.
7. All of us like to be appreciated.
8. Everyone has the freedom to express ideas, to experiment, and to fail.
9. Everyone prefers meaningful work to meaningless work.
10. Each individual is treated with respect.
11. Everyone needs to be informed as completely as possible on all matters.
12. Change, renewal, and constant readjustment are important aspects of an educational community.
13. Diversity and variation in thought and behavior are respected and encouraged within the mutually accepted standards of our institution. Human beings are never devalued in the process.
14. The use of threat, intimidation, and force are ineffective in working with others.
15. Lake Michigan College is a community of individuals with different areas of expertise and different roles but equal worth as human beings.
16. There is a management model in place at Lake Michigan College that assumes input from all areas of the college.
17. All of us want to make the environment as healthy as possible at Lake Michigan College.
18. The personnel of Lake Michigan College function as a team.

19. Goodwill exists among all members of the team; rivalry and jealousy are minimized.
20. Rationale for decisions is communicated to all appropriate audiences.
21. Decisions made are supported.
22. Decisions are made at the lowest possible level.
23. Decisions are made in a timely fashion.
24. All personnel assume appropriate responsibility in the decision-making process; the "buck" is not passed.

As I work with each of you, I commit to you that I will behave in ways that support these assumptions; and I expect you to tell me when you perceive that I am not functioning in such a manner. My expectation of you is that you will also behave in ways which support these assumptions. Thus, disagreement on issues will occur; such disagreement is accepted and even encouraged.

Mary Dee Wenniger

Revitalizing Campuses: Sometimes It Takes a Woman to Fix a Leaky Faucet

July 1994

As diminishing resources and public confidence are challenging and even threatening the very existence of some colleges, administrators are finding new styles of leadership to turn things around. And women are at the forefront.

Four years ago, Chicago State University was more than leaking, it was hemorrhaging. As student enrollment and retention hit record lows, so did faculty confidence and campus morale. Rumor said the Illinois legislature might close the campus. Enter the new president, Dolores E. Cross.

"People asked me, 'Why are you going to Chicago State University?'" she says. "There were real questions about whether this could be a viable, thriving university."

Students' Needs

Cross realized that the needs of the students were being ignored. She emphasizes that much of the student body, which is 85 percent African American, are first-generation students, often underprepared for higher education; many are single parents, many hold jobs. To help these students achieve success, Cross (who is herself African American) recalled challenges she had met as a vice chancellor at the City University of New York (CUNY).

Through research and experience, "we know what will make a difference for underprepared students," says Cross. "The ideas are there. The problem is whether there's a will to change." And will isn't enough by itself, Cross has found. All too often, "we tell people what do, we show them what to do, but we don't involve them."

Involvement Is the Key

Her first semester, Cross realized she couldn't just tell people "we must increase the enrollment," without involving them. Before coming on campus, she phoned professors. "Our first objective was to call every single student who has applied to Chicago State University. Make a personal call and find out what new information we can give them." Reaching out to students increased enrollment by 17 percent the first year, encouraging the faculty. "When people see an achievement through their collective effort, they're motivated," says Cross. As with this theory that worked in practice, Cross found other ideas also confirmed: (1) "Faculty are willing to get involved, but you must move beyond mere articulation of the problem to action." (2) "Key to improving students' success is improving the interaction between faculty and students." By giving people a role in revitalizing the campus, "the process becomes the product," says Cross.

Enhancing Faculty-Student Interaction

After meeting with faculty in focus groups to discuss goals for student achievement, Cross set up faculty innovation grants, making a startling offer: "If you have an idea to improve the success of students, we'll reallocate resources to fund it." Once again, she was "not only telling people and showing them, but involving them."

Next, Cross and her colleagues developed a three-point model for student success, which said that the university must be there for students in precollege programs before they matriculate, must support them once they are enrolled, and must create opportunities after they graduate. Cross stresses that "it's not just the model that's important but how we involve people in that model: through my visibility and my involvement, and through putting the responsibility for that model at the department-chair level." This involved Cross in working closely with department chairs, an unusual position for a president to be in, leaping several layers of administration.

Internal Validation Important

Although the indicators—rising enrollments, morale, and faculty-student involvement—were overwhelmingly positive, Cross sought an internal review process to determine how well the student success model was being communicated; to assess what people were doing differently because of it; and to uncover faculty, staff, and student concerns.

So she formed an action review team of junior and senior faculty who periodically interview campus members and report their findings to her.

Fastest-Growing Public University

Since Cross took the helm in 1990, student enrollment has skyrocketed 57 percent from fifty-eight hundred to over nine thousand, making it the fastest-growing public university in the state and perhaps the nation, says Cross. Other benchmarks of success are a 22 percent increase in the number of degrees granted, a pass rate of 100 percent for students taking the nursing exam, an acceptance rate of 100 percent for students applying to medical school, an increase in the retention rate of second-year students from 33 percent to 65 percent, an increase in the retention rate of Hispanic third-year students from 25 percent to 85 percent, and the university's awards for national excellence in retention in 1991 for nursing and in 1992 for math.

Perhaps most revealing are the intangibles. Cross observes, "There's a different feeling on campus. People feel better about the university, and they feel more involved." Nor have the changes gone unnoticed off campus. The *Chicago Tribune* refers to the school as "Success U."

Jennifer Hirsch

"I Don't Exactly Have Control. What I Do Is Instigate, Stir Things Up."

January 1998

Don't try to tell Theo Kalikow that a philosophy degree is impractical. She started her career teaching philosophy at Southeastern Massachusetts University in the 1970s and ended up as president of University of Maine-Farmington. As chief administrator, she still relies on skills honed in academia, mixing a Ph.D. in philosophy with her undergraduate work in chemistry.

"I got into the habit of analyzing what was happening around me, so I could take a step back and avoid getting caught up in academic craziness," says Kalikow. "My background made this job possible. It's possible for people to do a job like this without a faculty background, but I wouldn't recommend it."

Kalikow's father was an engineer who assumed she and her brother would end up in the sciences. Taking classes to meet general education requirements, she "ran into" philosophy—much to her father's dismay. "This was in 1960, and my dad told me, 'You're going to have to earn a living and you can't do that in philosophy, so you're going to be a chemist or I'm not paying the bills.'" She continued in both, mixing philosophy with quantum mechanics and animal behavior. She holds a bachelor's degree from Wellesley College in chemistry, a master's from MIT in philosophy, and a Ph.D. from Boston University in philosophy.

Now age fifty-six, Kalikow believes the eclectic mixture of academic experience helped her get where she is today: "As an administrator, I've done everything—work in the humanities and the sciences and the social sciences—and I know where they're all coming from. I'm sort of a garbage can for learning things."

She Stirs Things Up

Her varied background brings Kalikow a different approach to being boss. First, she believes it doesn't pay to work employees to the bone but advocates cultivating a life outside of work, advice she follows and passes on to associates. She likes to garden, read, cross-country ski, walk in the woods, and work out.

"I give lectures to people in administration about having a life," says Kalikow matter-of-factly. "I tell them to go home at 4:30. They didn't hire you to be an ATM machine. Don't turn into a crazy, depressed, nutty person." And if employees blow this off, she's there to remind them, just as she expects them to do for her: "We call it 'creative disrespect' around here."

Another rare trait for a top leader is not being adamant about getting her way. She learned this lesson at Plymouth State College, New Hampshire, as dean of the college from 1987 to 1994, with a year stint as interim president. "It was a contentious faculty, and they didn't always agree, and I didn't always get what I wanted. But if I got something I could live with and they could live with, that's what mattered."

Her university is now reforming the general education requirements. The vice president for academic affairs is getting public input via an e-mail discussion among faculty. About thirty are active participants in the electronic roundtable, and many more are "lurking"—reading what others have said and adding their ideas every once in a while.

What Does She Hope to Achieve?

"I don't care what it looks like, so long as it's better than it is now," she responds. "The more I get into this racket, the less I care what the results are. I don't exactly have control. What I do is instigate, stir things up." As Kalikow sees it, being a college president means getting academics, who are prone to acting like independent contractors, to want to commit to changing things. Then it's just a matter of exercising judgment—being able to separate the good from the terrible ideas. "A lot of times being a leader is getting the parade to start forming," she says. "And then you run in front of it and get the crap out of the road, so they can march along."

The Troublemaker

Kalikow had planned to be a faculty member until retirement: "I thought that would be my whole career. Nobody is born thinking they'll be a college president." She came to administration in an unusual way, not even realizing the risks she took or the direction she headed. She thought she was just advocating for her beliefs. She founded the women's studies program at Southeastern Massachusetts University, now the University of Massachusetts-Dartmouth. And as president of the college union, she fought to get a child care center and worked for women's equity. "I was a major troublemaker on campus," she confesses.

The actions got her noticed. When the president called her in, her first thought was, "What have I done now?" He surprised her by inviting her to be his assistant. Two years later, he nominated her for an American Council on Education fellowship in academic administration at Brown University, which led to her next job, dean of the College of Arts and Sciences at the University of Northern Colorado in Greeley.

Needless to say, she advises women in academia to speak their minds and come to the job as a whole person. "I know a lot of people are afraid to say what they think," says Kalikow. "They haven't been given permission to hear their own voice. I've never had that problem. It's not that I'm loud and obnoxious, but I tell it like it is."

She admits it can be risky but firmly believes if a woman builds a reputation, people will listen to her. "If you treat people reasonably, they'll listen to you when you talk," she says, adding, "Well, as much as they ever listen to women. Sometimes you have to say it ten times. But if you've built up a solid reputation, people aren't going to get crazy with you."

How do you build that reputation? Consistency and honesty. "You have to be there and say what you will do. And do what you say. It drove me bananas when people said they'd call or send you to a conference or fax you a paper, and it never happened. If I say I'll call you on Wednesday, I'll call you on Wednesday. Period. After a while, that's the reputation you get."

Living in the Fishbowl

Being an out lesbian appears to be one of the largest risks in Kalikow's career. "I've always been out," she says. "At my first institution, that was just the way I was, and I was too young and stupid to know the risk. And I had a very nice career there and made it up to assistant to the president. That's how I've been ever since, and it seems to work out just fine."

She admits nonchalantly that her frankness has probably lost her some jobs. In fact, when offered her current post, she turned to the chancellor and said, "You should know that I'm a lesbian. I'm coming here with my partner, and we're going to live together in the president's house. And if you don't want to offer me the job because of that, it's OK. I'm not going to sue you."

One reason for being so open, says Kalikow, is that the presidential house is a fishbowl, and what you aren't open about can be twisted or used as blackmail. Yet she doesn't make a big deal over her sexual orientation; in fact, she's told her media person she doesn't want to make a career of talking about it. But shortly after her arrival, a reporter asked about her personal life, and she mentioned her partner, a woman with a Harvard master's degree in education who practices Feldenkrais, an awareness of the body-mind connection.

"After the article was published, we waited for the crosses to be burned on the lawn, but nothing bad happened," recalls Kalikow. At Plymouth State, the rumor mill churned whenever she hired or promoted women, spinning assertions of her playing favorites. She laughs at the notion: "Sexuality doesn't mean I don't like men. It's just that for affection, I prefer women. Many of my male coworkers have been my buddies, and I've helped many of them along the way." And when she found herself having to fire a female, the accusations turned to her being unsupportive of women: "Sometimes you just can't win."

Kalikow pauses when asked what advice she'd give closeted lesbians in academia. "It's very far from my own experience, but I know a lot of people are scared." She suggests taking some baby steps, such as showing up at a basketball game with your partner, then maybe bringing her to a party. "A lot of times, people aren't looking," she says. "You get the feeling people are watching you and pointing, saying, 'There's that gay person.' It's not always happening. Just go ahead, and you be you, and maybe you'll find out it's fine. I think higher education is one of the more sympathetic places. We still have a lot of liberal thinkers around here."

As other advice to women administrators, Kalikow recommends "lots of degrees" and different job experiences. Her philosophy background kicks in when she suggests stepping back and looking at higher education in terms of what it is accomplishing, and identifying the big issues. Then dive in.

"Prepare yourself to lead, and don't wait for any permission," says Kalikow.

"It's not often that people get a mentor by someone saying, 'I'm here to groom you.' Present yourself."

In addition, she says women more than men tend to try something once, and if it doesn't work, throw up their hands and see it as a failure. Fight that feeling, she suggests. "Pick yourself up, analyze what happened, and go do something else. Be persistent."

Blueberry Fields Forever

Kalikow speaks her mind on many issues but knows that her high profile job has some limitations. "As a college president, you can't mouth off on all the social issues," although it's common knowledge that the issues near and dear to her heart are literacy and those surrounding building a community, such as jobs, poverty, and violence.

A strong supporter of women, she's proud that 69 percent of the two thousand students are women and 40 percent of the nearly one hundred faculty are women: "That's what affirmative action will do. It's great for women."

Kalikow plans to speak out even more after she retires in six years. "I'm going to grow blueberries and be a social activist in the Farmington community. I figure maybe people will listen to a former college president."

Melanie Conklin

Reflections on Being a "Twice-Failed" Administrator

November 1996
Lesley A. Diehl
Dean of Arts and Sciences, Eastern Connecticut State University
In January, I'll again return to the faculty at a school that has twice granted me leaves of absence to try out administration elsewhere. Although most friends and colleagues, both faculty and administrators, discourage me from calling myself a failure, the truth is that I didn't make it. And I'm rather proud of how I failed. In fact, I know now who I am better than I've ever known before.

My success at failing comes from my ability to focus on what I've learned in two posts, as a dean and as a vice president of academic affairs. Embarrassment prevented me from discussing my first administrative failure at the time, but now I feel encouraged to speak out. It's no coincidence that I'm a failed woman administrator, and my experience is not unique. Several years ago, a group of women proposed an AAHE workshop that explored factors in institutional climate leading to women leaving administrative positions. The workshop was not accepted.

I attribute my failure as a woman in administration in great part to higher education's refusal to significantly improve the climate for all women on campus. Too many campuses still consider women a problem to be addressed. Although they may set up guidelines to handle sexual harassment, often the dean is the same hierarchical, authoritarian naysayer who was there yesterday but who now may wear a skirt.

What happened to women's commitment to change the climate of our campuses? I fear that campuses have changed us instead and that some of us have been willing to be changed in order to be successful. I believe women who contemplate moving into administrative positions need to know what awaits them.

What I Learned

Not all institutions of higher learning are alike. Perhaps I might have been more successful elsewhere, but I chose not to continue seeking those places.

But they're more alike than different. Although I interviewed at a number of schools and was forthright about my administrative style, I found the campus climates difficult overall. And it's becoming less collegial for both women and men, as budget cuts force everyone to compete for a smaller piece of the pie, partially due to higher education's failure to win back the public trust. In addition, the separation between administration and faculty has widened; administrators are required to see their role as manager of the school's financial affairs. As administrators, we say "no" more often than we entertain, discuss, or consider academic excellence. Faculty see administrators as mere managers who fail to understand the reality of being in the classroom, trying to construct meaningful learning environments.

Consider leaving when your most precious talents and characteristics develop a downside. To my astonishment, I found that mediation, collaboration, and consensus building can be used negatively. Trying to mediate between faculty and administration, I found my position as the bridge sometimes actually encouraged each to assume ever more diametrically opposed positions. I began to feel like the wishbone at Thanksgiving, stretched to the breaking point. Soon, I became just the mouthpiece for each side, delivering bad news and uncompromising or absurd messages.

Experienced faculty even those with administrative skills don't necessarily make good administrators. In schools where the gap between administration and faculty has become an immeasurable abyss, administrators with strong faculty experience may find it difficult to prove to colleagues that they are team players. On the other hand, an administrator new to a school is not embraced by faculty as one of their own but is viewed suspiciously. My refusal to act like an administrator according to the faculty script sometimes resulted in my being lectured by faculty about how I *should* behave, although they disliked and distrusted the very behavior they were so eager for me to demonstrate!

Even after I produced a résumé showing nearly twenty-five years' experience as a full-time faculty member, they discounted my knowledge of pedagogy, program development, and student behavior. Many faculty treated me like an administrative stereotype, and many of my fellow administrators doubted my leadership savvy, especially when I spoke of collaboration in decision making. The combination of my faculty experience and my more feminine management style made them very uncomfortable.

Women especially academic women are more affected by the work climate. Although I believe my male colleagues felt as much stress as I did, everyone walked around as if "there was a dead horse in the room that no one was willing to acknowledge," as my partner noted. The few women in administration spoke among themselves about the work environment, but the men acted like tough guys. A top male administrator advised against my making any friends at work because "they will cut you off at the knees." I've found that women in academic affairs, especially those coming from faculty, expect to work in an environment that supports change. They generally expect their opinions will be heard and respected; when their expectations are not met, it's a question of how much they'll tolerate.

Administrators lose the connection to institutions based on students and the learning environment. Although faculty see both good and not-so-good aspects of the classroom, administrators tend to encounter only the problem students: those on academic probation, those who have flunked out, and those angry with their professors. Experiences with disgruntled students are rarely balanced by those with happy students.

Success at administration requires the right degrees and the right amount of arrogance. As a psychologist, I find my expertise useful in understanding quirks of human behavior; in fact, I've been encouraged to write a book entitled *The Administrator as Therapist.* I believe a dean needs a degree in law, as I have threats of lawsuits daily; an advanced degree in computer technology, so I can know with absolute certainty the exact specifications for each faculty member's computer; the general arrogance to believe that I know more than anyone else (except my boss); more arrogance to speak nonstop for a whole meeting; the absolute belief that I can tell anyone how to do her or his job better than she or he can do it (except my boss); a management style that punishes people for doing a job poorly and ignores competent work, while expecting them to eagerly volunteer for more work.

Positive changes in the climate for women in higher education vary between institutions. We want to believe things are improving for women, but the evidence is mixed. Having decided to leave administration, I've been flooded with notes from women who found negative climates on campus. Some women leaders continue to insist on a more collaborative, less authoritarian approach to resolving the issues challenging higher education. I personally know two women presidents whose styles have not changed. They steadfastly retain a humane and caring administrative approach, concerned about academic issues but aware of financial realities. These are the people we need to cherish. Their openness makes them vulnerable, and those who seek to create a new climate for women on campus need to join forces with them.

Before leaping into administration check on the climate at the school under consideration. One of the best sources is the networks that women have developed. But they can fail if potential colleagues live in a climate of mistrust and fear to speak the truth. Or if women fail to ask tough questions about climate issues such as, "Does my boss respect and like women? How do you know? Give me a few examples." Because I couldn't ask the questions I needed to ask and puzzled over answers to those I did ask, I decided to keep my safety net and accept a leave of absence kindly offered by the president of my home institution. It was the best decision I made. I returned to SUNY as faculty.

Women in administration must adapt to grow in difficult soil. Women are more likely to succeed in organizations that are nontraditional and nonhierarchical. Why don't I try another post? I'm leaving administration to be able to speak with the authority of my knowledge and experience, unencumbered by a reporting line, about what higher education can do to make the workplace less stressful and less hostile for us all, women and men.

We cannot grow creativity in soil made up of competition, arrogance, hostility, anger, and mistrust. These troubled times call for our most creative efforts, and women who are better prepared for the world of administration can contribute to an environment that encourages growth for all.

Frostbitten and Beheaded: A Cautionary Tale

October 1996
First, I felt chilly; then I caught a cold and got frostbitten. Finally, I was beheaded. As a healthy female administrator, I arrived on campus less than two years ago, rosy cheeked, energetic, and clear eyed, naive about the potential dangers of my new environment.

As a new vice president, I was outnumbered everywhere by men at the senior administrative level. I arrogantly ignored the chill, thinking it was irrelevant because I was so competent. Oblivious to petty power politics, I had more important work to do. Although the president enthusiastically welcomed me to campus, he never invited me into his inner circle.

I didn't fit in because I was task oriented, focusing on the challenges of my new position and embracing my mandate to be an agent of change. His hand on the thermostat, the president kept the climate very comfortable for the other senior administrators but never warmed it up much for me, the lone female in the cabinet.

Lacking the vision to face the challenges of today and tomorrow, they sought comfort in the current laissez-faire, chaotic, and uncoordinated environment. These political animals thrived in the warmth generated by their tightly knit circle. Although the president challenged me to bring order out of the chaos, when I tried, I was frozen out. Change meant sharing control, collaborating, and being members of a team. They preferred the autonomy of anarchy.

Symptoms of Sickness

I examined my symptoms, noticing often I was the only woman on a committee, council, or cabinet meeting, except a secretary. The only other female senior administrator had been fired a few months after my arrival. The others, predominantly males, developed or maintained long-term relationships with the president. Even administrators assigned to me went around me to the president, displaying passive resistance to my direction and communication along the paths outlined in the organizational chart. I felt the cold but thought I could accomplish my goals anyway.

But a new organizational chart confirmed the seriousness of my position. Seeking to make sense of my condition, I read an article, "The Three Levels of the Glass Ceiling: Sorcerer's Apprentice Through the Looking Glass" ("The Three Levels," 1991), describing the effects of the glass ceiling. At the top level, female executives feel like Alice in Wonderland, a place where the rules and relationships seem dramatically different.

Beheading Removes the Threat

Although some female executives succeed at this level despite the odds, many other high-performing women do not fit in and are perceived as threats, so they are stopped. But surgically removing these women from their positions sets off flashing lights, emergency warnings, and signals of crisis.

A less visible way to remove a woman at the top is to behead her. She keeps her title, office, and salary while losing her position, responsibility, and authority. Although the beheading superficially looks like politics as usual, there is a difference for a woman compared to her male peer who loses in a reorganization: usually, her career is over.

Checking the organizational chart and seeing her at work every day may lead one to believe she's still functioning in her former capacity, but imagine how difficult this is when her head has been severed from her body. Now, in addition to having frostbite from working in a very chilly climate, I find myself beheaded. And the climate gets chillier as I carry on in my new nonjob, collecting a salary, and pretending all is just terrific, while I am ignored and kept out of the loop.

As an energetic, talented, and committed administrator, I am forced to slow down my metabolism, ignore the signals my brain is giving to my detached body to move forward on the institutional agenda for which I have no role, and smile and stand erect while my emotions rebel. The normal channels and outlets for my energy have been blocked or rerouted to vapor space, causing great tension among the still-moving parts. Of course, I play the public role, contribute where I can, and find interesting things to occupy my time.

But the institution is hemorrhaging talent, failing to reap the benefit of my expertise, and demonstrating to women on campus that the climate is too chilly for comfort. Some women reach out to offer me support; others scurry away, fearing my condition may be contagious. They huddle for comfort and warmth, fearing they too might be frostbitten, beheaded, or maimed by a system that is dysfunctional and unhealthy for human beings of either sex.

Believing the condition isn't terminal, I seek a remedy to my accompanying symptoms of numbness, bewilderment, anxiety, and anger. I feel confident that relocation to a warmer climate can renew my health.

"Frostbitten"

"Been There, Done That," Administrator Tells Frostbitten

December 1996
I was an academic department chair for three years at a large American land-grant university and have been dean of faculty (college) for more than four years at a large comprehensive university in Canada. I, too, moved across institutional cultural divides to take both of these appointments and faced some extremely isolating experiences as the new and lone female unit head within a large College of Arts and Sciences, and subsequently, as the second-ever female dean in my current institution.

As a tenured professor in one of my departments, I'm now looking forward to a long sabbatical this fall at the end of my present five-year administrative term. I recently chose to avoid the option (humiliation?) of a reelection process for a second term. I enjoy a great many aspects of university administration but am also aware of its potentially devastating impacts on the psyche.

Although my own experiences and those of several other female administrators I know mirror those of Frostbitten in many ways, I believe she has made a few classic errors.

Assuming that new administrators especially women brought into formerly male cliques are recruited as agents of change. Any institution that is just now hiring its first female senior administrators probably is looking not for change but for comfort. An administration that is truly progressive would have appointed its first senior women at least a decade ago.

Assuming to paraphrase Barbara Mikulski that you can push the envelope before you know how the post office works. Frostbitten's best strategy as the new female administrator would have been to bide her time, make friends with her administrative colleagues in a supportive way, offer to assist their projects, and gain their trust well before embarking on changes that seem to threaten them.

Unfortunately, this is a tall order for most feminists. We feel muzzled and powerless as mascots and perhaps incapable of restraining our naturally dynamic personalities. Many of us are simply too busy to cultivate a social life with our colleagues. However, once an administrator is discredited as a loose cannon or as an opposition party, it's virtually impossible for her to gain or regain the trust of the other senior managers. Ask what have been the strategies of successful women, if any, in her administration. (Probably they behaved like honorary men or mascots. Oh, well.)

Assuming. Assuming that her institution's highest administrative values and principles are something other than loyalty to the *bruderbond*, particularly to one's president.

Speaking and possibly thinking in abstractions about the administrative climate rather than in tangible realities. No one can solve indefinite complaints couched in metaphors borrowed from meteorology. Problems and difficult incidents are resolved one by one. There are quite a few workshops and management books with tips on addressing particular irritants; none, so far as I know, on beheading or defective thermostats. Hopefully, Frostbitten's acknowledged task-oriented style can help her here to solve concrete, manageable problems.

Not quietly checking before accepting her position with knowledgeable insiders about the power structure on her new campus. Entrenched bureaucracies and old-boyism at the top are no secret to rank-and-file faculty and staff. Also, many campus climates merely reflect their local, regional, or possibly religious subcultures. Could these have been determined and analyzed ahead of time for a good fit with Frostbitten's experience and personality? For example, I learned only after moving to my present university that Anglo-Canadians tend to be far more reserved, group oriented, and conservative than the typical blunt Midwesterner. My own brand of individualism became a liability, rather than an asset, in my new setting. My university's administration merely expresses this reticent, group-solidarity subculture.

Becoming bitter. I used to be idealistic about what I hoped to accomplish as an administrator. Then I became hurt and angry. Now I'm merely cynical. Or possibly realistic. When colleagues behave badly, it helps to ask myself, "What did you expect? Of course they're going to act that way: it's human nature." Bitterness robs you of your motivation and self-worth, and gives your detractors an unearned second victory over you.

Can Frostbitten be saved? Yes, I think so. I prescribe the following treatment.

It's always imperative to have a life or lives outside of the university and family or friends who keep you sane. I unwind by taking long evening walks with my dog, who, unlike some of my fellow deans, is always happy to see me.

Strengthen your sense of humor. Laugh at your own foibles. Acknowledge your mistakes without berating yourself over them. Recreate your enemies in your mind as potentially OK people, even if you can't exactly turn the other cheek (let alone your back) to them. Be pleasant to people who avoid you or gossip about you.

Acknowledge the really good things about your job. Despite some residual misery, I like much of what I do and most of the people I encounter, and I try to savor the positive moments. Most people on the planet would be thrilled to have Frostbitten's vice presidential title, a nice office, and no crushing overload of work.

If Frostbitten came up through the professorial ranks, surely her research still beckons, and she will gain more respect among the faculty if they view her as a serious scholar. If she is in an academic support or staff position, surely she can consult with her president about some mutually agreeable new projects for her to develop or can gain recognition for herself and her institution through community service and outreach activities. If Frostbitten is not tenured, however, she should seriously consider new ways to make herself indispensable. Otherwise, she may lose more than a section of her portfolio in the next administrative reorganization.

Develop some street-fighting skills to deal with men who go behind your back or over your head. This is the oldest trick in the book, and they behave the same way toward other men, incidentally. One strategy for a brand new administrator is to get her boss to agree that he will pass back to her any attempted end runs around her prerogatives. Fiefdoms and turf are everywhere in universities, and people will instinctively try to protect them if they feel threatened. Try to show colleagues how they will benefit personally from cooperating and to make them think your plans were really their ideas all along. Do your homework: be sure of your facts, dates, and figures.

Frankly, I've had to deal with issues far worse than anything Frostbitten described. As dean, I've had colleagues who spread allegations about my supposed sex life and a supervisor (vice president) who encouraged me to resign as a consequence. When I formally complained to him of a poisoned working environment, he ignored my written complaint. (There is no sexual harassment officer on my campus.) Eventually, I negotiated a resolution with the university through my provincial Human Rights Commission, but by that point my reputation was toast. I've had department chairs misrepresent (lie about) my statements to their colleagues, then sit back in satisfaction when my proposals crashed in departmental and governing council meetings, or when coworkers became outraged by what the dean (reportedly) said.

A former dean once tried to tear a strip off me through a petition drive and personal attack in an open meeting. I've had to use "tough love" against an alcoholic professor and to initiate dismissal proceedings against a tenured professor who sexually assaulted a student.

When I was a department chair, competing heads of cognate units tried to duplicate the most attractive parts of my department's offerings and even to carve up and close my department so that they could absorb our programs and students.

My former dean promised academic employment for my (ex-) husband as an inducement for me to accept the department chair position and then reneged after my spouse had moved and given up his tenure at our first university. I had faculty who misrepresented their program's accreditation standards to try to get a bigger share of departmental resources and have been bullied by bigger men with louder voices than me more times than I can remember.

It really is true that anything that doesn't kill you makes you stronger. After these experiences, I cannot be surprised or intimidated by too much that occurs on university campuses. I think I'm fundamentally better off as a human being and as an administrator for being less naive. If administrative politics are not for fainthearted novices, they also badly need women and men who are committed to kindness, fair play, and moral vision. I don't claim that all or even most colleges operate in ways I've described. But some do, and the ability to withstand a swift game of hardball is unfortunately part of the shrewd administrator's repertoire.

Leave if the place is too toxic. With a vice presidential title, a nice c.v., and some decent letters of reference, Frostbitten could be off and working somewhere far more supportive than her current university. Just remember that publicly criticizing your former campus can reflect far worse on you than on the institution you criticize.

Best wishes, Frostbitten. Your goals, commitment, and vision of what a university should be like are in exactly the right place. Your recent difficult incidents have given you better judgment and more experience. And with sound advice like mine well in hand, your newfound sense of humor, hardheaded realism, and resilience should be real assets to your current or next employer!

Anonymous, of course!

Underwear Exhibit Brochure Spooks Trustees, Last Straw for President

June 1995

In a move that shocked the campus, Ophelia Garcia suddenly resigned last month after four years as president of Rosemont College, a small Catholic women's college in Pennsylvania. At issue was a continuing disagreement with four of thirty-six members of the board of trustees, culminating with their outrage over a brochure describing an upcoming exhibit reflecting on the cultural implications of women's underwear.

"Other cultures have bound women's feet," says Garcia, whose field is visual arts. "Our culture has bound women's torsos," to the detriment of their health and mobility. The faculty-led exhibit concerns cultural ideals linking beauty and restraint.

"An educational institution is one place we should be able to discuss issues we disagree about," Garcia says, but a few trustees dismissed the idea of the exhibit as "tasteless and inappropriate, terms they would just as easily apply to me." Garcia refused to cancel the exhibit, saying, "I don't cancel speakers, and I don't cancel exhibits." The exhibit ran. She referred to four years ago, when she invited a pro-choice speaker for commencement. "All hell broke loose," she recalls. "They have a capacity for rancor that is extraordinary."

A Question of Fit

Garcia came to Rosemont from the presidency of the Atlanta College of Art. Calling Rosemont "the most conservative Catholic diocese in the country," Garcia, who had attended a convent, "had expected that Rosemont, twenty years later, would be different." In some ways, the school is "caught in an image of itself in another time."

She said the board recognized the need for change, but they disagreed over particular changes. "The pace of change I thought necessary was too fast for some," she said. "I am Cuban. I grew up in a revolution, so I have a sense of urgency. I won't move at the pace of the slowest."

Another factor was her not being one of the gang. "I am neither Irish nor Italian," she says. "I know for sure that someone who is one or the other would not have had the trouble I've had."

A third factor was her style. "I am not well equipped in the land of euphemism," she says. She could see that they were in for "another round of nastiness," and she was "exhausted and had reached the point of diminishing returns." "I became radioactive," and whatever she became associated with caused controversy.

Her Future?

At age fifty-four, "I'm not sure whether I have the death wish to seek a third presidency," she says, "or whether I have carried the banner long enough." Garcia observed that the mortality rate for women presidents is higher than that for men.

"They really assume that we are just nice people when they hire us," she explains, and then they are surprised when women actually want to make changes for the good of the institution. As one educational leader said: "They want you to change everything but disturb no one."

Mary Dee Wenniger

SECTION THREE: SPECIAL PROBLEMS OF WOMEN IN DOUBLE JEOPARDY

You Go, Girl! African American Female Presidents Lead with Style

October 1998
Runae Edwards-Wilson, Ph.D.
Adjunct professor, Mercy College, New York

For women of color, leadership roles in higher education institutions have been fleeting at best. In 1991, white males held more than 65 percent of college faculty and administrative positions, according to the American Council of Education. "Women and minorities have been systematically excluded from participating in mainstream higher education since colonial times—minorities even more drastically than white women," assert writers Wilson and Melendez.

Research on African American female leaders in higher education reveals that they adopt the leadership characteristics of the culture at the institutions where they serve. Josephine Davis, former president of CUNY's York College, reports that these women are astute practitioners of the leadership behaviors that facilitate their tenure in higher education.

Study of Twenty-Seven Presidents

The study I conducted on the leadership styles of twenty-seven African American female college presidents at four-year public and private schools supported Davis's findings. Among my respondents were the first African American female president of a New York State University, the first African American female leader of a statewide higher education system, the first African American female president of one of the elite Seven Sisters schools, and the first African American female president of a Big Ten university. Looking at the respondents, one sees a myriad of characteristics that have combined to produce America's top female leaders in higher education today.

Respondents provided background information about themselves and their schools and writing samples, and twelve agreed to be interviewed. The study found that African American women successfully hold leadership positions in American colleges and universities across the spectrum of higher education institutions. Although they all hold Ph.D.'s, their backgrounds are highly varied and collectively represent many years of experience in national and international higher education.

The twenty-seven presidents' self-reported leadership style was participatory and team oriented, in contrast with the traditional presidents' directive style. This finding agreed with those of other researchers. An analysis of the presidents' writing samples indicated the majority were clearly aware of the existence of segregation of and discrimination against African Americans. Discussing school desegregation, one president said: "Cultural marginalization and psychological stigmatization, the last two elements of the structure of racism, are more obscure, covert, subconscious, and less obvious, although just as significant as the other elements maintaining the structure of racism."

The president of a large midwestern college wrote: "For most black Americans, one of the most important and challenging changes has been their struggle for freedom and equality in the area of education."

Who and Where Are They?

More than 70 percent of the presidents surveyed were in urban settings, well above the national average of 28 percent of colleges being urban, as reported in *Peterson's Register of Higher Education* for 1997. The concentration of African American female college presidents in the survey is in predominantly historically black colleges and universities (fifteen respondents) or urban environments (twelve respondents), where there are large numbers of minority group members, which also intimates segregation.

For most of the schools, the enrollment was between one thousand and five thousand students. Two presidents said they got their jobs because of their schools' needs at the time; they became the first African American presidents after their schools had changed from serving white students predominantly at their founding in the 1970s to now serving mostly African Americans or females.

The presidents' average age was fifty-seven, with the largest number of them being fifty-nine, somewhat older than the average white male college president, who is fifty-four, according to the 1993 American Council on Education report *The American College President* (Ross and Green, 2000). This age difference suggests that it takes longer for women to climb the professional ranks to a college presidency.

Like their white male counterparts, the majority of the respondents were married. This finding suggests that marriage and family did not negatively affect the careers of these women and their ascension to college presidencies, which concurs with a 1977 statement by O'Leary that African American women and men view a commitment to work as compatible with the traditional female role.

Considering economic status, the study indicates that adverse financial circumstances during their childhoods had not deterred these presidents from successful careers. Three presidents told of overcoming dire economic situations, including one who came home from school to discover she had nowhere to live because her mother had spent the rent money. Another president's biography recounts how her family "barely eked out a living by raising cotton as tenant farmers." Motivation and help by church groups or individuals were significant factors in the success of these women.

Two presidents told of instances in which the benevolence of others helped provide food or shelter for them. Presidents also mentioned receiving help in their careers from teachers. One president attended school as an undergraduate because a teacher got her a scholarship and another gave her clothes to wear at college.

Definitions of Leadership

In defining *leadership*, the presidents used these terms: displays vision, inspires, is a team player, provides resources, and empowers others. When describing themselves as leaders, the presidents used these terms: change agent, participatory, hands-on, intuitive, humanistic, communicative, charismatic, high energy, and supportive. Service and community work were very important to their sense of self. A president of a historically black college said: "You must believe in yourself and have a vision; I have a strong service orientation."

Presidents saw themselves in a precarious position requiring a balance between power and empowerment, authority and support. These presidents viewed leaders as those who work with their administrative staff to help them make the best decisions for their schools. They appreciated being well informed and usually received information through both established and informal channels. They saw their administrative staff and other subordinates as most helpful when they worked with them as allies to benefit the students and the schools.

About her own leadership style, the president of a Texas college said, "The end results and the accomplishments [of her leadership] demand careful, meaningful planning and strategizing." Another CEO said, "There is no one model of successful leadership that fits all circumstances."

Areas where the presidents reported exercising the most leadership were in governance, planning, strategic planning, enrollment, and budgeting. These tasks may require team participation and are very structural, so presidents often acted as directors to get them done. Again, they reported using more than one leadership style to accomplish their goals.

The overall success of these women as leaders appeared to depend on how well they balanced varied characteristics like creativity, organization, and working with others. The presidents generally practice a participatory, team-oriented leadership style. Being administrators on predominantly African American, female, or urban campuses, they have a personal awareness of minority issues that helps them to resolve many campus problems.

Assorted Adaptations by African American Administrators

November 1998
Janice M. Edwards
Associate Dean of Students and Director of Multicultural Programs,
Wittlenberg University, Ohio
African American women in leadership positions at white colleges and universities face distinct difficulties unique to them, which pose a very real threat to their well-being, both personally and professionally. Based on Janice M. Edwards's 1997 Ed.D. dissertation, this article discusses the issues and coping strategies of three women administrators, each of whom she shadowed for a week at their public midwestern schools.

Challenges for African American Women

Although women in general face tremendous challenges in managing patriarchal conflicts at many schools, African American women must also deal with the complex intersection of race and gender. They have long been socialized to juggle family and community commitments with outside work; the very foundation of the African American community depends on this ability. Although admirable, these women often provide this salvation at a cost.

Although women from all racial backgrounds dominate at lower levels of administration, a disparity exists between the number of women who enter the system and those who ultimately reach the upper strata. Despite a pool of competent African American female educators and legislation aimed at correcting past inequities, higher ed administration remains predominantly male. African American women at white schools perceive that they work harder for their promotions than do their white colleagues; often they must sit idly by as their counterparts receive promotions at their expense.

Tokenism. African American women are at once more visible and equally isolated due to racial and gender differences. The token woman often finds herself in situations where she is made aware of her unique status as the only African American female present, yet feels compelled to behave as though this difference did not exist.

Sexism. Institutionalized systems of sex bias often create impenetrable barriers that halt women's progress and stifle their professional development. Though sexism can severely affect the lives of all women on campus, racism and sexism compound the impact for African American women.

Racism. Systemic racism may be one of the most covert but virulent forms of racial oppression facing the African American community. Although doors have recently opened and African Americans have obtained greater educational and occupational opportunities, there has been no fundamental change in the principles and ideologies that fuel racism.

Mentoring. African American women face an interesting challenge in searching for a mentor to monitor their progress and facilitate their professional development. The scarcity of African American women in first-line administration on campus makes it difficult to find enough mentors to meet demand. As a result, a functional but ironic professional alliance has often been formed between African American women and white men.

Balance and family. African American women often feel stretched to their limits physically, emotionally, and psychologically as they try to find and maintain a balance between personal and professional lives. They will not forgo their work and cannot abandon their communities. Balancing these equally important but conflicting factors continues to be a goal that often eludes their grasp.

Competence and confidence. Although confident of their abilities to lead, African American women too often find their competencies questioned by peers. These inquisitions do not seem to affect their sense of assurance, value, and worth, but the questions continue to contaminate their professional experiences. Despite the difficulties, many African American women aspire to and maintain leadership positions at predominantly white colleges and universities. What motivates them to pursue and persevere as leaders, which creates such hardship and discomfort in their lives? How do they cope with the oppositional environments?

Internal and External Motivations

Care for communities. Internally motivated to juggle their professional responsibilities with community commitments, African American women want to improve social and economic conditions for other African Americans and women in their schools and communities. They also work for the welfare of African Americans and women in their professional capacities.

Leave a legacy. African American women speak at length of wanting to make a difference and leave a legacy for other African Americans and women. They don't expect to directly benefit from their efforts, but they struggle for others who follow. Indeed, this nation's history is replete with African American women who were catalysts for extraordinary social change. Likewise, these contemporary women educational leaders see themselves as mechanisms for social and institutional change.

Justify their competence. African American women often must justify their professional abilities more frequently than their white and male colleagues. Whether confronted overtly or covertly, these women feel the frustration and degradation from having skills, abilities, and credentials questioned, accusations often motivated by misguided assumptions about the leadership abilities of women and minorities.

Perform without support. Although mentoring is necessary to the upward mobility of African American women aspiring to educational administration, few opportunities for support and guidance exist within the three women's schools. Given the absence of institutional efforts to correct current conditions, colleges and universities that employ these women clearly expect them to perform with equal skill and efficiency, despite less than equal support and assistance.

Adaptations to Manage Their Environments

African American women leaders demonstrate several internal coping mechanisms to resolve the conflicts they encounter and allow them to manage their lives.

Perceptions. Although issues of racism, sexism, and tokenism are very real problems for them, they do not affect these women personally, for they have chosen instead to change how they think about the issues. Most do not perceive racism and sexism as obstacles. Instead, they see them as issues and challenges to overcome. These women do not perceive race and gender as something that limits or confines them, either personally or professionally. They acknowledge the reality of the issues and decide to move forward.

Attitude. Similarly, although African American women's lives have been confounded by issues of racism, sexism, and tokenism, these women leaders do not develop a pessimistic attitude about their opportunities. They acknowledge racism and sexism as real and set forth to deal with both. This strategy is clearly adaptive, given their educational and professional aspirations; had they seen the issues as obstacles, they would have been unable to achieve their current success.

Family. Family commitments and support have emerged as one of the most critical variables to African American women's overall success. Whether the support comes from mothers, husbands, siblings, or children, these women felt they would not have risen to their current levels without the unwavering confidence of their families.

Community. Although community involvement created an additional layer of complexity in their lives, African American women in educational leadership often indicated that they could not imagine functioning otherwise. With built-in positive reinforcement, encouragement, and affirmation, their community responsibilities allow these women to persist professionally. They serve on boards and committees; they're highly sought and welcomed with open arms, a far cry from what usually happens at their schools. What sense of assurance and esteem their colleges take away, their community replaces.

Spirituality. The church has historically been and still remains one of the most critical components of the African American community. In a society in which minorities are frequently devalued and women often marginalized, African American women rely heavily on the church and spirituality for encouragement, guidance, training, and fellowship.

Presence as resistance. Many African American women leaders actively resist the notion that they must denounce their race and gender in order to reach high leadership positions. Further, they resist frequent assaults on their self-esteem and self-worth by immersing themselves in their communities, families, and churches—locations where they receive messages to the contrary.

By purposefully placing themselves where they were valued and respected, these women resisted the potential internalization of negative racial and gender stereotypes. They clearly and consistently resisted with vehemence and passion anything counterproductive to their health and well-being; their will to resist allowed them to persist as leaders.

Implications

If African American women are to get and keep leadership jobs in higher ed administration at predominantly white colleges and universities, they should

- Seek opportunities for involvement and leadership in communities external to their schools.
- Develop the ability to perceive racism and sexism more as negotiable challenges than as immovable obstacles.
- Seek opportunities for internal support both from other African American women and white men in higher ed administration. External sources of support are also critical for these women; family and spirituality stand as the most important resources.
- Not expect to receive traditional rewards for their work. Rather, there will be times to recognize and accept the rewards found in working for the greater good.

Conclusions

Although it's been more than thirty years since the passage of antidiscriminatory measures such as Title VII, Title IX, and affirmative action, it appears that very little progress has occurred. African American women continue to struggle with racism, sexism, and other policies and practices that exclude them from the very highest strata of higher ed administration.

Educational leaders across racial and gender lines must become more fully aware of the challenges that confront women and African American administrators at their schools. As we move toward a new millennium, it becomes critical for administrators to think carefully about how demographic changes will affect their schools and plan accordingly.

What Does It Take to Crack Higher Ed's Adobe Ceiling?

February 1999
Virginia Lopez Hansen
Associate Dean, Student Support Services, Southwestern College, California
"The awakening of the bicultural voice . . . is significant, given the forces of hegemony and cultural invasion at work in the manner that bicultural [administrators] perceive themselves, their communities, and their ability to participate in the world" (Darder, 1991). The number of women of color in higher education leadership is still significantly low. As a Latina administrator in a community college

pursuing a Ph.D. at the Claremont Graduate University, I wondered what factors contribute to my leadership role, style, and success. To learn more about my style and the styles of other women of color, I reviewed the literature and developed a conceptual framework: the college environment, persistence despite nonperformance barriers, and a bicultural identity influence the style of bicultural educational leaders.

The old boys' network works against women and people of color by excluding them from the informal settings where careers are made and broken. To advance, one must also project the right image and meet cultural norms. Black administrators refer to being stopped by a concrete ceiling that you can't see through or break. Women refer to a glass ceiling, a barrier so subtle that it's transparent, yet so strong that it prohibits women from moving up in administration. In Catholic colleges, it's a stained glass ceiling. Latinas call it the adobe ceiling, a term coined by Cecilia Burciaga, assistant dean at Stanford University. You can't see through it; it doesn't crumble; it's thick, dense, and made to last for centuries.

How have Latina administrators cracked the adobe ceiling? (I say cracked because it hasn't been broken.) In the fall of 1996, I interviewed seventeen Latina presidents and vice presidents of California community colleges to identify factors contributing to their success. Their voices reflected enthusiasm, tension, and commitment to their role of supporting students. Interviews centered on three areas: college environment, persistence factors, and bicultural identity.

College Environment

I examined the Latina administrators' perceptions of how the college environment affects their leadership role through the lenses of diversity and the problem-solving process. Three patterns of tension emerged.

1. The culture of governance of most community colleges was autocratic, whereas most Latina leaders used a participatory style in problem solving. Culture and cognitive differences were not discussed openly at the colleges. In addition, existing racism and sexism affected their participation in the decision-making process. Latina administrators adapted to their colleges' environments even if it meant living with tension.

2. The style differences between the Latina leader's participatory leadership style and the college decision-making process created a political tension, due to a struggle over who has the power of decision making. Tension occurred when the leader's participatory style, seeking collaboration and dialogue, contrasted with the political nature and structure of the college.

3. Embedded racism and sexism in institutional practices and behaviors also created tension. The hiring of bicultural administrators in key positions during

the last few years has resulted in shifts of how community college employees participate in governance behavior.

Successful Latina leaders either converted their leadership style to that of the college at the expense of their biculturalism or worked to transform their college's culture of gender and ethnic bias as well as problem-solving style.

Persistence Factors

Nonperformance obstacles included time required by their jobs and balancing work and family, political decisions and personnel issues that go against personal values, racism and sexism, pressure to make decisions along ethnic lines, difficult people, and decisive versus preemptory decisions.

Persistence strategies included support of family, personal values, working with and around instead of through racism and sexism, working harder than others and being competent, focused goals and objectives to obtain education and leadership positions, and self-confidence.

The Latina administrators' motivation to continue their leadership role was primarily their ability to influence the direction of their colleges for student success. They also liked their positions.

Bicultural Identity

They said their biculturalism required developing the abilities to

- *Integrate their culture* and that of the college into their leadership role.
- *Separate the home and college cultures;* only one felt she integrated both cultures into her unconscious behavior, whereas the others behaved only in the context of the Latina culture or the college culture.
- *Remain fair* in their leadership role and not just advocate or make decisions based on biculturalism.
- *Provide different perspectives,* values, and perceptions to their college governance structure.
- *Maintain bicultural identity* as leaders; a few indicated a need to change bicultural identity for success.

As women and people of color assume top leadership positions, they bring to the campus their biculturalism, leadership styles, and diverse problem-solving styles, which directly affect a college. Their leadership styles don't always mesh with their college's problem-solving styles, which results in the tension to either change or adapt to the college environment as a survival strategy.

The voices of the Latina leaders in this study expressed their struggles, desires, motivations, sacrifices, and rewards—all factors in becoming successful leaders.

Tribal Culture Supports Women in Campus Presidencies

December 1998
Bernita Krumm
Assistant Professor of Educational Leadership, North Dakota State University

In the past, leadership studies were generally studies of men; gender was rarely considered an important component because only men were thought of as leaders. In the twenty years from 1975 to 1995, women leaders of two- and four-year schools increased from 5 percent to 16 percent, and women led 27 percent of independent two-year schools, according to the American Council on Education's 1995 survey. But the woman leader is still an anomaly in most campus work arenas. In the tribal college, however, women fill many leadership positions. Women led ten of twenty-eight (39 percent) American Indian Higher Education Consortium member colleges in 1992 and ten of thirty-one member schools (32 percent) in 1996.

My Ph.D. study at the University of Nebraska examining the experiences of American Indian women tribal college presidents emphasizes their understanding and perceptions of their leadership roles. Models of leadership generally have common elements; they define a leader as one who has a vision, focuses on a mission, serves as a role model for others, and enables others to take action or perform their roles.

The four women leaders in my study possessed a trust that enabled them to open themselves to scrutiny by another person. Their trust, however, was not necessarily a trust in me; rather, each possesses a self-trust—a belief in herself, the people she works with, and the mission of the school she leads. They described it as faith, confidence, empowerment, and commitment.

Faith

Having faith in oneself is of primary importance in leadership. A leader must not only envision a distant goal but also believe herself capable of achieving it. Worrying about failure is counterproductive. The leader must take calculated risks and learn from her mistakes as well as her successes. She must build on the strengths of others and have faith in their abilities and expertise.

Janine Pretty On Top, founding president of Little Big Horn College (Crow Agency, Montana) stresses the value of giving others "ownership" and "voice" in decision making. She recognizes others' contributions to the success of the college and credits them for their achievements. She values teamwork, utilizing the skills of others and investing "confidence and faith and the resources" in others.

Confidence

Confidence gives a leader the tenacity to act on her faith despite adversity. Verna Fowler, founding president of College of the Menominee Nation (Keshena, Wisconsin), says her job as a leader is to be the "one who has a vision and has a direction worth heading. My job is to persuade the others to follow me in that direction." Fowler believes a leader must have high standards, high ethics, and a strong value system, and must model a sense of pride for others, "so others know you know something and have confidence in you." She prefers to give others "the opportunity to give their viewpoints," emphasizing the value of listening to others and allowing people to make their own decisions. "My role is to have faith, confidence, and trust in the faculty person."

Empowerment

Empowered is how followers feel when leaders have faith and confidence in them. Tanya Ward, president of Cheyenne River Community College (Eagle Butte, South Dakota), works to actively involve faculty and staff so that they develop a sense of ownership. She empowers others by sharing responsibilities and affirming their worth through recognition of their contributions. She views her presidential role pragmatically. "I don't see the position really as glamorous or as prestigious. It's doing the work."

Commitment

Leaders must not only be committed to their work and to those who work with them but also know how to create commitment in others. Value and respect for others help to create commitment. Margarett Campbell, former president of Fort Belknap College (Harlem, Montana), believes in the importance of value and respect for others. When leaders work hard and function well with others, they "enable others to do the same." She believes good leadership is "inclusive and participatory," involves a "broad base of opinions, values, and expertise," and is "encouraging." She admires a leader who is able "to make others believe in themselves."

Gender and Leadership

Social scientists generally contend there is no empirical basis for concluding that gender affects leadership style. Others believe women leaders are more concerned with interpersonal relationships and task accomplishment, value intimacy and nurturing in interactions with others, and use a more democratic and participative leadership style than do men. Women use communication to gain understanding and work to achieve consensus; men use communication to acquire power and to maintain majority rule.

Women view the leadership position as lonely and remote and would rather be in the center of things. Women leaders generally need to be extremely well qualified, have records of high accomplishments, and be overprepared for their positions.

The women in this study hold differing perceptions of the influence gender has on leadership. Tanya Ward believes there is a big difference in how men and women operate and are perceived as leaders. Women "have to work twice as hard" and show they are capable of leading. Verna Fowler contends that "men are more aggressive" and able to leave their problems at work. Margarett Campbell believes women are less authoritarian than men. Women are caretakers.

Women "tend to be more conciliatory, more participatory," and "morale within the institutions that are led by women tends to be higher. There's more cohesiveness, more unity . . . that whole family concept." Janine Pretty On Top analogizes: "Higher education is like housework; as soon as you get it done, there's just as much. It's like an avalanche, sweeping an avalanche. Scads to do."

Tribal Culture and Leadership

Cultural factors may provide some basis for the higher percentage of women in tribal college presidencies as compared to other higher education institutions. The tribes of the leaders in this study did not appear to create barriers that prevented women from assuming leadership positions. Janine Pretty On Top explains that women leaders may not be subject to the same criticism as women leaders in other cultures because Crow society is matriarchal and matrilineal. "So the line of the woman and leadership role of the woman in the family and decisions that are made in the family are very powerful. In some others, there could be criticism, I think, for so many women being administrators, or in particular my being an administrator. I think that it's going to be less so here."

In Crow society, leadership in education is congruent with the role of woman as caregiver and nurturer. "It's just a very important responsibility. It's not culturally in conflict; it's very complementary to the cultural role." However, Ambler cautioned in a 1992 article "Women Leaders in Indian Education" in *Tribal College Journal*, "The high-profile leadership of Indian women at tribal colleges does not necessarily reflect the status of women throughout Indian society. Education has always been a more acceptable avenue for female leadership and, as could be expected, the role of women varies among different tribes and cultural groups."

For the four women in this study, leadership is a lifestyle, an expression of learned patterns of thought and behaviors, values and beliefs. Culture formulates the purpose, process, and product, and the schools themselves; therefore, leadership is not separate from their culture.

To Be a Leader

Not all who lead choose to be leaders. In their 1987 book *The Leadership Challenge*, Kouzes and Posner wrote: "People who become leaders do not always seek the challenges they face. Challenges also seek leaders." None of the women in this study set out to be leaders; however, each stepped forward to answer a challenge and fill a need. Each has the self-trust that enables her to build faith and confidence in others, empowers her to act, and inspires her commitment.

In the spring 1995 issue of *Winds of Change*, in "American Indian Leadership 2000: A Community Road Ahead," author N. S. Hill wrote: "Great things are accomplished by ordinary people who are consumed with a dream. With no dreams and no vision, there can be no development. But energy and persistence will conquer all obstacles."

Lesbian Administrators Make Deeply Personal Choices

July 1998

You've just been appointed to a dean's committee. If you let the group know you're a lesbian, they may hear everything you say in terms of their stereotypes instead of listening to you seriously. On the other hand, keeping quiet means constant mental gymnastics balancing conflicting outward and inward conversations. What do you do?

Coming out as a lesbian is a calculated risk, HERS Mid-America Assistant Director Betsy Metzger learned. She interviewed fifty-five lesbian college and university administrators for her dissertation research at the University of Denver, where she'll get a Ph.D. in August. Neither age, rank, geography, nor school type emerged as a predictor of individual decisions about whether, when, or how to come out. Lesbians are quite diverse and their decisions deeply personal, she said at the NAWE conference in Baltimore in March 1998. Metzger believes lesbians at higher administrative levels are less likely to be out. About 90 percent of male presidents are married, whereas about 55 percent of women presidents are single. Reasons to be reticent are real.

Professional Discrimination: The Lavender Ceiling

Feeling out the institutional climate convinced some that their lesbian identity might stand in the way of being hired or promoted. "If I have to be something I'm not, then I don't want that job. But when you've trained all your life for something, it's hard to give it up." In 1995, Susanne Woods decided not to assume the presidency of the College of Wooster, Ohio, after media reported her being listed in a school directory as the partner of a woman who identified herself as a lesbian. A woman was interviewed but not offered a dean's job at SUNY-New Paltz last spring after a conservative state legislator called a press conference to label her a lesbian witch.

Stereotyping

Women who are openly lesbian must deal every day with comments, stereotypes, discomfort, or morbid fascination. Some decide it's not worth the bother.

Boundaries, Culture, and Personality

Some feel they can be more effective professionals by maintaining clear boundaries between private and professional lives. Some come from cultural backgrounds that emphasize personal privacy, and some are introverts who prefer not to talk about themselves at all.

Reasons for Coming Out

Although their environments rarely affirm their sexual orientation, each of the fifty-five administrators was at least somewhat open about her lesbian identity, or she couldn't have been included in the study. One said, "You have to give this some thought. You have to exercise a certain amount of caution because it's not always safe to be openly lesbian. It's not like you get some benefit from sharing this information." Still, in certain times and places, each decided the benefits of coming out made it worth the risks.

Motives Ranged from Political to Personal

Politics. For feminist lesbians who associate their sexual orientation with politics, coming out is necessary to change society. Many who came out during the civil rights movement are now in their forties and fifties and in top administrative positions.

Education. Some came out to counter widespread stereotypes of lesbians and gays. Although a lesbian who doesn't fit the stereotypes can easily pass as straight, she may decide that's all the more reason to go public.

Support for students. An openly lesbian administrator can make the campus feel safer for lesbian students who feel they're not alone and there's someone to talk to.

Relationship. A lesbian who lives with a partner must come out to claim domestic partner health benefits or to have her partner share the president's house. Before accepting the presidency of the University of Maine at Farmington, Theo Kalikow asked trustees if her female partner living in the president's house would bother them. (See Kalikow's article earlier in this chapter.)

Cultural heritage. An administrator with cultural links to the Holocaust felt she must not pass (as straight) because of the evil that's possible when good people don't come forward. The risks she ran personally as a lesbian frightened her less than the prospect of letting homophobic mores dominate the environment.

Peace of mind. The strongest internal motive was personal integration. Lesbians described this as "to be honest to myself," "to have my life be all of a piece," "not to have to remember who I've told," "to make my relationships with others more real."

Repeated Decisions

Unless you're Ellen DeGeneres, coming out isn't a one-time decision. Because sexual orientation is usually invisible, the decision arises over and over. Professors must come out to their students every semester. People who change jobs must decide whether to let their new employer know early in the application process, near the end of the process, after they get the job, or not at all. Many test the waters, sizing up people and schools before deciding how and what to communicate. They reveal themselves most among other lesbians. Some are open everywhere except at work. Some tell supervisors but not colleagues; some tell colleagues but not students. Lesbian mothers tend to stay very closeted to their children's teachers.

"People can accept and deal with anything, as long as you don't say 'lesbian.'" Just as there are diverse possible ways to express a lesbian identity—activities, relationships, spirituality, political activism, professional life, appearance, symbols, or artifacts—there are many different ways to communicate or obscure it. Without making a formal announcement, a lesbian who chooses to be out may

- Name and label her partner
- Be open about her activities and relationships
- Practice self-disclosure in general
- Bring a partner or date to events
- Invite colleagues to a shared home
- List her partner's name in the directory

One who decides to stay closeted at work can take advantage of other people's assumptions. To camouflage her orientation with silence or ambiguity, she may

- Use neutral pronouns
- Be vague about activities and relationships
- Avoid self-disclosure in general
- Come alone to events
- Present her male companion as a date
- Look and act different from stereotypes
- Chat about children, pets, or her ex-husband

Suggestions for Straight Colleagues

"I would like to be able to come out at work and not have it be a political issue at all. It's just a factor of my life. Just like I drive a maroon Subaru. I'm a lesbian," one interviewee said. "You talk about the fact that maybe I drive a Subaru and I really like a Subaru, and do you like it better than your Mazda or something like that. But it's not, 'I drive a maroon Subaru,' and 'Gasp! My god!' and people go running out of the room."

What they wanted most was honor and respect as individuals; being a lesbian is just one of many identities. They suggested ways that both institutions and individuals can improve the campus climate.

Voice your support. Express your offense at gay-bashing comments or jokes. Display a "safe space" triangle sign or magnet in your office; wear a button that says "Straight but not Narrow." Attend gay, lesbian, bisexual, and transgender events on campus and get other heterosexuals to go; it can mean a lot to students. Support gay causes and gay-owned businesses financially.

Acknowledge your lesbian colleague's life. Inquire about her partner as you might about family members. "The people that I appreciate the most are the ones who can incorporate who I am and who my relationship is with into their thought process without stumbling over it," one said. Don't ask her to take her partner's picture off her desk; no one calls heterosexuals flagrant when they display family pictures and wear wedding rings.

Include your lesbian colleague socially. An invitation that says "and guest" is more welcome than one that says "and spouse." Don't make assumptions based on stereotypes; she might enjoy "shopping with the girls," after all. Make sure the inclusion is sincere and not for effect; "I don't want them to use our relationship as an opportunity to get their political correctness cards updated."

Don't shun contact. Being gay is not contagious, and most lesbians have no romantic interest in heterosexuals. "I want my straight friends to feel that they can hug me without it being misinterpreted. I want them to feel that they can be comfortable in my home, even if it's just the two of us for dinner."

Don't assume a heterosexual norm. Identify yourself as heterosexual sometimes to show that you don't assume everyone is. If you mention a lesbian mother in a discussion on parenting, identify someone else as a heterosexual mother. Try using *partner* for a mate of either gender. Don't assume that a single woman who never mentions relationships is available for overtime.

Treat lesbians as individuals. "I would like to be treated as just a person. This is just one dimension of my identity, not the most important." Lesbians are very diverse, with no single cultural norm; don't let the image of "lesbian" overshadow every other aspect of her identity.

Recognize your heterosexual privilege. "I want them to understand the deliberateness with which I need to lead my life. And I don't want them to treat me any differently because of that. I don't want them to patronize me because of that; I just want them to know that it's a little bit harder for me to do what I do. And that they have a role in making that a little bit easier, because they are part of the dominant culture and how they advocate for me, and how they talk about me with their children, and how they talk about me in professional contexts is part of what they *can* do to change the world. That they as allies carry a separate set of powers that I can never have, being a lesbian, and I want them to use those powers to make the world a better place."

Sarah Gibbard Cook

Stained Glass Ceiling Challenges Women in Catholic Schools

August 1994

It was quiet subversion, a group of about two hundred women working in eighty Catholic institutions of higher education, swapping ideas and encouragement to improve the status of women in their traditionally patriarchal campus environments. At Loyola University of Chicago last month, the second conference of the new National Association for Women in Catholic Higher Education met to reclaim respect for the past contributions by women religious and shape the future of women in Catholic higher education. Never have so many women named Mary assembled, a product of their ages and their faith.

Claiming the Past

Women religious have been stereotyped as toiling in obscurity for centuries. In reality, they "developed creative strategies to become more independent of bishops, spiritual directors, and the male branches of their respective congregations," according to Florence Deacon of Cardinal Stritch College in Milwaukee.

Her research on early sisterhoods in Wisconsin showed that the needs of immigrant Catholics in the early nineteenth century demanded the sisters' individual talents and skills and gave mothers superior a source of power in conflicts with bishops or clergy. She notes: "By 1900, mothers superior might be responsible for the well-being and ministry of over 2,000 members, real estate worth over $600,000 or investments of $150,000. They were CEOs in all but name, and the essential services sisters performed made them valued partners of bishops and priests."

Keeping Women in Math, Sciences

According to Kelli J. Armstrong, a Ph.D. candidate in education at Boston College who studied women in the 1993 first-year class, there is evidence of "a negative relationship between students raised in traditional Catholic environments and persistence in the math and science fields." Introducing role models and advising in math and science early in the college experience can increase persistence. Any solutions, say Kathy Vargas and Janet Kerner of St. John's University in Jamaica, New York, must consider both the lack of relevant courses for girls to take in high school and the view many women have that careers in math and sciences are antisocial in nature—both increase what the two call "leakage in the pipeline." Among the solutions are exposing students to the challenges of science and technology, showing how they help solve human problems, and making role models and mentors readily accessible.

Nonreligious Leaders

Laywomen now lead more Catholic schools. From 1986 to 1990, the percentage of women religious presidents dropped from 35 percent of all women presidents to 25 percent. Only 8 percent of the new appointments were women religious.

The change is happening by the design of the orders and by the necessity of the colleges. Lucy Morros, president of Barat College, Illinois, offered ideas to preserve the founding spirit and rich heritage. She suggests: Vigilantly maintain the number of religious representing the founding congregation on the board, as set in bylaws, and orient all new board members on the history, tradition, and role of the congregation. Tap into alumni who provide the school's oral history and make fine mentors. Involve the congregation by inviting a member to serve on the president's cabinet to focus on mission integration. Help faculty and students stay connected to the school's tradition and spirit through orientations, workshops, and activities that focus on the school's mission. Link students to national networks for summer or service projects. Cancel classes for all-school events to emphasize core values. And look to similar schools for ideas.

Of Lions and Lambs

Patricia McGuire, president of Trinity College in Washington, D.C., noted that in the biblical reference "The lion shall lie down with the lamb," nobody mentions how much sleep the lamb got. She called on the group to become powerful lambs, to assure that "there shall be no sleep for the lions. The last thing we need is lambs huddled together bleating in the field, too scared to go to the edge and bring back their lost ones."

Catholic higher education is now a diverse environment serving adult learners, people of color, and those of different faiths, McGuire noted. (An estimated 25 percent of the conference participants were not Catholic.) "The model of the last 125 years just doesn't work very well."

Future leaders in Catholic higher education must balance strong constitutions with prudent recklessness, restore belief that faith and culture can be balanced, and rescue a crumbling infrastructure. Asserting that there is "more caution than creativity and more foreboding than freedom" in Catholic higher education today, she asked, "If we keep heading in the same direction, who's going to want the leadership jobs? And if you want the job, doesn't that mean you're too dangerous to have it?"

Transformational changes must occur within the schools, she warned, requiring passionate leadership and vision by those who must be aggressively faithful, and those leaders are likely to be women. "With women heading Duke University and the University of Pennsylvania, how long will it be before a woman sits in the president's office at Notre Dame?" she asked.

To do this, leaders must "talk like a scholar and think like a gambler," she said with tongue in cheek. "Know every student by their first name, talk with the gardener, and never be seen as controlling, decisive, vacillating, angry, or tired." Future leaders will hold positions throughout their schools, "not at the top of pyramids but at the center and edges of interlocking circles."

McGuire urged women in Catholic schools to keep their credibility not by playing the role of outsiders or victims or by being silent, but by "finding ways to be at the table and speak up, creating change from within." The goal is to help women be the best they can be, she reminded. "We are educating the next generation of leaders." McGuire said she wants to be remembered for "ensuring that there shall be no sleep for the lions."

Tough Questions Answered

How do you remain true to yourself, impact the institution, and do the job you're paid to do, without being co-opted by the structures that are inherently hierarchical and patriarchal? Create alternative communities within the institution, such as women's studies programs or departments led by women on campus. (Marilyn Frye, in *Willful Virgin*, says people who believe in equity and women's rights can conscientiously hold and use their positions within the establishment if they are "simultaneously cultivating skills, attitudes, identity, and an alternative community" so that eventually they can function without their positions and meanwhile stay honest.)

As women, how can we be role models for our women students to remain in Jesuit-Catholic schools when they see women marginalized there? We have a duty to teach our women students to be critical consumers of knowledge and reach their own conclusions. One said, "Our mothers didn't defeat the dragons, but they made sure we'd live through their fire breath."

Why not just leave? Wouldn't you be happier away from ecclesiastical ties? One woman answered: "Why should I leave, and leave them [men] all the churches and schools and great works of art" that women helped create over the centuries?

Mary Dee Wenniger

Advice on Being the "Other" on a Catholic Campus

October 1998

On any campus with a religious identity or well-entrenched cultural norms, some experience themselves as different or "other." It's rarely as comfortable as being in the majority. Barbara Deck says women who feel marginalized on campus can reposition themselves closer to the center without compromising who they are. With a Ph.D. in the history of ideas from Brandeis University and an M.B.A. from Harvard, Deck describes herself as a "freelance feminist liberal activist." She's executive director of the EIKOS Community Centers in Newton, Massachusetts, and does training in peer counseling and leadership skills, with an emphasis on women and "recovering Catholics."

At her workshop, "Being the 'Other' on Catholic Campuses: Not Only Non-Catholics" at the June 1998 conference of the National Association of Women in Catholic Higher Education (NAWCHE), she invited participants to ask themselves the following questions:

- How do you feel different or "other"?
- Why are you at a Catholic school?
- What's positive about the experience?
- What's difficult about it?
- How might partnerships and allies help?
- What can you contribute as an ally?

To her surprise, two-thirds of the women in the workshop were Catholic. Religion was not the main reason the women felt like an "other" at their schools; neither was sexual orientation. Instead, women who feel out of place on a Catholic campus often say it's because they're feminists. Although the church's traditions of social justice support feminism on some campuses, elsewhere feminism seems to violate the cultural norm.

Colleges Founded by Women

Deck opened the workshop by asking participants which kind of Catholic college or university they're affiliated with. Women's experience of being "other" varies tremendously according to whether the school was founded by women or men. Women who teach at colleges founded by women's religious orders tend to feel a great deal of support. "Most nuns are feminists themselves," she said. Nuns have chosen to live in a community of women. They're in the forefront of efforts to include women within the church. They're movers and shakers for social justice, associating feminism broadly with fairness toward all those oppressed.

A feminist may feel very much at home at a Catholic college led by women with feminist sympathies. If she's part of a minority on campus because she is Protestant or Jewish or African American, she benefits from the ideals of acceptance and inclusiveness affirmed by leaders. Feminists at such schools may be so comfortable that they don't realize how much the women at some other colleges and universities need their support.

Women on the Margin

Colleges and universities founded by male religious orders or a diocese aren't always so supportive. Patriarchal traditions still run strong. Negative images of women color the response to those who aren't quiet and submissive. Women's studies and women's centers are lightning rods for patriarchal reaction. Unlike the nuns who equate feminism with justice in the broadest sense, some male religious leaders associate feminism with sexual issues like abortion and homosexuality. Trash has been swept into the women's center on at least one Catholic campus.

A student or faculty member who finds herself the only woman in a theology department full of priests may feel doubly marginalized for her gender and her theology. Not all priests understand or welcome the feminist theology that has blossomed since the 1970s. The isolation may feel even more acute if the priests went to seminary together, forming a kind of old boys' club. Similar issues can fester in departments like history or English, where feminists appear to violate a secular canon. A complicating factor is *Ex Corde Ecclesiae,* the 1990 papal declaration authorizing bishops to make sure that what happens on Catholic campuses is consistent with Catholic doctrine. Academic administrators and faculty of both sexes risk punitive action if they don't comply.

"To be a feminist is becoming an occupational hazard at some universities," according to Sharlene Hesse-Biber, NAWCHE executive director, who attended Deck's workshop. "The sad thing is that people felt they couldn't speak. They've lost their voice in the silencing of difference."

Moving Toward the Center

Deck encourages women who've been pushed to the margin to try to find a powerful and positive approach to regaining the center. Quite apart from any feelings of victimization, she suggests looking for common ground with the university's leaders and stated ideals. To the woman whose offices were targeted for harassment, Deck suggested that instead of treating the university president as part of the problem, she could approach him positively by saying, "Father X, I expect you to be my best ally." He may share her dislike of interference from the bishop, whether or not he's willing to say so. He probably dislikes disorder and vandalism and feels some responsibility for what happens on campus.

"Claim the high ground," Deck suggested. Make the most of the high ideals in whose name the school was founded. If you're at a school established by Franciscans or Dominicans, study the values of St. Francis or St. Dominic and find ways to present yourself as the true Franciscan or Dominican. Women who feel comfortable and secure on Catholic campuses need to recognize the problems of those who don't. Catholic and non-Catholic women need to form alliances. Women who support each other can counter the loneliness that's sometimes the most painful part of being "other" on a Catholic campus.

Sarah Gibbard Cook

CHAPTER THREE

DRIVER'S ED: DEVELOPING LEADERSHIP SKILLS

Because women leaders on campus are often strangers in a strange land, trying to survive and thrive in alien territory, it's useful to have a crash course in driver's education. Although today's women in academia may complain of a bumpy road, the pioneer women on campus would respond, "I built that road."

Leaders have found two effective strategies to end their isolation in alien departments and schools: networking and mentoring. By gathering together to share stories, observations, strategies, and tactics, they can support each other and a common goal of gender equity. Conferences, publications, associations, mentoring, and campuswide gatherings are effective tools to help women become leaders on a campus that may be chilly or downright hostile.

This chapter deals with how women can build on their inherent leadership skills by first defining leadership in a much broader sense. Leaders can be those who have the powerful titles or those whose personal power propels them into becoming change agents for a campus, no matter what their nominal job on campus.

Section One deals with general leadership concepts: What is leadership? How does it differ for women? What survival strategies serve women administrators? How do you use mentoring and your current environment to develop leadership skills?

Section Two offers coaching in specific skills that women need for success on campus: a list of competencies helpful to community college presidents, information on how to choose your battles, instruction on how and why to play politics, advice on how to negotiate and use humor, and tips on how to get around those in your way.

Section Three features first-person narratives by those who have been there, to help new leaders survive their first days and months in their new jobs. Because critics are harder on women leaders and less likely to forgive their mistakes, this section is especially important to block the revolving door and increase the critical mass of women in campus leadership positions.

SECTION ONE: GENERAL LEADERSHIP SKILLS FOR WOMEN

What's Leadership? The Ability to Influence a Situation

October 1999

It's a piece of cake to identify those with big titles as campus leaders. But what about the librarian who was able to end the reign of a terrorist community college president? Leadership involves getting passionate about an issue that's important to you and putting in the energy to affect the outcome. "Leadership opportunities exist virtually everywhere for everyone," said Anita M. Pampusch, president of the Bush Foundation, a nonprofit in Minneapolis, who keynoted the annual conference of Wisconsin Women in Higher Education Leadership in La Crosse, Wisconsin, in September.

"Leadership is the ability to influence a situation. It can be large and visible, or it can be more modest, like in a classroom or an office or a task force or a local school board," she said. "It's not limited to just a few charismatic individuals."

Management Versus Leadership

Pampusch differentiated between management, a task-oriented approach that focuses on keeping the in-box empty, and leadership, which demands creating time for reflection on the big things. "Leaders must look ahead, establish a vision, set goals and strategies, and get others to help achieve them," she said.

Although higher education is now more amenable to women leaders than before, it's still based on a male model. The expectation is that the (male) academic makes a lifetime commitment to the career, his job is his first priority, and he has set times to move to the next step; the role of a woman is to be the trailing spouse who remains responsible for care of the home and children. "The model is not changing as fast as the composition of the workplace," Pampusch said, although higher education offers more flexibility than business, especially on the teaching side, where to some extent women can choose where and when they work.

Women Making Progress on Campus

Now women are about 18 percent of college and university presidents, she estimated. "I remember when it was 1 percent." There are more women faculty, although they are still concentrated in the arts and humanities and lag in engineering and the sciences. More women are administrators, although they are much more likely to work in public relations, fund-raising, and student affairs than in finance or the computer center.

Nationwide, women are the majority of students at 52 percent and have reached parity with men in earning bachelor's and master's degrees, but not yet doctoral degrees. Pampusch applauded the "growth in how people see the world and use the talents of women" and advised women that the best way to advance is to "make small changes in our own behavior" rather than trying to change the entire system.

How did she come to administration? "I've always liked to talk and been interested in ideas," she explained, having assumed she'd wind up as a philosophy professor. Instead, she got involved in a lot of committees, where her leadership talents emerged. "It's also true of a lot of undergraduates," Pampusch said. "They think their job will be in their major discipline, but it's the totality of what you bring" to the table that determines where you will contribute.

Lessons Learned

Pampusch shared what she has learned over her three decades as a leader in higher education.

Grab the opportunities that come along. Besides your current job, consider committees, professional organizations, and interim positions as opportunities to grow. "Oh, no, I don't have the qualifications" is a typical woman's response to being asked to consider applying for an advancement, she said, whereas more than one businessman has told her, "After I retire, I'd like to be a college president."

Pampusch recalled her first administrative job, as acting dean at the College of St. Catherine in St. Paul, where she got to "try it out to see if I liked it" after the dean left. She did and stayed. The same thing happened later when the president left, and she got to be acting president. Because she wasn't a member of the religious order, she was ineligible to be the real president. But when the presidential search failed and the board dropped that qualification in 1984, she got the job.

Hard work is essential. Do your current job well, and do your homework, especially for committees and task forces, which are how higher education gets things done. Don't be like the man who admits in a committee meeting, "I haven't read the proposal, but I think . . ." Instead, she recommends reading up on the issue, thinking about it, talking to people, and contributing to the meeting.

Don't defer to others when you have something to say. Research shows that in mixed groups, women don't speak up. Even at the prestigious Harvard Institutes for administrators, women have a tendency to revert to high school behavior—staying silent and letting the men control the discussion. If you do speak up, most of the time you'll find that others will tell you later that they agreed with your statement but hesitated to say anything.

Master the art of public speaking and thinking on your feet. "The best ideas won't go anywhere unless they're expressed," Pampusch said, noting that both Mount Holyoke and Smith College in Massachusetts now require a course in public speaking.

Pick your fights. "I'm the kind who wanted to fix everything," Pampusch confessed, but she's finally learned to figure out what's important and worth putting her life on the line for, and learned to live with other things that aren't right. The basic question is: What are the overall consequences of the decision? She gave two examples: a faculty member who didn't get tenure because he lacked a Ph.D. then sued for bias based on national origin. Although school leaders were ready to capitulate, she advised them not to because it would set a terrible precedent for the school in giving tenure. In another case, an independent alumnae association was resisting closer coordination with the school, with an important capital campaign looming. She met with alumnae leaders regularly for a year, especially twenty who were committed to the current structure, and finally was able to resolve the issue to her satisfaction.

Establish a professional network and use it. "You need to be able to call and ask for advice," she said, which most people are flattered to be asked for. "Think of it as asking for a consultant." She described how, as head of the Bush Foundation, she routinely uses that technique in evaluating grant proposals. "Find out who's the best, and talk to them about it," as she recently did about a proposal to increase minority retention.

Establish a personal network and use it. "When the going gets rough, you need to have friends you can rant and rave to," she advised.

Find balance in your life. "What's important to keep you functioning optimally?" she asked. Some say exercise and health, some devote themselves to their family, some focus on spiritual values. Whatever trips your trigger, go for it. You're not being selfish but taking care of yourself. Membership in several groups of women helps Pampusch regularly discuss things of importance to her.

Play to your strengths. Nobody can be your exact role model, she said.

"I'm a conceptual person, and I need help at taking ideas and finding pathways to make them happen," she admitted, recalling a vice president at St. Catherine's who was excellent at this. Don't be a square peg in a round hole without a carpenter around. "Otherwise, you won't be happy and productive," she advised.

Be faithful to your values. They are part of your inner life, be they moral, work, intellectual, personal, or religious values. "It's important to remain consistent," she said, "which is called integrity." Some assume a lack of integrity goes with the job of being an administrator, she said, recalling being told, "You're not devious enough to be an administrator." Instead, Pampusch cited a book called *Habits of the Heart,* in which U.C. Berkeley sociologist Robert Bellah reported that the happiest people were those who liked their work and felt it contributed to the community.

Whatever you do your attitude is important. Again citing Bellah, she said people can look at their work as a job, where they just punch in and punch out; as an occupation, where they focus on how to get promoted; or as a calling, which requires commitment and service. He found those who considered their work a calling had the most personal passion, happiness, and satisfaction. Pampusch said she hoped each woman would consider her own job a calling to leadership in higher education.

Mary Dee Wenniger

Fencing as a Metaphor for Women as Leaders

May 1998
With a leap and flick of a fencing foil, Barbara Baxter Pillinger started an engaging discussion of similarities between the sport of fencing and women as leaders at the NAWE annual conference in Baltimore in March. "Through athletics, we learn to win with grace and lose with dignity," she said. "That's also part of leadership. Sometimes we're the captain, sometimes the first mate or the deckhand. And sometimes we sit at the end of the bench, waiting to be discovered."

A women's fencing coach before becoming a professor of student development and athletics in the department of educational policy and administration at the University of Minnesota, Pillinger demonstrated fencing moves as she spoke.

Timing Is Everything

"In fencing, as in leadership, timing is everything," she said. "It's vital to know when to go all out, when to hold your ground, and when to retreat." Before the bout begins, opponents take time to acknowledge each other with a salute of their foils. Leaders should too. Pillinger said that, like chess, fencing is both an art and a science. And like leaders, participants must be in a ready *en garde* position. "You're not exactly going anywhere, but you're ready to move: loose, light, and fluid."

Demonstrating the lunge, she said its key components are keeping a vision of the target, deciding when to move, moving quickly and decisively, and recovering. "After a lunge, whether or not we hit the target, we need to recover back to the *en garde* position," she said. To reinforce the need to keep an eye on the target as part of a big picture, both in fencing and in leadership, she recited: "As you wander on through life, whatever be your goal, keep your eye upon the doughnut and not upon the hole."

Plan Your Next Move

Pillinger demonstrated some subtle, indirect attack movements that fencers and leaders use as tools.

- *The cutover coupé,* where you cut over your opponent's blade, takes you indirectly from point A to point C through point B. For leaders, point B could be another person or group.
- *The disengage,* cutting under another's blade, is another indirect strategy for testing the waters, feeling out the situation before deciding on a path.
- *The double disengage,* which may confuse your opponent, returns you to the original line of attack.
- *The ballestra* is a very aggressive combination jump and lunge used to surprise the opponent. "People do not respond well to surprises," Pillinger said, so the move should be used quite judiciously.
- *The parry* deflects an opponent's thrust, which leaders perform by using a clever or evasive reply or remark to ward off criticism or hostile questioning.
- *The riposte,* a sharp, swift thrust made after parrying an opponent's lunge, is an offensive action that absorbs the motion. In leadership, a verbal riposte can be very effective.

"Women often fail at the fencing and chess aspects of leadership because they fail to plan and anticipate their next moves," Pillinger noted. After your move, you need a plan to counter your opponent's response and a tertiary counterattack move as well. "After the thrust and lunge, when we're parried, we tend to stop there," she said. "We need to learn to counter and come back, maybe straight back or maybe with a disengage. Leaders do a lot of parrying back and forth."

Often, women leaders fail to riposte by speaking up. Women hold it in and tend to get angry, she said, which can lead to "good old, middle-aged depression." She advised them instead to go ahead without fear.

Fencing and Leadership Are Solo Sports

The fencer and the leader who sets the tone for the organization are really alone, Pillinger noted, and each must choose her own countermoves, unlike team sports where members huddle to plan the next move. "Women need to prepare mentally by getting into a pattern and practice of leadership," she said.

Participants suggested that women can learn from previous contests if they engage in a healthy "constructive reflection." Instead, women often get mired in "rumination." They dwell on the issue too long, beating themselves up for their perceived failures and refusing to disengage. In contrast, men say, "The game's over, let's move on"—which is why competing male attorneys can go at each other's throats in court, then share a drink afterward.

Ellen Plummer, head of the women's center at Duke University, observed that today's women are learning to play sports with teammates "who are not my best friend." The skills they develop in team sports prepare them for the real world, where teammates are not always buddies, contests are impersonal, and players get practice at winning and losing and coming back at it another time.

Women in leadership roles find the game is never over and they continue to carry their baggage. A woman said, "I had to lose with dignity, learn to recover, so I could go back with a clean slate, saying 'OK, you won yesterday, and today's my day.'" Humor works well to lighten the exchange.

Course Joins Theory to Practice

Pillinger uses fencing terms to join theory and practice in an honors colloquium on women and leadership in the College of Liberal Arts. Last year's first class of seventeen female students had guest speakers, films, and a closing celebration. In the biographical approach to leadership, students read and orally report on outstanding female leaders including Margaret Mead, Eva Perón, Margaret Thatcher, Madeleine Albright, and Eleanor Roosevelt. Like women in leadership, Pillinger said, foil fencing relies on disciplined, subtle movements. "If you use wild and wondrous moves like Zorro, your opponent will definitely prevail."

Mary Dee Wenniger

Survival Strategies for Women Administrators

August 1994
Sometimes it's not a matter of advancement but simply of survival to balance the conflicting demands, lack of time, and limited resources available to women

administrators on campus. Participants at a session at the conference of Catholic Women in Higher Education at Loyola University in July shared their ideas on how to get it all done "in jobs where the desk is never clear and the phone always rings."

Facilitator Carol Hurd Green, associate dean of the College of Arts and Sciences at Boston College, finds support from an associate deans' roundtable, a group of middle administrators from fourteen institutions in the Boston area. Meeting regularly, group members share problems, solutions, and support.

Other Specific Suggestions

Work late one night a week. Free from phone and personal interruptions, you can get as much done in one evening as in a whole day. And it assures that the other four weeknights, you can walk away from it all without the slightest feeling of guilt or temptation to take anything home with you. "I never take work home," one woman stated.

Prioritize demands on your time. Try to separate what's really important that *you* need to do, what you can delegate, and what you can lose that nobody really cares about. "I make it a point not to do some things until I'm asked for them twice, which shows that somebody really wants it done," one administrator explained. Delegation is the key, another said. "If they can do it, why deprive them of the chance?" A third described listing all the individual tasks done in her department, including answering the phone, teaching, writing the syllabi, contacting alumni, and so on. By deciding who can do them most effectively, department members were able to reorganize the workload and spread it more efficiently between department staff, faculty, and the chair.

Take time to play. One administrator attributes going cross-country skiing almost every lunchtime in winter to improving her mental health. If you allow yourself to burn out, you're no longer any good to anyone.

Become involved with other groups outside the school sharing information on work and career with others from different kinds of schools, organizations, and interests. It gives you a new perspective on your own situation.

Go out into the community for power. By becoming a force in the community, you command more power within your own institution. And you develop skills and contacts helpful on campus.

Meet with new women faculty regularly to keep them on track and help them learn the organizational culture so that they can succeed, a department chair suggests.

Publish a newsletter each semester to communicate vision and concerns for your unit. Getting the message out in black and white leaves little room for errors in interpretation.

Establish a forum for conversation with women at all levels on your campus, across all employee groups, to remove the isolation some women may feel.

Fight to stay focused on two or three things that you really want to accomplish in your area. You can't do it all, so concentrate on what is most important to you. Consider both personal and professional goals. The corollary is being willing to let go of those things that are peripheral to your main focus. Refer to your school's mission statement. Ideally your priorities will contribute to the mission, so it becomes another source of support. If not, work to rewrite the mission statement so that it shows a respect for humans, not dogma or patriarchal values.

Choose your institution carefully. "I knew there were problems there," one administrator said. "My mistake was in thinking that the higher-ups wanted to correct them." Check it out before you check in.

Take time to reflect on the impact of your decisions before you make them. New administrators particularly may tend to see the trees, without taking time to step back and examine their vision of the forest. One new chair found that her predecessor became a friendly mentor and helped her to step back from the details to see the bigger picture.

Remain true to yourself and your values not co-opted by patriarchal structures within the institution. Some find it important to develop their own spirituality and work to change the focus of the school to one of service and spirituality.

Remember that being in administration offers you a chance to make a big difference, giving you the resources and voice to turn your vision into a reality. A few dark days and too much work are part of the price you pay for the privilege of changing the world, one little corner at a time.

Mary Dee Wenniger

So You Think You Wannabe an Assistant Dean. . . .

August 1998

For many faculty women, the job of assistant or associate dean seems like a good starter position, a way to test the waters of administration before making the leap. Carol Hurd Green, associate dean of arts and sciences at Boston College, reflected on the role of midlevel administrators at the biennial conference of the National Association for Women in Catholic Higher Education, held in Washington, D.C., in June.

"An assistant or associate dean is charged with the academic care of students," said Green. Her multidimensional job is advising students, faculty, parents, and other administrators. "As midlevel administrators, we stand at the interface of several constituencies, not as policy makers but as those who nurture, advocate, interpret, and facilitate," she said, a common role for women.

The Role of Nurturing

"Students come to us with problems, and they expect to be listened to seriously and their problems to be solved," she said. The core of her students at Boston College are traditional, full-time residentials ages eighteen to twenty-one. Advising has become a real problem, Green notes. Complaints about advising have skyrocketed in recent years as students have become obsessive about their demands.

The Role of Advocating

"We are the critical advocates for students, petitioning on their behalf to the faculty when it's appropriate," Green said. There are huge gaps in the analysis of requirements, and a student may have this or that problem with a faculty member or administrator. Credibility with the faculty is crucial, she warned: "Be awfully careful that you're trusted by the faculty" or your effectiveness will suffer.

The Role of Interpreting

As the academic middlepersons on campus, assistant and associate deans spend a good deal of their time interpreting and explaining the rules to everyone, the faculty to the students, the students to the faculty, the culture of the school, everything to the parents.

The increasing number of adjunct and part-time faculty need even more help to understand their students, Green said. On campus for less time, they're less likely to understand or communicate a school's culture and tradition. Even full-time faculty require help because they're under heavy pressure to produce more. Some may have just one office hour a week.

Meanwhile, students are becoming astute consumers: "We're paying for our education, and we expect certain things in return." In response, Green says midlevel administrators must be aware of the need to listen to students and recognize their rights. Letters from administrators may sound clear to the authors, but often students simply don't understand what they mean.

"Parent advising" also takes time because parents see the dean's office as representing the school. "We're the people they have access to," Green notes. "Our phones ring constantly, and appointment books fill up with parental concerns like 'Why didn't you know he hasn't been attending class?' or 'Why can't you stop the professor from harassing my child (that is, making him do the work)?'"

The Role of Facilitating

Dealing with so many constituencies brings many different viewpoints to the table, so midlevel administrators often find themselves negotiating between them. "We have to know the rules," Green warned. "As women in a Catholic institution, we should see what we do as not only representing the institution but within the frame of social justice," Green said. "In these encounters, we need to ask ourselves what are the prejudices and privileges we bring to the issue. We need to genuinely see the need in each party, which can be a way to understand what we do, what women have always done."

But sometimes she's torn between doing what's best for the school and what's best for the individual. "The research suggests that once you get to a certain level, you have to make choices and trade-offs. I made a lot of decisions I do not feel good about on a personal level, yet the good of the institution must come before the good of the individual."

She suggested the 1960s viewpoint of faculty seeing administrators as their enemy is inaccurate today. Socializing new faculty to the joint responsibilities of faculty and administrators to serve the school's mission is far better.

What's the Role of Women?

Participant Patricia Ann Matthews, vice president of academic affairs at Marywood University, Pennsylvania, noted that unlike Green's, her job deals with "the hard things" that directly affect the school's bottom line: reading computer printouts, administering an annual budget of $27 million, and hiring and firing people.

To get more women into top administrative jobs like hers, she's tried to prepare and mentor several women who have ultimately rejected the role. "They don't like it very much. It doesn't fit into their idea of a good, whole, well-balanced lifestyle," Matthews said. "They don't want to spend their time doing the kinds of things I do."

But that's exactly where more women are needed, making policy decisions that affect more than just one person. Green said that a recent meeting of thirty-five policy-making administrators of New England colleges had only seven female participants; women dominate in the advising area. She suggested the shortage of women in policy-making jobs may be a matter of access as much as choice.

Mary Dee Wenniger

Thinking About Becoming a Dean?

October 1996
Mary Ann O'Donnell
Dean, School of Arts, Manhattan College, New York

I always wanted to be an orchestra conductor. I find deaning is not terribly different. Sections are all different shapes, sizes, sounds, and especially temperaments. You must get them to talk and especially listen to each other and convince them to take some direction (God forbid), even from you.

Trumpets do not like to talk to second fiddles. As conductor, you have to hear the whole opus all at once, trying to control the section that wants to be the loudest, to develop the weakest sound so that it has a voice, and to cope with one or two players who are always out of step or out of tune. The fascinating aspect is that the conductor must always be one full beat ahead of the orchestra so that her mind hears the melody not as it is played but as it is about to be played. The mind is always in the future as the eye and ear are always in the present. All this must be done with style and grace, and in public.

More women, and more laywomen, are planning for administrative careers now that more jobs are open, especially in Catholic colleges. As you consider possibilities, look for opportunities to test your resolve in handling problems—because it's almost all a dean does—and to assess your ability to motivate faculty, leading the disparate orchestra. I've been told: "The job of the faculty is to think for the college; of the president, to speak for the college; of the dean, to keep the faculty from speaking and the president from thinking."

If you aspire to a career in administration, test the waters early to see if you have the interest, skills, and resolve to manage. Consider how you interact with others and your potential to keep presidents from thinking and faculty from speaking.

When to Become an Administrator

Consider switching from the classroom to the administrator's office either early in your career or after teaching about fifteen years. Becoming an administrator at age forty-five offers little time to go higher: provost, academic vice president, or even president. The average shelf life for a dean these days is about eight years: all the bad decisions we make in our first three years come back to haunt us in year eight, and it's time to move on, up, or out. Returning to the classroom after deaning is problematic because you know too much about your colleagues and may have made some painful decisions about them. Can you then rejoin them?

There is value to coming to administration after about fifteen years of teaching. You are at least an associate professor and an established scholar. If you choose an administrative career early, even right after graduate school, plan carefully. Today's wisdom is to get tenure before moving up; I've seen good candidates for dean blocked because they hadn't gone up for tenure. Some feel they couldn't understand the process without having undergone it; others are seen as trying to escape tenure by switching to administration.

A new breed of administrator chooses not to be tenured, and more schools offer nontenure-track administrative jobs to outsiders. This can set up a dual system, with deans from inside keeping tenure and those from outside having no chance to achieve it. Or schools may ask inside candidates to resign tenure to become administrators.

Where to Become an Administrator

Taking an administrative job at another school gives you a clean slate and no baggage, but every special interest group and self-involved person will be chewing on you even before you reach your new assignment. You must quickly sort out shades of truth and varieties of reality. If you move to another school, be sure of the fit. Understand its problems, ethos, mission, as well as what it thinks is its mission, and what it suggests is its mission through its actions, which sadly are not always the same. If you don't fit, don't move. It could end your administrative career. If you stay at your own school, few can scam you, but your ties and friendships may fade as your relationships with faculty and top administrators change unalterably.

Preparing to Become an Administrator

Observe other administrators realizing your target has more information than you do. Watch for style and how to deliver good news and bad.

Chair a department or a division as one of the best training experiences for deaning, although I admit it's the single toughest job I've ever held.

Chair a committee to learn about your own skills and resolve. Early in your career, volunteer for some hardworking committees. (Before tenure, avoid controversial ones.) Search committees for faculty, deans, and other administrators can be revealing, as you see colleagues from other departments in action, meet interesting job applicants, and get a sense of what works and what doesn't work in interviews, and of the questions interviewers can throw.

The athletic committee is one of the best if you're in a Division I NCAA school. There you will see raw power, big bucks, bigger egos, pressure groups, gender equity issues—more than you bargained for. Try to make a difference for women athletes while mastering all this.

Find a mentor. A major asset is a mentor willing to assist you. Better yet, find a whole raft of people, each with expertise in a certain facet of administration.

Get an internship. Some schools have administrative internships. The American Council on Education has fellowships, if your school will carry your annual salary while you intern elsewhere.

Attend an institute on leadership. They're a good place to start learning administration, but most schools send faculty only after they become administrators. Check the Council of Independent Colleges, the Institute for Educational Management, the Management Development Program at Harvard, the National Institute for Leadership Development, and the HERS institutes.

Learn about numbers. Learn to read balance sheets, and take a course in statistics. You'll spend a lot of time assuring the college's money is well spent and trying to stretch a few hundred dollars farther than you ever thought possible. Many statistics will come your way: enrollment figures, changes in SATs, numbers of sections of required courses. Make them work for you, not against you.

Read publications widely. Keep up with trends through *Change, The Chronicle of Higher Education, On Campus with Women, About Women on Campus,* and *Women in Higher Education.*

Use computer networking for discussions in your discipline or on academic issues in general. Deans have available two great listservs: the American Conference of Academic Deans and the Council of Independent Colleges.

Attend conferences such as AAHE, AACU, NAWCHE, and those on legal issues at the University of Vermont in fall and Stetson University in winter.

Administration Has Some Drawbacks

Can a woman have a marriage, children, and an administrative career? Yes, but very few women can do it all. Shirley Strum Kenny, president of SUNY-Stony Brook, earned a doctorate and had a family early, putting administration on hold until her five children were in school. She sees a new pattern of women having children posttenure, noting this often puts their "careers on hiatus at a time when they would advance within their departments to positions such as graduate director or chair," she wrote in *On Campus With Women,* Spring 1996.

Women Administrators in Catholic Colleges

Does an ethos deter women's advancement to administration at Catholic colleges? First, consider the notion of marriage. I suspect there's still the fear that children somehow disable one—not the male parent, just the female parent. I've been at meetings where a faculty member has declared that *he* must leave to meet the school bus, and no one flinched. When *she* has to meet the school bus, "Well, isn't that typical?"

In some Catholic circles, women are cute, interesting, sweet, but never motivated, decisive, straight-talking. Some still think of women administrators as Samuel Johnson thought of women preachers: "Sir, a woman preaching is like a dog's walking on his hind legs. It is not done well; but you are surprised to find it done at all" (Bartlett, 1919).

I've also encountered those who fear women are too liberal on issues like ordination, contraception, and abortion. How will this translate in her administration? I detect a shift to the right in some traditionally more liberal schools, as Catholic colleges struggle with identity and related enrollment problems.

Some Catholic colleges have failed to groom new administrators from their sponsoring orders. Others have no new talent in the pipeline. This will lead to more positions available, but it can lead to a power struggle as the old guard (and even older alums) fear lay leadership as somehow selling out, losing identity, betraying the founders and the mission. Some schools willingly accept laypersons, even non-Catholics, into administration. In fact, some non-Catholic leaders are more respectful of and less paranoid about the college's mission than some older Catholic faculty and administrators.

Are Catholic colleges willing to identify early and develop our own homegrown leadership, with the real possibility that homegrown leaders could leave to head another school? To ignore the potential for women leaders is to ignore about 30 percent of the possible pool. If Catholic higher education in this country is to survive and keep its identity, values, and commitment to academic freedom, we must identify and develop young administrative talent, looking to young women faculty as leaders in the century to come.

Financial problems especially plague Catholic colleges. As funds become more scarce and salaries fail to keep pace with other private or state schools, more women will be hired as administrators. Schools tend to offer women less in salary and benefits, and women tend to accept less. If salaries fail to keep pace, there will be less respect for administrative jobs.

Expectations for Women Administrators

Academic deans are expected to carry out policies of higher administration, represent the needs and opinions of the faculty, and reflect administration's needs and opinions to the faculty. Janus-faced, but not two-faced, the dean looks in both directions at the same time. It is not by accident that the bidirectional Roman god was also related to keeping the peace.

If a dean promoted from within was perceived as a strong leader while on faculty, faculty might expect a leader who will constantly buck top administration, whether or not its policy is reasonable. A woman dean might be expected to champion women faculty, no matter what, or be seen as a betrayer of her sex.

Simple Advice for Aspiring Administrators

Expect to work as usual, at least 110 percent to be perceived as passably fair. Grow a skin thicker than your head, because "No good deed will go unpunished." Keep your hand in teaching whenever possible; it renews you while draining every last bit of energy. Keep your research projects going to divert your mind and to set the standard of excellence for faculty by example. If you return to teaching after administration, you can't be dried up as a scholar.

I find what makes a good teacher and scholar is what makes a good administrator. Responding to letters, memos, phone calls is just like getting papers and exams back to students within a week. Staying on top of issues and problems is not unlike staying on top of your discipline. You listen to students as a teacher; you listen to faculty and students as an administrator. Getting students to voice their questions and aspirations is not unlike mentoring young faculty. Administration can be painful yet exhilarating. If you think you want to try, go for it. But go prepared.

Mentoring I: The First Steps Are Casual, Informal

December 1992
Geneva Lopez
Assistant Registrar, Stanford University, California
[Many women have identified mentoring as a key variable in helping them gain career success. The word *mentor* comes from the Greek leader Ulysses, who went to fight the Trojan War, leaving his trusted elderly friend and adviser Mentor as guardian to his son. Today, many schools have begun programs to mentor women faculty, helping them gain tenure. Women administrators on campus also can benefit from a wise, faithful counselor.—*Editor's note*]

When you start in your career, you generally learn the hands-on skills or day-to-day information. You usually learn the hard way about those things that are an important part of the learning experience. At this stage of your career, you think you can learn a great deal on your own and don't need to learn much from anyone else. You may even feel frustrated because you think you know more than the boss about skills needed in your job.

What you don't realize at this stage is that the boss doesn't need to know everything that you know or in the same way that you do. You move along in your job, where what's important to you is the skill building and information gathering.

It's the Little Things

But when your supervisor calls you on such things as your tone of voice, lack of protocol, or approach, or confronts you with other comments from staff or clients, you've reached another stage in your career. You discover that the knowledge bank you've built up is not valued in the same way and that gaining further knowledge depends not only on your ability to learn but on tone of voice and relations with people.

When you feel frustrated that you've been treated unfairly, you probably go to someone you can air out your feelings with. Sometimes that someone is a peer, a more experienced staff member, a spouse, a relative, or a friend who gives you advice or a different perspective on the situation. They encourage you to either "just do your job" or they advise you on how to approach your supervisor or peers, how to handle a particular situation if it happens again, depending on what and who you've asked.

You want to continue gaining as much information as you can on your own, but you begin to realize that the information others can provide can be valuable and that there are different kinds of helpful information.

You've Been Mentored

Mentoring is happening, but you may not realize it because it's been so informal and casual. You begin to see that in order to advance, you need to be aware of people and situations, know what's behind the scenes, who the players are, and how the game is played. You seek out someone you trust and with whom you feel comfortable.

Where do you look? Usually outside your immediate office because of the safety and objectivity that kind of contact provides. You haven't asked someone to be your mentor; you've gotten someone to mentor you. You've consistently asked for their perspective on a situation, for advice on how to handle a problem, for suggestions on steps to take.

More Is Better

Traditionally, a mentor has been a person who serves many roles: tutor, supporter, sponsor, master teacher, or adviser. But as work styles and environments vary, one mentor can't fill the bill. So you begin to draw from different people, and the number of contacts you begin making depends on the breadth of your goals and the different aspects of your job.

Can you get ahead without a mentor? You can answer the question by looking around at who's recommended you, who's suggested that you participate in a certain group, who's introduced you to key people, who's pointed out a mistake you've made. Who's opened doors by doing these things? Has one person or have several different people done this consistently? If the answer is yes, you've been mentored in some way, but you've just hit the tip of the iceberg.

There's more to be taught and learned along the way. In the next stage of mentoring, you will continue not only to learn the ropes but also to share your knowledge with others as well.

Mentoring II: A Network of Advisers for You

February 1993
Geneva Lopez
Assistant Registrar, Stanford University, California
[Women new to their schools or their jobs need a different type of mentor than those who have been around awhile. Later in your career, it becomes a question not only of knowing the name of the game but learning about game-playing techniques. You become more adept at the game, more selective about skills you want to develop, and even about where you want to work. As you get to know people in different units or across campus, you begin to identify key players you can learn from. And you may have even outgrown the mentor who helped you get where you are. The problems are more complex and varied, and you need a wider range of skills, contacts, and viewpoints at your disposal. It's time to create your own personal board of directors.—*Editor's note*]

At the middle and advanced career stages, advice may come to you only at crises, key turning points, or on key decisions you need to make. Sources of support become many, including peers, and not necessarily or exclusively workplace elders. And relationships become much more informal.

At this stage, advice and guidance give you the confidence to express your ideas, views, or "takes" of a situation and help you develop the strategies to approach a person or situation, or to conduct yourself in face-to-face discussions.

A Network Replaces a Mentor

Instead of relying on just one person for advice or support, create a network of supporters and advisers. They provide better feedback on how you're perceived, whom you should be aware of or alerted to, what associations are beneficial or detrimental, when the climate is right for making a move, or what's becoming a campuswide issue.

By "hiring" a network or board of directors, you actively take control of your career rather than continue the more passive role of a protégée. Of course, you let your network know your work-related concerns and problems so that they can advise you in the proper context and support your goals. Advisers can be on campus or out in the world.

Networking requires investing time and energy, precious commodities for those busy promoting their own careers, so you respect their value. In addition, building a relationship with another involves taking risks. To merit the time and risk invested, your potential and personal abilities and skills must appear worthwhile.

Although others' careers may even benefit because of your successes, beware of problems that may arise at these levels: you may be perceived as a competitor, or your peers may feel you have an unfair advantage.

A Two-Way Street

Seek out associations that provide an opportunity to cultivate not only skills but mutual respect, those in which you can make both professional and also nurturing connections, where you can feel safe in voicing not only ideas but also doubts and fears, and admit ignorance.

How do you make the connections and create your own midcareer advisory network? Become active on a committee on campus, in the community, or in a professional association. Make a special effort to get to know people you admire or respect, or who appear to be particularly good at one facet where you feel inadequate.

Call, see, or write them occasionally, or even regularly, asking for advice on a particular problem or passing on some information useful to them. Try to build a symbiotic relationship, in which both parties contribute and both receive benefits. Or call a few colleagues and arrange a lunch, perhaps turning it into a regular event to swap ideas and career plans. Keep it positive.

Look around for others to add to your circle of advisers, perhaps even younger women and men whom you respect. Their viewpoints and concerns can give you a broader perspective. And vice versa.

Mentoring III: Women as Academic Administrators

March 1993
Miriam Shillingsburg
Associate Vice President for Academic Affairs, Mississippi State University
Although women are earning Ph.D.'s and gaining faculty positions at a rate equal
to men, they tend to remain in the lower ranks, with lower pay and status, for
longer periods of time than do male faculty. To advance, when an administrative opening occurs, women must have positioned themselves to compete with men
who may appear to be better qualified by virtue of their earlier promotions.

Many barriers prevent women from rising in academic administration. First,
there is a reluctance to value the nurturing role often played by women, such as
advising students or handling departmental social obligations. Also, an institution's
need to display token women in committee assignments may limit a woman's ability to perform the tasks necessary for promotion at a pace equal to that of males.

The so-called pipeline issues, often used to excuse pay and promotion inequities, also prevent women from acquiring power and prestige in the academy.
This problem may be particularly acute for women seeking to make the transition
from faculty to administration.

Mentors Can Help

To leap that professional gap, women need mentors. A role first acted out by
Athena, goddess of wisdom cleverly disguised as a man, Mentor was a wise and
powerful friend who guided and sponsored the youthful Telemachus while his
father Ulysses was at war. Women can help others by dusting off this ancient model
and applying it in their schools.

Institutions that are serious about promoting women into the administrative
stream can take affirmative action to identify and train suitable candidates. An intern program used at Mississippi State University has helped several women break
into administration. Although the mentors were the president and provost of a
large university and both males, the plan could be adapted for deans. Benefits to
the intern include opportunities to (1) make known her interest in administration,
(2) try it out without making a full commitment and abandoning her scholarly discipline, and (3) position herself to apply for slots that may open up in the same institution or elsewhere.

Women who have passed through the application process will have realistically assessed their own interests and abilities and been screened by others. They
will have little to lose and much to gain, and at least would fail at no higher rate
than their male counterparts.

Schools Benefit Too

Benefits to the institution as a whole include (1) better communication with the faculty, (2) a larger pool of competent people from which to select future administrators, and (3) a diversity of genders and backgrounds influencing the institution's administrative decision making.

To start the program, an administrator sends departments an invitation for internship applications, best in the early spring, outlining the requirements, including academic rank; whether it is a minority or female-only program; time commitments needed; and other considerations. Minimum requirements should include having been an associate professor with three years' institutional experience. The one-year position should be a half-time assignment, with the release actually paid to the department if at all possible, to assure a buy-in by the departments.

A screening committee, including faculty members, interviews at least two or three of the candidates. Making clear in the announcement that the program does not guarantee entry into administration anywhere, and particularly not at that same institution, can save later trouble.

Wide Range of Responsibilities

The duties of the intern may vary widely. The most successful internships are those in which the member gets as broad a view of the institution as possible. The intern meets and works with as many administrators as feasible and yet has some genuine responsibilities: ghostwriting letters and memos, serving as a member of search and screen committees, advising the dean on promotion and tenure, or writing minutes of meetings. She needs to be both learning and doing.

If given realistic tasks, the intern will be seen as a team member, a knowledgeable colleague, a resourceful and competent leader. She will extend the effectiveness of her mentor at little cost, and the unit will maximize administrative resources and forge better alliances with the faculty.

Of course, if the intern is unsuited for administrative work, she may be seen as uncooperative, incapable, not a team player, disorganized, or uncreative. But both she and the institution will have made the discovery in a low-risk, high-potential-gain situation. Not all women are interested in administration, nor are all men, but most can succeed if given the opportunity.

Mississippi State Program

In the fall of 1987, Mississippi State University's president and provost started the program with an intern in each office. Of the five interns, all but the most recent have already moved into academic administration. The president's office mentored a white female who became associate dean of a college, a black female who moved to a vice presidency at another institution, and a white male. The provost's office mentored a white female who became associate vice president (me) and a black male who became head of a large department at another university.

For this year, the program has been on hold; its office space and budget have been assigned to the director of reaccreditation self-study, who is getting many of the experiences that the interns previously received. As the first intern selected, I am now in a position to become a mentor. At a lunch I recently hosted for tenured women, they suggested reviving the internship program, which I will propose to the provost and president for next academic year.

Tips to Help Build Leadership Skills Wherever You Are

November 1999

Whether or not you know what you want to do next, your present job probably offers good opportunities to learn valuable leadership skills. At the Wisconsin Women in Higher Education Leadership conference in September, Marie Wunsch, who is provost and vice chancellor for the two-year University of Wisconsin Colleges system, suggested how to do it.

There's no reason to wait until you're ready to move before you work on your leadership skills, she said, asking participants to choose how they'd describe where they are now from the following list:

- I've made a firm decision to move up in my career area.
- I'm thinking about it, but am not ready or able to move now.
- I'm satisfied and fulfilled in my current position.
- I don't know where I am or where I am going.

It's perfectly all right to be in any category. If you know where you're headed, you can work on specific job skills; by the time you get the position you want, you will already be doing most of the things it involves.

If you're happy in your present job, you can keep it fresh and interesting by taking on new challenges. Leadership skills are not about just preparing for job change. If you aren't ready to move just now or don't have a clear vision of what to aim for, you can use your present position to learn skills that will help you wherever and whenever you go.

Some barriers are more self-imposed than real. Women especially are apt to say they would like to advance but can't because they are place-bound or tied down by kids, husbands, or parents. "You can still be acquiring new skills. Kids grow up faster than you think," Wunsch said. "Why waste all that good day-to-day experience?"

What Leadership Involves

To be a leader is to make a difference, to stand up and stand out, to influence people and outcomes. Opportunities for leadership are everywhere. Part of leadership is to take advantage of where you are. Develop "an analytical attitude" to see the potential for growth and development in whatever situations may come up. An analytical attitude is one of the most important qualities that sustains leadership, Wunsch said.

You also need to be willing to reflect. Some people keep busy to avoid reflection. Can you distance yourself from a crisis enough to analyze what's happening and recognize what is important? Learn to keep a clear head, to stand above the situation.

It helps if you're always in a learning mode. You gain confidence in yourself and a better understanding of what others are going through. Leadership involves ambiguity and risk. The further up you go in an organization, the less structure it provides, and the more your success depends on people and events you can't directly control.

High stakes, high visibility, and the opportunity to shape things mean the opportunity to fail. Some women also fear success: if you do something well enough, you may be asked to do it again.

Developmental Jobs

Many jobs have features that offer rich possibilities for developing your capacity for leadership. These features involve risk, change, dealing with difference, and understanding the context of the larger organization. Most jobs contain one or more of these features; the key is to recognize them. Examine your position to identify the components that offer opportunities for learning. In *Job Challenge Profile*, C. D. McCauley (1999) described components of a developmental job.

Adapting to change. Has your job changed during the time you've been there? The best jobs do. Transitions caused by circumstances beyond your control can result in unfamiliar responsibilities very different from what you did before. As you adapt successfully, you learn flexibility and how to transfer old skills to new situations. You gain self-confidence as you realize how often you've picked up new skills and adjusted to changes.

Creating change. You can hone your skills in bringing about change whenever you are responsible for starting something new in your organization, making strategic changes that will affect your school, or fixing problems that existed before you took the job.

People are among the biggest barriers to change. Creating change offers even greater learning opportunities when it involves problems with employees who are inexperienced, incompetent, or resistant to change.

Managing at high levels of responsibility. The stakes are higher if your job has features that make success or failure clearly evident, like clear deadlines, pressure from senior administrators, high visibility, or responsibility for key decisions.

Another form of high-level responsibility is when the sheer scope of your job is large, involving responsibility for multiple functions, groups, products, or services.

Managing boundaries. One feature of leadership is dealing effectively with people who do not report to you. A job where you manage the interface with important groups outside the organization, such as customers, unions, or government agencies, can teach you how to handle external pressure. You can learn to handle responsibility without authority in a job that requires you to influence people over whom you have no direct control, such as peers, upper administration, or staff in other parts of the school.

Dealing with diversity. An important leadership skill is knowing how to work with people who are different from those you've dealt with in the past. Individuals do things in different ways. One locks herself in her office; another comes out every two minutes. Some differences reflect ethnic, gender, and cultural diversity. Does your work group include people of both genders and various racial and ethnic backgrounds? Do you have on-the-job interactions with people from different institutional or ethnic cultures or with those in other countries? Treat them all as learning opportunities.

Increasing Your Opportunities

Wunsch suggests reflecting on ways to enhance the learning potential of your current job. Ask yourself these questions: How is my job already helping me develop leadership skills? What components of my job could be developmental? How can I take better advantage of them? What new strategies can I try? What obstacles will I have to overcome?

You Can Take Firm Steps to Increase Your Opportunities

Articulate your goals and intentions. Many women find it hard to say, "I am interested, I am capable." If people know what you want, they can help you get there. Use the word *leadership* in conversation at least once a day. Opportunities come to those who want them and work for them.

Take incremental risks. You can choose to do something differently. What will help you move from ideas to action? Start with baby steps; you don't have to try everything at once. Take small risks before moving on to bigger ones.

Ask for feedback. Ask what you did right, not what you did wrong. Positive feedback affirms you, so you'll do the same thing automatically next time.

Develop supportive relationships. Women need to learn the skill of giving constructive, supportive feedback. Keep it specific: What worked? What was effective? Keep it positive: "You do this really well. Can I sit in a meeting when you do it next time?" To encourage a habit of reflection, ask, "What was going through your mind when you did that?"

Work with a mentor. Find someone who has the leadership skills you want to learn, understands your school, and is willing to offer you guidance. Most people are flattered to be asked for help.

Take advantage of training opportunities. Evaluate and make use of opportunities for training and professional development. Women tend to put everyone else's needs first. Value yourself enough to invest time and money in developing your professional skills.

Help others advance. Helping others will build networks, improve your understanding of other people, and show you how much you already know.

Wherever you are, whatever you have done, you have probably learned more than you realize. With analysis and reflection, you can always keep learning more.

Sarah Gibbard Cook

SECTION TWO: SPECIFIC LEADERSHIP TIPS FOR WOMEN ON CAMPUS

What Do You Need to Be a President or Other Academic Leader?

August 1997

Leading an academic institution always has been a by-the-seat-of-your-pants job, with only subjective measures to determine success. Now comes the first study to academically define twenty-two specific competencies that a community college president needs to succeed and to connect the campus to its environmental climate. With more women leading community colleges each year, the study can be especially useful to help women learn what they must achieve and learn to be successful.

Carolyn Desjardins, former head of the National Institute for Leadership Development (NILD), initiated and directed the ten-year project to define and interpret what it takes to successfully lead a community college in today's and tomorrow's environment. "There are no preconceived ideas of what presidential competencies would be," she explained in a session of the American Association of Community Colleges convention in Anaheim, California, in April.

The list of twenty-two competencies was created from two-hour recorded interviews with seventy-four presidents nominated by people in the field as high performers; the interviews were begun in 1986 at Harvard University and updated by in-depth discussions with six of the presidents in 1995. "Added strength and accuracy" characterize the instrument, compared to a simple paper-and-pencil questionnaire, Desjardins said. "The probing reached many more awakening and awareness levels than would have happened if someone was filling out something." This is the opposite of methods used to create most standardized tests like the SAT, where white males use no empirical data to decide what students need to know.

Desjardins said the research found the presidents with the most competencies were less hierarchical and had inclusive and horizontal management styles. The results of this study can help search committees select the best candidates for jobs, trustees evaluate top leaders, presidents evaluate themselves, and potential leaders determine what competencies they need to develop. Although focused on top leaders in community colleges, the data can be useful for assessment in other types of schools and other levels of administrators as well.

Published by the NILD, the project's concluding report has three components: a list of the resulting twenty-two presidential competencies, including a narrative on its origins and direct quotes from presidents interviewed; an assessment questionnaire for presidents and wanna-bes including a development planning guide; and an assessment questionnaire for her or his supervisor, employee, or other evaluator.

Sheila Huff, a consultant with twenty-five years' experience in competency-based research and applications, analyzed the original interviews and conducted and interpreted the 1995 interviews. Her final report is entitled "On the Leading Edge: Competencies of Outstanding Community College Presidents." Colleague C. Ann Carver created both assessment questionnaires.

New Climate Demands New Competencies

The study found that today's environment for higher education has created five types of new challenges for leaders: shrinking government funds, demands for more accountability, demographic shifts, globalization, and an age of information technology amid a changing business culture.

Each challenge forces leaders to develop new competencies, Desjardins explained. For example, shrinking government funding is driving leaders to find new revenue sources, increase productivity, and make hard choices. As a result, presidents need to maintain perspective and manage finances proactively, foster creativity and innovation, enhance productivity, influence strategically, and communicate effectively. For clarity, the twenty-two competencies are italicized here.

Leadership Competencies

The presidents felt responsible for creating a *high-involvement leadership* situation, where they are very visible on campus, especially in times of transition, and people in the employment community are very involved in strategic planning. Their job is to *create a shared vision* of what the college wants to become as a strategic plan and help people see how their daily activities connect to it. To move their schools forward, they must *champion change* yet manage it in a way that questions how the change affects all stakeholders. Some changes can be immediate and visible, but some must be planned over several years, rather like moving a mature tree by cutting a few roots at a time. Leaders must be sensitive to where their people are and back off when they find changes are not appropriate.

A president must *maintain perspective* by keeping the big picture alive and looking out for the whole school in the long term. For example, if it's important for faculty to attend graduation because taxpayers or students expect it, an administrative fiat may be required.

They define *maintaining equilibrium* as delegating judiciously, balancing work and play, keeping a sense of humor and a support network, matching career goals to venue, maintaining serenity in the face of turmoil, and knowing when to move on. "Leadership is just another word for helping people fulfill their potential, individually and collectively," a top president said.

Culture and Climate Competencies

First and foremost, a leader must continually remind administrators, faculty, and staff that the quality *education of students* is its central mission. This involves setting challenging yet realistic goals for students, considering the effects of all decisions on students, seizing opportunities to get to know the student body and leaders better and broaden their world as global citizens.

Recognizing that a college is a key member of its geographic *community*, a leader must consider the community's needs, processes, and values. By becoming a visible, connected presence in the community, the leader kindles mutually beneficial relationships.

In this age, a leader must *value cultural pluralism* and exposure to diverse cultures as vital to the school, using community demographics as a benchmark to set goals. Recruiting practices, personnel policies, and internal procedures should support the goals.

It's up to leaders to *create cohesiveness* on campus, rather than allow empires of fractious and fragmented faculty. By breaking down hierarchies and cross-functional barriers, leaders can build new alliances in pursuit of common goals through joint ventures. Staging events to celebrate the completion of major projects can help.

A good leader *prevents crises* instead of reacting to them, by staying alert to signs of adversity and creating a culture where people can debate and disagree without disaster. By staying visible in tense situations and facing rumors squarely with full disclosure, a leader can dispel fear and discord.

By *empowering others,* leaders can nurture and bring out the best in people so that they can rise to the occasion. Giving people as much latitude as possible helps them grow. "Being president is not a solo performance; this is an orchestra," one said.

Leaders who *foster creativity and innovation* are more likely to succeed, they reported. By creating an organizational culture encouraging people to experiment and take risks, they find unconventional solutions to problems and new opportunities.

If a leader is sure to *recognize and reward excellence,* those models are likely to be repeated. It costs nothing to say thank you and acknowledge contributions to success, and it makes people feel noticed and appreciated, especially with a personal touch.

Influence Competencies

Long-term results come from a president's being able to *influence strategically* those whose buy-in and support are needed. Like it or not, politics is a key factor on campus, and presidents must play the game, investing time and energy to gain influence. "If you pay attention to politics, you can do it just as well as anyone. Just don't pretend it's not there," a female president advised. Governance is polycentric, no longer in a straight line, but shared with many others: students, business, industry, other schools, accreditors, special interest groups, and the federal government, which one president called "the largest school board in the world."

Effective communications help share information in all directions. By listening, responding to inquiries promptly, making professional presentations and valuing regular communications, presidents can assure that people have the information they need to take initiative and make wise decisions. "Communication at my college is costly but well worth the expense," a president said.

Without *effective board relations,* a president may have a short tenure. One of the best ways to prepare to be a school president is to have been on a board somewhere so that you learn what it's like to be on the other side, responsible to constituents. Presidents must invest time to educate the board and develop social or informal personal relationships with board members. "In the end, goodwill is the terrain on which we all operate, and without that, the dynamics can turn in a direction that is not very positive," a president said.

Business Management Competencies

The president who *maintains high standards* shows that the school is a real class act, in everything from hiring quality people to maintaining a strong customer service orientation. By conveying the philosophy that anything worth doing is worth doing well, the president stresses quality in all aspects of operations.

As finances dwindle, presidents must *manage finances proactively* to maintain a strong fiscal position. This means a president must thoroughly understand fiscal foundations: investment portfolio and rationale, historical funding patterns, cash flow, and monthly reports. By developing new or expanded funding sources, sharing financial information with faculty and staff and partnering with others, a president makes financial stability possible.

Without *investing in staff development,* a president is stuck with the status quo. "Often other things need to happen before you can do the sexy thing you want to do," a female president explained. Especially in leadership and diversity training, it's important to involve a whole group so that there's widespread support. Keeping up with technology is crucial.

A president who *strengthens the infrastructure* understands the connection between campus appearance and identity image. By attending to the physical and organizational systems, the leader can improve the comfort level and pride of the campus community. Again, information technology is important.

Doing the little things that eliminate time-wasters will *enhance productivity* on campus: reduce red tape and bureaucracy, stay focused on priorities, solve problems that irritate people, and find techniques to respect people's time.

Discussing the need to *correct performance problems,* a female president called it "one of the most difficult things we do." Presidents make enemies when they have to remove people who are unwilling or unable to perform competently, so they must maintain legally defensible processes. Becoming comfortable giving corrective feedback in a constructive, nondemeaning way means explaining what must change and by when. When the good of the school is at stake, the president must be tough-minded and firm. One of the worst ways to handle performance problems is reorganization, a common solution on many campuses.

Mary Dee Wenniger

How Women Administrators Choose Their Battles

May 1999

"Choosing a battle is a conscious decision. It has to be a strategic battle. There are always battles going on every day that I turn my back on and walk away from. You know, I can only choose so many. They're exhausting, and incredibly demanding. It is the way, I think, administrators make change." That's how one woman described her approach to the conflicts and disagreements that challenge administrators daily. Stephanie Clemons told the 1999 NAWE conference in Denver what she learned in her doctoral research through face-to-face interviews with ten women deans, chancellors, presidents, and other higher education administrators.

All but one agreed that they chose their battles; the woman who did not agree said her presence as a woman in a male environment was a conflict in itself. One cited the Kenny Rogers song about poker and life: you have to know when to hold them, when to fold them, and when to walk away.

Taking tough stands comes with the territory. "Many women hesitate to make a decision. They say they'll sleep on it," Clemons said. "While you're sleeping on it, men are gathering their forces and making their decisions." Whatever decision you make, some won't like it. Then you face a second round of decision making: Which decisions are worth fighting for?

Battles Pro and Con

Many women disliked talking about battles. "I don't like the word *battle*, but there are some battles. My preference is to think in terms of negotiating, and so the primary part of my work is to select the ways in which I will negotiate for what needs to happen. There are occasional battles, but for me what has been most successful has been to negotiate, negotiate, negotiate. And if there are battles, they had best be very, very, very significant."

Responses varied by level in the organization. Presidents spoke of always resolving disagreements by negotiation. Those at lower ranks used war terms more readily; soldiers in the trenches see conflict differently from officers in the war room. One said, "I think *battle* is not a bad word. I think it is pretty accurate. There are battles. There are winners and losers sometimes."

Conflict resolution sounds less loaded. They agreed conflict is inevitable; if you try to avoid conflicts, they often fester underground. But the women differed sharply on whether conflict is good or a necessary evil. To one, "It's pretty hard when you're on the 'con' side . . . to see any benefit in conflict at all. It's not a pleasant situation to be in . . . where you're being beat up for a particular situation. I'm sure there are positive sides to it, and you can see them after the fact, but you can't see them when you're going through it."

Another emphasized the educational potential of conflict: "If we truly believe that institutions of higher learning are learning institutions, then you would make the assumption that every time we're in conflict as an institution, whether internally or externally, that we are in the process of learning. From that standpoint, I would say it's all positive."

The Process of Choosing

You can't fight for every issue. It's demanding and exhausting and may distract you from issues that matter more. One preferred to wage one battle per year but might enter up to three if necessary. "There are many different levels of figuring out whether I'll be part of a battle or not. What political agendas are operating? What do I have to lose? What do I have to gain? How will it personally impact me? How will it impact the people I feel I'm advocating for?"

The women chose their battles deliberately, cautiously, and carefully. Although their styles varied, Clemons identified a common pattern and use of the same tools in the prebattle phase as in the midst of a fight: silence at strategic moments, active listening, noting others' successful strategies, persuasive arguments, attention to relationships, taking time to ponder, and keeping communication channels open.

They noted that men use more logic and data to make decisions and are more casual about relationships. That anecdotal evidence is hard to confirm because Clemons found no research on how men choose their battles.

The Prebattle Phase

Whether the administrator initiates the issue or it's brought to her, there's a prebattle phase of trying to find a win-win solution. It starts with active listening to identify the real issue, get the facts, communicate with diverse stakeholders, and hear all sides of the issue. Several mentioned having backgrounds in counseling or psychology that helped them understand multiple realities.

As they begin to search for common ground, they seek old and new allies and advisers with a variety of perspectives. They observe the dynamics to decide how they can best be heard. As the only woman and the only minority in a group of ten or fifteen white males, one found her comments in meetings were totally ignored. She developed the strategy of whispering her idea to the man sitting next to her, who repeated it aloud, and everybody paid attention.

If the period of listening and negotiation fails to bring a win-win solution and the conflict moves toward a fight, it's still important to have established the strongest possible relationships. Some said committees run everything, so don't sever your relationships on a committee. "I think for me, I truly believe that to be able to win your fight . . . it's based on relationship building. If you go in to fight a battle and you haven't established a relationship previously—one of respect, trust, and knowledge—I think your ability is certainly lessened. A lot to winning is having that relationship cemented even before you negotiate."

Is This Conflict for Me?

When negotiation fails, it's time to decide whether the issue is worth a fight. The criteria are complex.

Personal Values. An issue that doesn't involve truth, justice, equity, or other values is rarely worth a fight; stop and walk away. One that revolves significantly around your core values may carry a moral imperative that outweighs any strategic considerations. "It was for me, in terms of my value system . . . the right thing to do—morally, professionally, ethically. I have even taken on a battle knowing that there was a possibility that I could lose in a very, very big way. And that it would impact me adversely professionally." Most issues fall between the extremes, so the decision depends on institutional and personal context.

The Odds of Winning. Most agreed that the only battles worth taking on are those one might win. One said, "I think I spend a lot of time determining whether or not it's worth my energy. I think for me, I measure whether it's an area I have control over." How much influence do I have in this area? Who is on my side, and who is against me? What will be gained if I win?

The Price of Losing. An unsuccessful battle may cost a leader her platform and voice, hurting the very people she tried to defend. Who will be hurt if I lose? Will my career or influence suffer? What's the worst-case scenario? Is this an issue I can move forward by taking a stand, even if I don't succeed this time around?

Occasionally, they enter battles they know they can't win. "Some have done kamikaze stunts, but they move the initiative forward," Clemons said. On the other hand, "Sometimes you need not fight to win. You've planted the seed and can step back for now."

Costs and Fallout. Regardless of who wins or loses, the fight itself exacts a price. What will the battle cost, in energy and impact? Will it hurt my position or reputation? Will it divert attention or resources from other things?

Timing. The personal and institutional contexts may make an issue worth a fight at some times but not others. How many other battles am I waging? How ready is the institution to deal with this? Are the battle participants ready to engage? Is this the best time to address this issue?

"There are times when you're in the middle of a skirmish. And you say, 'You know, maybe that's not the best quality [of the task], but we're going to be dragged into the mother of all battles on this, and the issues are going to be blurred. I'm just going to put that on the side for a while. We're going to get this one thing taken care of and maybe come back to that other issue one day.'"

Preparing for Battle

Having decided to take a stand, they prepare, assembling their weapons of facts and observation. "Power in a battle is based on solid arguments. Always remember to think before you speak. Be very knowledgeable about the issues and corresponding facts," one woman said.

They also assemble their troops. Who should be recruited as combatants? The president? The board? Does the case need both experts on the facts and people who speak with passion? What will be the battle regalia? Trial attorneys know it matters how combatants dress.

They review the terrain. What is the institutional context? Where is the opposition coming from? What political agendas affect the environment?

They review the rules of courtesy or engagement. "I think there are some rules of engagement in these kinds of battles. The rules are that everybody gets a chance to speak and everybody's belief is valid. I think the biggest thing is getting everybody engaged in the conversation and discussion and being honest and not being hurtful."

Battle and Beyond

The women administrators go into combat guided by personal battle philosophies, such as

- Trust the process.
- Fight fair.
- Respect multiple opinions and truths.
- Understand the big picture.
- Consider alternatives: plans B and C.

- Realize different roads can reach one goal.
- Be aware that only so many cards may be dealt.
- Know that some won't agree with you.
- Know that the battle may be lost.

Their strategies vary by battle, depending on the situation. Some have gone outside their school to ask for help. Some use special maneuvers, such as staying cautiously in the background. If the battle became too personal, sometimes they've chosen to find another advocate.

Favorite tools of battle include persuasive arguments, conflict resolution techniques, and open channels of communication. During the fight, they strive to think critically, speak honestly, avoid arrogance, cut to the issue, and deliver a clear, direct message. They attempt to preserve relationships; this year's opponent may be an ally on the next issue. Battle lines may shift during the conflict. So may goals, as combatants see they may not win and begin to consider compromise.

Whatever the outcome, after the battle they look back on the costs and fall-out. Sometimes they're beat up and in pain, showing physical wear and feeling like failures. Relationships may be damaged as colleagues feel gun-shy, angry, or discouraged. Their professional track record and reputation may have deteriorated or improved.

The postbattle phase is the time to repair relationships and assess the new situation. Soon, another issue will arise, and it's time for another decision. Is this issue worth a battle?

Sarah Gibbard Cook

Women and Campus Politics: Don't Do It *Their* Way!

January 1996
Barbara Gellman-Danley
Vice President of Educational Technology, Monroe Community College, New York
Many years ago, someone told a young graduate student she was lucky to be in higher education because there are no politics there. The naïveté of the assumption by those outside our world is innocent, but for the tens of thousands of women in higher education, it can be deadly. Politics is really all about power and positioning. Although the perception is that some win and some lose, ironically, those most adept at politics realize that if everyone wins, there is a far greater success in the long run.

What Is Politics?

Webster's defines *politic* as "characterized by shrewdness in managing, contriving, or dealing." To women, this definition may seem too harsh, conflicting with our upbringing and traditional role. If you're an academic, think back to graduate school. One young student worked desperately to finish a Ph.D., only to be caught between combating forces on her committee. Another managed to get the best assistantships and sail through her committee. Does this have to do with politics and what Webster calls "dealing"? You bet it does.

Politics Can Be Positive

Women often see themselves at a political disadvantage. As women, we are not taught how to maneuver politically, so we assume it's a role sanctioned only for men. If we participate in politics, it must be on their terms, acting just the opposite of our inclinations and how Mother taught us. Not so. Although all men are no more alike than all women, there are some trends in the male model of politics that women do not want to imitate.

Consider the John Wayne mentality. Some men position themselves by taking the most macho stance and actually speaking as if they were about to reach into their holster and take aim! Rather than try to imitate it, women should step back and enjoy the humor of the behavior and relish the reality that we do not have to buy into this old style.

A New Model

Politics is really about getting what you want and making sure that you are not left behind or taken advantage of as decisions are made within your college or university. Instead of buying into the old male model of politics, you can help create a new model that can be just as effective but lacks the negative elements. Following are some ideas to help you define your own role within a political environment.

The Politics of Ethics and Values

Don't get into battles with other women. This suggestion falls at the very core of ethical and value commitment to other women. As women move up in the organization, nothing is more enjoyable to our detractors than pitting us against each other. Don't buy into it. Ever. You not only lose ground in your own professional development, but you give others far too much ammunition to blame conflict on gender-related issues. Decline to join in, saying, "This is a dangerous conversation, and I don't feel comfortable with it.

Focus on we versus me. In an effort to achieve (or overachieve), don't focus on a personal agenda that supersedes the agenda of the institution. If you keep yourself directed toward the mission of your college or university, your own agenda will fall into place behind it. Getting the order confused will hurt your own reputation permanently.

Don't leave any dead bodies along the way. It hurts to be betrayed by people you trusted. To repeat their behavior yourself is unforgivable. Politics need not translate into moving ahead with your agenda at the expense of others. You can succeed based on substance, not form alone. Over time, hurting others along the way will only hurt you the most. Because not everyone plays by these rules, I've learned to always walk away facing people until I can trust them. I used to turn my back, but I've gotten more savvy (and cynical) over the years.

Have faith that people who are politically vicious will blow themselves up eventually. You don't have to do it for them. In other words, let it go. Competitive, assertive leaders find it difficult not to take on someone who is manipulating around them. But in reality, the most prudent approach sometimes is just to walk away. There can't be a battle if only one person is fighting. Eventually, you will win by not participating in a no-win scenario. You will have taken the high road.

Do not espouse modern management theories and strategies unless you are willing to use them. It is very disappointing to staff when their manager promotes a certain philosophy (total quality management, reengineering, or participative management) but then fails to practice it herself. If you position yourself as supporting it, you will be expected to act according to the rules of that game. Don't be a hypocrite. If a certain theory does not fit your style, it is far better to bypass it than to halfheartedly embrace it.

Be willing to trade off but not trade yourself in. Politics (and life in general) is all about compromise. You don't have to win every time. Be willing to give in, trade off, and wait for the next opportunity to deal. Engaging partnerships and allies for the future will serve you best across the span of your career.

The Politics of Knowledge

Do your homework on an issue. Become knowledgeable not only about the current situation but about similar ideas on other campuses and the history of the idea at your school. You can then attack with facts.

Be aware of the networks around you. Chart the informal lines of communication and authority around you: who talks to whom, who owes whom a favor, who's likely to oppose an idea and why. Use this information to plan your strategy.

The Politics of Communication

Be open and honest. If women have a gender advantage, it's in the arena of open communication. Although you don't want to give away confidential information, your staying open and accessible enables others to see you as approachable and, most of all, honest. Sometimes people take the position "I know something you don't know," which just aggravates the communication channels. By letting others see that you don't feel you own the information of your institution and are willing to share it, you will gain the greatest political asset of all—trust.

Communicate about offenses. Hearing inappropriate or offensive statements, women often think that it is best politically not to say anything. Beyond the implications for sexual harassment, many other assumptions can offend. For example, women may openly express their feelings about certain decisions in the workplace and be told by a male supervisor, "You are just being sensitive." Women see this as a red flag, comparable to implying that our emotions are driven by monthly cycles. But men may not. It is advisable, therefore, to tactfully point out the offense and how it makes you feel. Or simply state, "Thank you for noticing I'm sensitive; I consider that an asset in my position."

Let them *do the bragging.* To succeed within the politics on campus, all participants are under incredible pressures—to publish or perish, serve on a variety of committees, earn more degrees, and, in general, to excel. Allow your hard work to speak for itself, or better yet, find subtle ways to get credit for your ideas and efforts. If you have to blatantly blow your own horn, it implies that you are not self-confident and need reassurance.

Another variation is the pervasive political game of "who stays latest at the office." One administrator may brag that he was at the college until late the evening before a big meeting. My feeling is that those who announce their hours likely are camouflaging some other deficiency.

Sometimes, women are disadvantaged by child care responsibilities. If you find you are being questioned about your time commitment (face-to-face or behind your back), use other methods to creatively demonstrate your commitment. For instance, as a night owl, I use the technique of e-mailing people late at night because the message notes the time sent. This may seem petty, but many women's careers have been hurt by others trying to point out a lack of "readiness for management responsibility" due to their time commitments. With today's computers and modems, *time at work* can no longer be defined as "time in the office."

Use management by walking around. Although not at all new, this style still works. To gain a strong position at your school, walk around to visit people in their offices. Engage an honest open-door policy, and be seen and not heard. One female executive walking into a staff member's office was told, "You're the first VP I've seen in twelve years." It makes all the difference.

The Politics of Style

Don't buy into **their** *style of politics*.   Each person has her own style. If women want to move up the career ladder, dealing with politics will be part of that progression. But do it on your own terms. Knowing your own style and gaining recognition for your individuality are much greater assets than imitating the style of others. Particularly if the other is a traditional male model that does not fit well into your own management style.

Stay focused on the learner.   Remember that the purpose of everything we do in higher education is to serve our learners. Consider them your lighthouse on a dark night, with a stormy sea surrounding you. The waves are the political situations you must manage throughout your career; focusing on the lighthouse (the learner) can serve as a critical reminder that students are our primary customers. Keeping that sense of direction will help you make decisions that are learner-based and not primarily political in nature.

Give in to your instincts; it's OK to be female.   As major retailers are advertising, it's perfectly acceptable to call upon your softer side. Sometimes the strength of women in political circumstances are traits that tend to be more gender-specific: empathy, good listening skills, and sensitivity. Why emulate men when you can call upon these assets? Don't apologize for being a woman; take advantage of it.

Appear demure then attack with facts.   Men in power battles seek positions of strength and dominance. Let them. Sometimes in a meeting, it's best to lie in the weeds, allowing others to posture and position. Be a good listener. Then, and only then, you can gather up the information and come back at a future time filled with enough facts to roll over any weak arguments.

Trying to take on a strong male during a meeting may only cause you to present your side without sufficient backing. This applies to those spontaneous political moments, not those for which you have prepared in advance. Patience is indeed a virtue, as is a willingness to wait; come back later in a position of greater strength. As you bite your lip in the meeting, take comfort in the knowledge that at no time does putting someone down in public gain you political advantage or respect. In fact, the opposite is true.

The Politics of Strategy

Learn only the positive techniques from men.   Although many of the above ideas are tailored for women, don't ignore the excellent political strategies you can learn from male colleagues. If most campus leaders are still men and many are skilled "politicians," why not learn from them? Take their best, not the worst, and adapt it to your own style.

105

Read extensively about gender communication. To a large extent, politics is based on good communication. Many of the reasons why men and women cannot communicate easily are gender-based. By reading about them and learning to apply the ideas of experts, you'll learn to overcome one of the great obstacles to successful politics.

Read **The Prince** *and leave it out in your office.* Although written in the early 1500s, Machiavelli's well-known treatise is full of profound suggestions on politics. Despite its advice that contradicts the management style most women embrace, we cannot afford to ignore its brilliance. Buy this book, and keep it visible in your office. Let others know you have read it, even if you never use a single suggestion that Machiavelli offers! *They* will then know that *you* know, and perhaps be deterred from playing their games.

Make it **their** *idea.* Perhaps the greatest compliment to an author is to see herself in a footnote. The same is true of idea development, at any stage. Recognize that if you cannot advance an agenda that's good for your students, it may be advisable to let someone else advance that agenda. In the long run, people will learn whose ideas are making a difference.

Remember people's birthdays and occasions. When it comes to recognition, get personal. Unfortunately for our male colleagues, many acts of kindness and gratitude seem inappropriate for men. But not for us. In our sexist society, women can clearly take advantage of their gender in this situation. Acknowledge birthdays, special occasions, and achievements via notes in your own handwriting, cards, flowers, or other symbols. Write a poem. By reaching out to tell people you care, in a way that is memorable, you're telling them that you value them for more than just their job. You value them for who they are.

Is politics a game? In a sense, yes. But politics is an integral part of the everyday workings of all colleges and universities. Women need to move beyond feeling they simply cannot play the game, to learn ways to become active participants.

Keep your focus on the learners, keep the agenda away from yourself, and behave in ways that make you proud to look in the mirror at the end of the day. Over time, you'll find that you not only can play the game but you can win—and enjoy it.

Let's Play the Negotiation Game!

October 1994

Although many consider negotiation a male-dominated skill, women actually engage in the process as often as men, asserts Audrey D. Hawkins, director of education talent search at Paris Junior College, Texas. At the 1994 Women in Higher

Education conference sponsored by the University of Texas, Hawkins discussed how to negotiate and get what you want by planning, listening, and acting.

Who Plays the Game?

Hawkins cites a survey of one hundred female and male administrators in Texas public schools, colleges, and universities reporting their negotiating activities. Whereas 64 percent of the men say they negotiated more with their supervisors and colleagues than with anyone else, the same percentage of women report negotiating more with subordinates, students, and family members. Negotiating with subordinates is virtually always less threatening than with superiors, so women are more inclined to do it. Both women and men report negotiating most frequently at work over schedules, salary, staff evaluations, subordinate grievances, federal grants, and working with other offices and units.

The Role of Gender

Women feel that gender plays a significant role in the negotiating process. Almost three-fourths of the women surveyed (73 percent) remembered being in a professional or personal negotiating situation in which they considered gender to be a factor in the process or affected its outcome. Only 2 percent of the men recalled being in a similar situation.

A woman administrator at a historically black college writes: "My gender has proved to be both a benefit and a hindrance. In many cases, I had to utilize other skills or abilities to prove my point. It might have required me to: (1) be more assertive or aggressive; (2) arm myself with knowledge; or (3) outthink or outsmart my opponents. I've had to use similar skills in dealing with situations where race was an issue."

Another woman administrator writes: "I think the most difficult kinds of negotiations take place with people who don't see reality the same way you do. I deal with male students who originally came from Middle Eastern countries like Saudi Arabia. My experience is that they are unaccustomed to negotiation with women at all. They will reject from a woman the same suggestion they would readily accept from a man."

Chicago attorney Laurel G. Bellows, past president of the Chicago Bar Association, says women are seen as more intuitive and detail-oriented than men, good at building relationships and consensus, and being creative. Although these assets work well in nonpositional negotiation, where the parties are using creative and cooperative methods to come up with a plan that helps both sides, Bellows notes that many of today's negotiations are more adversarial and confrontational. When women go to the bargaining table "they want to make friends," she says.

Although being friendly may make the session feel more pleasant, without a solid strategy you sacrifice effectiveness.

Choosing Your Battles

Although almost everything is negotiable, says Hawkins, it's best to choose battles according to your own personal values:

- Determine your level of comfort in a particular negotiating situation.
- Assess your needs to determine whether they will be met through this process.
- Decide whether the benefits are worth your investment of time and effort.

Keys to Success

Having established your goals and determined that they're worth the effort, it's time to prepare. According to the *Black Book of Executive Politics* (National Institute, n.d.), these smart preparations will help:

- *Keep things simple.* Condense your ideas into a few sentences, minimizing paper at the session.
- *Structure your presentation.* Present your biggest idea first. If it is well received, go on to make your second and third points. Don't preamble your ideas; it weakens your stance.
- *Anticipate objections.* Predict how others are likely to react to your proposal, based on their treatment of similar proposals in the past. Anticipate likely objections and prepare effective responses.
- *Build in some sacrifices.* To protect what you really want, add in a few things you'd like but are willing to part with. This gives you room to bargain without giving up what means the most to you.
- *Don't try to score all the points.* Your position will be stronger and more likely to gain cooperation if you accept some ideas from your critics, getting them to buy into the idea. Establish what you want, but also consider what others want.
- *Meet resistance flexibly.* We tend to overreact when anyone raises questions about a project we care about strongly. Resist the temptation to get defensive; it's best to treat objections lightly and try to foster an atmosphere of cooperation. This plan makes it seem your project is already under way. If negotiations stall completely, try to figure out what aspect of your proposal is really bothering the other side, by reading between the lines. As a last resort, consider giving up one of your sacrifice chips.

- *Don't give away the store.* Retain your core values. It's OK to accept modifications to your plan or idea, as long as what's important to you or to the project stays intact. If it looks as though you'll lose what you're most committed to, offer to withdraw the entire proposal for further development. Otherwise, you may find yourself supervising a project that's not yours anymore.
- *Rise above politics.* Try not to consider who your opponents are when you're actually making a presentation. Don't betray any aggressive feelings toward your opponents or act condescendingly toward them, even if you think they are stupid—and even if they are. The more important your proposal, the more vital it is to appear to have the interests of the entire organization at heart.

Dianne Jenkins

How to Confront, Rather Than Avoid, Conflict

September 1994

Lila's been at her school for fifteen years and a director for eight of them. Naturally, she thought she'd get the big corner office in the new building. But rumor says that spot is going to a director with less seniority but at a higher profile program. She's incensed at the injustice and all the more furious because making a fuss would make her look petty.

Lila is a candidate for *constructive conflict management,* defined as "how to be constructive when we feel we've been unjustly treated," explains Joan Hrubetz, dean of nursing at Saint Louis University Health Sciences Center. In their workshops on conflict management presented in July at the National Conference for Women in Catholic Higher Education, Hrubetz and her partner Noreen Carrocci, undergraduate dean at St. Thomas University, Minnesota, provide tools and insights to help campus employees resolve conflicts.

First, Know Thyself

"Self-reflection is critical so that we know what our hot buttons are and can control them before others do," Hrubetz says. For example, Hrubetz admits she can't stand whiners. She realizes that although whining doesn't mean a complaint isn't valid, it does mean she won't be able give it a fair hearing. So she stops the whiner tactfully and suggests that she or he describe the problem very specifically, in writing.

Similarly, maybe Lila's reacting so strongly because long ago, her older sister always got the bigger bedroom. If Lila realizes this about herself, she'll be able to make a more cool-headed decision about whether the issue's worth pursuing. "We also need to analyze the ways we manipulate others," especially patterns we fall into with each gender, which we learned growing up, says Hrubetz. Ask yourself:

> **With male colleagues** do I revert to a compliant, submissive, peace-keeping behavior? Or do I pull a helpless little girl act?
>
> **With women** do I use emotional ties to manipulate? Or do I expect women to be agreeable and resent them if they're feisty or outspoken?

"Looking at our behavior with fathers, brothers, husbands or boyfriends, mothers and sisters" can reveal patterns that influence our professional relationships and interactions, Hrubetz says. "Ask yourself: 'Why is this making me so upset?'" Perhaps your own emotional baggage really is upsetting you.

Is It Really a Conflict?

If Lila's anger stems from ancient turf wars with her sister, it's probably a no-win situation not worth pursuing. Acting out those old feelings will only make her appear unprofessional; even if she wins the corner office, she'll never win the old battles with her big sister.

But suppose Lila doesn't have a big sister and her supervisor had hinted she'd get the office. She feels betrayed. Should she confront her supervisor? Maybe. But she needs to act on more than rumor, so she should check out the new office assignments. If she confirms the rumor and feels enough is at stake—and it may not be the office so much as her dignity, if she thinks she's being taken advantage of or discriminated against—then she should speak up.

Not Just Picking a Fight

Constructive confrontation is "a deliberate attempt to help another person examine the consequences of some aspect of his or her behavior, to present the person who is being confronted with an invitation to self-examination" and a chance to change their behavior, explains Hrubetz.

To be successful, the confrontation should avoid making the other person defensive. She advises:

- Be descriptive, not accusatory.
- Try to see things from the other's viewpoint.
- Be specific and to the point.
- Convey a real interest in the other's welfare.

- Be polite and tentative, not angry or hurt.
- Avoid the urge to create a winner and a loser.
- Listen carefully and respectfully.

Listening is critical, says Hrubetz, especially "listening beyond the words" to the tone, body language, and facial expression. "If these contradict the words, it may be appropriate to point that out: 'You say you're not angry, but I sense some anger over this. Can you tell me more how you're feeling?'" she suggests. Non-verbal language can also indicate whether the person is receptive to your concerns and indicate whether to press your case or drop it.

Compromise and Conciliation

If you can't get what you really want, settling for something else can be a positive resolution. Suppose Lila's boss says, "I know you really wanted that office, but it was beyond my control. But I did get authorization for that laser printer you've wanted." Her boss acknowledges Lila's been let down and regrets it. The consolation prize is graciously accepted; nothing more need be said.

To a supervisor, the experience illustrates several key tenets for avoiding or resolving conflict:

- Don't promise what you can't deliver.
- Make sure your staffers get bad news directly from you so that they don't suspect you're the cause.
- If you are the cause, share your reasons. They don't have to like it, but they do deserve an explanation.
- Offer an alternative.
- Offer an apology. The words "I'm sorry," sincerely delivered, do much to soothe angry or hurt feelings.
- Do something special to affirm the staffer's value to your unit: take her to lunch, or send a card or perhaps a package of gourmet coffee or tea.

Trust Is Fundamental

Unfortunately, many supervisors believe that being boss means never having to say you're sorry. In dealing with disgruntled employees, what do you gain by giving bad news in person, sharing your reasons, and apologizing or compromising?

In a word, trust. "Trust is absolutely fundamental to building really good work relationships. Trust makes people a joy to work with," and the opposite holds true as well, Hrubetz stresses. It also reduces potential conflict because with trust comes the assumption that people "have good reasons for what they do."

Conflict is inevitable in all institutions, no matter how well run; Hrubetz notes that although it is painful, conflict can bring about creative change and improvement. "The strength and animation of an organization is judged not by the absence of conflict but by the way in which conflict is managed."

Conflict Management Strategy Self-Test

These proverbs describe different strategies for resolving conflicts. Rate how well each proverb describes how you approach conflict: 5 = Very closely; 4 = Frequently; 3 = Sometimes; 2 = Seldom; 1 = Never.

____ 1. He who fights and runs away lives to fight another day.

____ 2. Might overcomes right.

____ 3. Soft words win hard hearts.

____ 4. You scratch my back, I'll scratch yours.

____ 5. Truth lies in knowledge, not in majority opinion.

____ 6. Stay away from people who disagree with you.

____ 7. Fields are won by those who believe in winning.

____ 8. Kill your enemies with kindness.

____ 9. A fair exchange brings no quarrel.

___ 10. No person has the final answer, but each has a piece to contribute.

___ 11. The best way of handling conflicts is to avoid them.

___ 12. Put your foot down where you mean to stand.

___ 13. Kind words are worth much and cost little.

___ 14. Better half a loaf than no bread at all.

___ 15. Frankness, honesty, and trust will move mountains.

Scoring: High scores on these items indicate

#1, 6, 11: You tend to withdraw from conflict.

#2, 7, 12: You tend to force your position on others.

#3, 8, 13: You try to conciliate.

#4, 9, 14: You try to compromise.

#5, 10, 15: You try to integrate different viewpoints.

The test indicates how you tend to function in conflict and is a stimulus to examine your style, says Hrubetz. No one strategy is necessarily best; success depends on the situation. "The better you are at adapting your style to fit the situation, the more effective you'll be," she says. It's easy to see how conciliation, compromising, and integrating viewpoints can help resolve conflicts. But with-drawal and force have their place as well, says Hrubetz. For example, if you're angry because your colleague did something that reminds you of your mother-in-law, withdrawal is probably the most appropriate strategy. And with someone who avoids conflict through denial, you may need to force your position.

Jennifer Hirsch

Take a Risk: Add Humor to Your Campus Workplace

December 1999

Choose your favorite title for the luncheon talk on humor by Betsy Morgan, chair of psychology at the University of Wisconsin-La Crosse, at the fall Wisconsin Women in Higher Education Leadership conference:

> *Academic:* "Humor and Leadership: An Anecdotal and Empirical Approach to Engendered Epistemological Issues in Higher Education"
> *Male:* "Women's Leadership: Doink!"
> *Seinfeld:* "What's Up with Women and Leadership?"
> *Pop psych:* "Funny Jobs and the Women Who Love Them"

Despite the assigned title, "A Funny Thing Happened on the Way to Lead-ership—How to Keep Humor in the Workplace," Morgan doesn't believe the cam-pus workplace has much humor to keep. And that's a shame. The longer you're in administration, the more humorless it gets, she believes, showing a graph of laughs per semester as a function of years in administration, which was a straight line forty-five degrees downhill. "Higher education people tend to take themselves very seriously. Sometimes what we do is not all that serious," she said. We may be trying to affect brains, but it isn't always as complex as brain surgery.

Humor Can Be Risky Business

We avoid humor because we think it puts us at risk, which it does. We're afraid of losing face, of not being taken seriously. Cultural differences may make our jokes fall flat. Much of what administrators do is mediation, and the situations we mediate just aren't funny. Humor can cause pain and reinforce stereotypes. Not everyone has a ready retort like Dolly Parton: "I'm not offended by dumb blonde jokes because I know I'm not dumb, and I also know I'm not blonde."

On the other hand, you can't usefully sit around all day trying to figure out what will or won't offend someone. "So far, painting my door blue was the only thing I've done here that got a rise out of people across the board. I couldn't have predicted in the whole world what would put people off here," she said. Be aware, but don't worry too much. "At some point, you just have to live your life."

"They Drool, I Rule"

One of the top reasons department chairs give for taking the job is that they think they could do it better than their predecessor. That's not stepping up to leadership; it's stepping into a vacuum. The dangerous conviction that they can do everything best has women stepping up to vacuums—and dishwashers and changing tables, and curriculum planning and memo writing, Morgan warned.

Overload results from taking oneself too seriously and undervaluing the skills of others. Women take on too much and delegate too little. "Psychologists call it the 'They drool, I rule' syndrome. There is no known cure. That's not funny," she said.

Irony Without Cushions

Irony is one thing that makes administrators laugh:

- The psychology department faculty who can't get along
- Historians who can't recall what happened last time they tried that policy
- Bacteriologists who don't wash their coffee cups
- Economists who can't balance a checkbook
- Physical education faculty who are out of shape
- Postmodernists who reject every other position
- Communication profs who can't structure a lecture

Funny, right? Only from the outside. "Irony is hard, with no cushions," she said. Administrators know there's nothing funny about administrators who won't give up the floor when talking about consensus.

Humor is easiest to see in someone else's workplace. Remember the joke about how many feminists it takes to screw in a lightbulb? The answer: "That's not funny."

Distance and Perspective

Humor requires a distance and perspective, having less to do with other people than with our own worldview. The ability to laugh at oneself is good for mental health. How many times have people told you to lighten up? (They don't say that to men, of course.) How do you lighten up? "For me it's Miss Clairol #103, but for most people it's a more labored process," Morgan said.

A research design teacher once showed his class a survey Morgan had written, as an example of poor design. She vented her anger by writing him an e-mail saying he should have consulted her first. "I have done much poorer quality surveys you might have used for your example." She did not press the send button. There's something wrong when we can't get enough distance to see what's funny about our experiences. Humor is a reality check and a healthy reminder of one's own humanity.

Funny Things to Do at Work

- Page yourself on the intercom; don't disguise your voice.
- Send colleagues e-mail to keep in touch: "If anyone needs me, I'll be in the bathroom."
- Use "Xena, Goddess of Fire" in your e-mail address.
- When asked to do something, reply, "Do you want fries with that?"
- Put a garbage can on your desk and label it IN.
- Develop an unnatural fear of staplers or paper clips.
- Finish sentences with "in accordance with the prophecy."
- Skip at work rather than walk.

Sarah Gibbard Cook

Tips to Circumvent Alien Gatekeepers

September 1993

Through the network, I meet a wide variety of women on campuses. Here I've assembled their best techniques for dealing with recalcitrant colleagues. Try some at your own risk.

Make them think it's their idea. You've had the experience of proposing a new or creative idea at a meeting, only to have it politely ignored or dismissed. Later, perhaps even in the same meeting, a more powerful or prestigious colleague restates your original idea and meets instant approval, gaining even more status. Instead of getting mad, evaluate whether you most want the credit or want your idea accepted. As a reader said in the *Guide to the Universe of Women in Higher Education* (Haber, 1994), "You can accomplish a great deal if you don't care who gets the credit." If you want the credit, say something like, "Al, I'm glad you see the merit in the suggestion I made earlier. Perhaps we can work together on it."

If you are proposing a truly radical idea, tone down the differences by saying, "I agree that John's idea is a great one. In fact, I believe we can make it work even better by . . . " In planting the seed of ownership in someone else, you hitchhike on their accumulated goodwill; they may assume ownership and work to get the idea accepted.

Divide and conquer. A meeting is not the place to win friends and influence people, or to sell an idea. The old gang will stick together, presenting a united front in the face of your challenge to the old ways of thinking and doing. Approach those who seem educable one-on-one in a comfortable and relaxed situation where clubhouse rules do not prevent an opening of the mind. As one chair says, "Don't do your committee work in committee." Do it before or after.

Use their kind of reasoning and their own key words to argue your points. If you are dealing with those who trust only numbers, it would be foolhardy to present your idea as a hunch. Rather, present a logical argument dealing with all aspects: historical perspective, numerical analysis of past-present-future data, quotations from interviews with the key players if possible, likely scenarios for alternative courses of action, diagrams and models, charts and graphs, whatever you expect will trip their trigger. As a colleague remarked, "When men say they have a hunch, others assume it is based on logic. No such assumption is made of women's hunches."

Adopt a nonabrasive but assertive style. Unless you are assertive, you will not be taken seriously. If you are perceived as a threat, they will stop at nothing to thwart you. The biblical caveat "Be cunning as a serpent, harmless as a dove" also applies to those who would be effective on campus.

Get personal. One reader described a colleague with a reputation as a rotten-tempered ogre who opposes everything. She gets through his negative office persona just by asking "How's your mother?" before discussing a mutual concern.

Question their authority. One woman needed quick approval of one of the doctors on staff to place ads in a publication. Her asking "Do you have the authority to approve this?" met with an almost instantaneous positive response.

Avoid sexual overtones by ignoring them. An engineering grad student passed on this tip for dealing with a technician whose help was necessary in getting equipment to work for her experiment. By staying on task, ignoring casual invitations to go out for a beer, she gained the reputation of being cold and impersonal. She may not have gained his friendship, but she didn't seek it. All she wanted was his help in doing what he is paid to do and nothing more. She got it.

Deal with the "what" and not the "who" of a situation. Take care of the task at hand and forget personalities, politics, and bygones.

If you lose a battle the first time repackage and rename the same idea and present it again.

"Know when to hold know when to fold " recognizing that not all battles can be won, and not all jobs are worth the stress. Be ready to move on.

Mary Dee Wenniger

Tips on How to Increase Your Personal Effectiveness

October 1999

Personal effectiveness is the key to superb job performance, according to Brigid
McGrath Massie, who presented at the AAWCC/NILD conference on Righting
the Standard in June. She defines *personal effectiveness* as having the right information and acting on it. We will each have many different jobs in our lifetimes, so we
need to be able to move out of our comfort zones and work on effectiveness.
Massie based her presentation, entitled "Find Out What They Say When You
Leave the Room," on this quiz:

1. *Most of the feedback that personally effective people get at work
is negative.* True.

About 70 percent of all job feedback is negative, a sad state of affairs. She
called compliments the lubricants of our relationships, helping us feel comfortable, important, welcome, and understood. To be effective, compliments must be
specific, sincere, and timely. Your body language must match what you're saying,
or no one will buy it. Give compliments right away, not "Remember last year when
you . . . "

Handing out business cards is another way to make connections. She suggests
being able to quickly find business cards, which must be free of handwriting (new
area code, title, address) to look professional. Bring enough so that you don't run
out at a crucial time, like at conferences.

Confident self-talk is another way to be a positive force in a negative world.
Don't belittle yourself by saying, "I'm just a. . . . " Be proud and optimistic instead.
Surround yourself with people who are as good as or better than you, and learn
from them. Screen your input by protecting your mind and attitude from the bom-
bardment of negativity. Stay away from negative people; we all know who they are.

2. *If you enter competitions for awards or promotions you will be
labeled as an egomaniac.* True.

Entering competitions for awards or promotions makes people think you
believe you're good, according to Massie. They'll be jealous and may want to keep
you down, but you can rise above their hostility. Mediocrity breeds mediocrity; excellence breeds excellence.

3. *Gossiping (spreading personal information that's almost always* *negative) is expected if you are going to be popular at work.* False.

Gossip can hurt you now and when you apply for a new job. A blabbermouth past won't help when someone in human resources asks of you, "Would you hire this person again?"

4. *To manage your time well you have to eliminate most fun activities.* False.

Too many people live like the lyrics of the song "It's Getting to the Point Where I'm No Fun Anymore." It's important to balance family, leisure, health, and career. The number one mistake is not budgeting enough time for activities. Get a handle on activity versus productivity. Because there's always time for the important things, take time to have fun.

5. *Controlling your moods is essential to personal effectiveness.* True.

It's exhausting to be around people who are on emotional roller-coasters, Massie pointed out. The biggest cause of crankiness is sleep deprivation, so make sure you're getting enough. Having the TV in the bedroom steals an hour a day, she advises, so get it out of there. Also, don't necessarily go to bed and get up with your partner; set a sleep schedule that fits your needs.

Daily exercise helps your body relieve stress. Often, we're mentally exhausted at bedtime but not physically tired, which keeps us awake longer. Massie also suggests creating a positive reward system to encourage yourself. If you don't love and appreciate yourself, neither will anyone else.

6. *People learn twice as much from your example as from your advice.* True.

Identify what you want, and do it. Identify what's stopping you and get rid of it. Start taking actions that reinforce your desire to become more personally effective.

7. *Sharing highly personal information at work is OK if you are really upset.* False.

As Sergeant Friday said, "Everything can and will be used against you," and at the worst possible time, she said. Personal information can come back to haunt you in professional situations, so be careful where and how you share it. Sharing personal information at work implies that you're lonely and have nowhere else to share your news, she said.

8. *Seeking out influential people based on their ability to help your career is an effective thing to do.* True.

Some people are powerful, as important as brand names, so work to get in touch with them. Some may see your actions as sucking up, but we need to get over that. Once you've sought out influential people, listen to their feedback. But then do what you want with it, depending on what's in your best interest and your heart.

9. *Given an impossible situation at work or home your alternatives are to change accept or leave.* True.

A popular conference seminar is entitled "How to Work for a Jerk." Realize you're not alone in your situation, and ask yourself if you contribute to it. You can be an agent of change where you are rooted, or you can leave. If you choose to leave, remember to take your entire being with you wherever you go.

10. *Most people are aware of what is said about them when they leave the room.* False.

The magic of personal effectiveness is preparing for the event. So be aware of what's going on within yourself and your surroundings.

Although Massie never really answered the question of how to find out what they say when you leave the room, with work and diligence her tips can help women increase their personal effectiveness. As the Chinese proverb says, "Regardless of your past, your future is spotless."

Diane S. Grypp

How to Maximize Your Personal Power on Campus

January 1999

To maximize your power, know yourself and the powers that you have, Sister Joel Read advised. The charismatic president of Alverno College, Wisconsin, led a discussion entitled "Speaking Your Voice" at the Wisconsin Women in Higher Education Leadership conference in Appleton, Wisconsin, in October.

Your power doesn't depend on your formal position but on what's inside you. Power is the vision that inspires people to shed their doubts, trust, and follow you. It means knowing how to nudge and influence, to shape the way people look at the world. Some with impressive job titles don't have influence; they usually don't keep their jobs. On the other hand, people of character and influence don't need the job title. They need people so they can work through others, but not to tell them who they are.

Know Yourself

The essence of power lies in knowing and liking yourself. "Speaking your own voice is knowing who you are and accepting that you're a very powerful person."

Determine what's important to you. What do you believe? What would you die for? When you believe something, you don't ignore challenges to it; you take action. An idea you'd give up easily isn't a belief, just a provisional opinion.

Be clear about who you are. It shows in how you dress, walk, and talk.

Know what you like and dislike. When someone purports to quote you, know whether or not that's something you could have said. Most people aren't clear about who they are. Your clarity protects you from being misused or pulled off balance.

Assess your tolerance for ambiguity. Administration is full of ambiguity. You lose the power of concentration that you enjoyed as a faculty member. You never know when the next phone call is going to wipe out everything that happened last week. You get into situations you couldn't predict and can't control.

Recognize your level of resilience your risk quotient and your limits. "I don't believe stress is in the job. Stress is in the person," Read said. "Worry is interest paid on trouble before it is due."

Know the Powers You Have

Alice Walker said women give up their power by thinking they have none. We all have countless powers.

Knowledge. Put your antennae up. Know not only yourself but your school and its politics. Know how to make things happen. Learn to read body language. Learn who talks to whom. Know the whole pecking order on campus. Cultivate street smarts.

Interpretation. One person may see more than others who have had the same experience. With imagination and perspective, you can take something everybody knows and help others see it in a new light, like the nurses who redefined care of the sick as health care. Because people don't hear new ideas the first time, learn how to say the same thing in ten different ways.

Relationships. This power lets you build a campuswide network. Know who you can trust; sometimes women are too naive and trusting. Learn to be friends with men in a way that's not sexually charged. "You can assume everybody likes you, even if they don't. It helps you to be fearless."

Judgment. Sometimes the academy overrates the right answer and underrates judgment. A good professor has her students think aloud, so that both can hear the process and not just the result. Being right isn't as important as what goes on in your head; you can always apologize for a mistake, but people will know if the apology is insincere.

Teamwork. Most work gets done in teams; in fact, teamwork is the heart and soul of the educational process. It requires you to lead and follow simultaneously, switching easily from one to the other. Know how to get people to talk, how to summarize, how to keep anyone from dominating a discussion. We need to teach our students teamwork, which we'd been taught to call cheating.

Developing others. This power means changing the climate of the organization by inviting people to share your ideas and values. It offers a long-term opportunity for power regardless of your level. Once you work a change through the organization, it gets institutionalized so that it can't be line-item vetoed.

Example. People who act with integrity are critically important although they may be unaware of setting an example. We all know certain people with character or backbone whom we'd trust in a pinch. They sustain the school. If they're missing, anything goes.

Kindness. Everyone has opportunities to exercise this power every day. The more difficult the situation, the more it matters to act with generous heart and spirit. Kindness lets you deflect the irate with a smile and pull the rug out from under them.

Stories. Ancient bards had the power to determine which stories were told and remembered. So do you. There are many good, interesting, significant things happening all around you. Use e-mail to inform others; preserve the stories in conversations and speeches.

Organization. Politics is the art of the possible. One person can make a difference if she understands the group and has an idea how to make it more effective. Learn to read people; you can't make them do anything against their will. Whoever creates the agenda runs the show.

Commitment and perseverance. With commitment, others cannot talk us out of what we believe. With perseverance, others cannot prevent us from finishing. Commitment requires conviction; perseverance requires courage.

The list goes on. There's the power to communicate, to convene, to articulate. Know and use your powers. "You'll see your risk quotient go right through the sky. You won't be afraid of anything."

Sarah Gibbard Cook

SECTION THREE: HOW NEW LEADERS CAN SURVIVE IN AN ALIEN ENVIRONMENT

What I Learned in My First Six Months as an Administrator, or Has Anyone Seen That Missing Iguana?

February 1997
Claudia A. Limbert
Chief Academic Officer, Pennsylvania State University DuBois
As a nontraditional student age thirty-five who finished B.A., M.A., and Ph.D. programs while raising four children, I find my life hasn't followed a logical se-

quence. My first academic job was as a tenure-track assistant professor of English at a Penn State University campus. Six years passed as I worked toward achieving tenure and promotion, extremely busy years of teaching, doing research, publishing both scholarly and creative work, and being very active in campus service.

It was campus service that got me thinking about moving into administration. I began compulsively reading material on higher education, management, and administration. Although I had no budget or real power, I often chaired committees, facilitated difficult meetings, wrote reports, and did semiadministrative work. To my surprise, I found that I enjoyed doing this and was told that I was highly effective in such roles.

The first time a supervisor mentioned my moving in that direction, I remember being frightened by such an idea. Why would I want to do that? Why take on something new and move into unknown territory? And the faculty member in me asked: "Why in the world would I want to be one of them?" As time passed, I realized I wanted to be an administrator because I wanted to form policy rather than react to it. But was there a way to learn more about administration without totally committing to it? At Penn State, there was. Supervisors suggested I apply for one of the three highly competitive, one-year administrative fellowships for women and minorities at our main campus, a fellowship that would put me under the guidance and mentorship of a top administrator. Having received tenure and promotion, I applied for a fellowship.

On August 15, I reported to our main campus as an administrative fellow. My new mentor told me he was committed to teaching me in twelve months everything he had learned about being a good administrator during his thirty years with the university. Evidently, he did a good job; only eleven months later, I was hired as chief academic officer at Penn State's DuBois campus.

Stunned is hardly the word for how I felt entering my new office. Pistol-whipped is better. I was analogous to the dean of a small college, responsible for forty-three full-time faculty members in all disciplines, about thirty adjunct faculty, and the academic integrity of all our programs. I administered a large budget, and was second in command to our CEO, a retired rear admiral. However, there was a lot I didn't know. In my first six months, I discovered theory has very little to do with reality when one becomes an administrator. Did I ever learn.

Some Serious, Job-Related Things I've Learned

You must in some way separate yourself from the person who held that position before you no matter how wonderful that person was. Why? Because people need to realize there's a new person with new ways of doing things. And because half the people probably loved the former administrator and the other half probably hated that person, it's best to start on neutral ground. I'm very different in personality and work style than my predecessor. I signaled that difference by changing the work space—filling it with light, plants, personal possessions like a robin's nest, favorite books, and artwork, as well as moving the furniture so that the room looked simple, uncluttered, and informal.

If you're an academic officer you may find that in the past the faculty who now report to you have been abused: disciplined criticized and given too many responsibilities. But they may not have received much respect and, at best, may feel ignored and neglected. As my ex–rear admiral CEO said when I was hired: "The faculty need someone to love them." After six months, almost all the faculty have come to visit me. Most aren't asking for anything; they just want to tell me about themselves and what they do.

If you are the chief academic officer nothing can possibly prepare you for all the tasks you'll need to do. For example, I have helped deal with the realities of a wheelchair-bound student whose program was held in our only inaccessible space, authored responses to accreditation visits when I had never even seen one before, restaffed courses one week before classes began, held the hand of a person who tearfully talked about a marriage ending, and had appointments fill my day until I sometimes felt like a deli worker.

Controlling your budget enables you to control your office. I've spent more time learning how to manage my budget than anything else, but I now know to the penny what is being spent on each unit and person reporting to me. Next year, my first budget proposal will be grounded in reality. It's especially important for a female administrator to be good with budgeting. In another job interview, I was asked: "Can you do math? Could you define an algorithm?"—questions that clearly would not have been asked of a male candidate. My answer: "I have always balanced my own checkbook and have never lost a penny. How about you?"

When communication is poor trading often inaccurate gossip is how information gets passed along. Information hoarding as a form of power control becomes rampant. I began an electronic campus newsletter for all full-time faculty; it now also reaches all staff members, as they wanted access to the same information to work more closely with the faculty.

Don't automatically think you know best. You probably don't. Instead, try working with teams and bring the best of everyone to the table. At such meetings, do a lot of listening and watching body language. Ask lots of questions. Yes, you're still responsible for making the final decisions, but those decisions now will be informed decisions.

You'll need to encourage creativity especially in these times of limited resources remembering that creativity historically hasn't been highly valued in higher education. We too often tend to fall back on old ways of doing things, even when those ways no longer work. You may need to physically signal that creative thinking is welcome; I put creative toys like Legos and Toobers and Zots on my office conference table and found it very interesting to note the various responses. To stimulate creativity, I say things like "Think big"; "Don't self-edit"; "What is something new that we could try that might solve this problem?"; "What would you do if you could do anything about this situation?" But I'm amazed at the collective brainpower now being brought to bear on problems and the truly innovative solutions being proposed for those problems.

Don't just sit behind your desk. By the time information reaches you, it's so filtered that it's totally useless, and a small problem assumes crisis proportion. I do what some faculty call "Claudia's walkabouts," visiting faculty and staff in their own offices, because I find that people are more comfortable talking on their own turf. You may ask the faculty if they want you to sit in on their classes to acquaint you not only with disciplines other than your own but with the reality of their teaching lives and classroom needs. But unless it involves a disciplinary action, don't enter uninvited.

Learn as much as you can about technology as higher education is heading that way. My administrative fellowship year really introduced me to computers, as technology had been very limited on my previous campus. I remember being amazed by a color monitor in my new office.

Some general rules for working with those who report to you: Never show favoritism; treat everyone with respect; offer sincere praise when something has been well done; offer constructive criticism and help when something hasn't gone as well as hoped; build a supportive environment where all are valued; do what is right, not what is easy; and always model the professional behavior you expect in others.

Some Personal Things I've Learned

Set short-term and long-term goals for both your unit and yourself. Where will I be and what will I be doing in three, five, or ten years? Only after we identify a goal can we begin working toward it.

Give serious thought to professional development. At Motorola University West in Phoenix, all employees regardless of position must have at least forty hours of classroom instruction per year, whose cost is part of every budget. How much continuing professional development do we give administrators? Zero? Is that why so many of us either burn out or ossify at the same level as we entered administration?

Expect stress in any new job particularly those first few months. I could rarely sleep more than four hours a night, waking up with my mind racing, worrying about the million things that needed doing the next day. Complicating this was what my daughter labels the Charlatan Complex. It's that feeling deep down inside that many women share: we are impostors, and someday someone will surely find us out, suddenly leaping out and yelling, "Charlatan!" and everyone will know. I'm still working on the Charlatan Complex, but I found a way to get around the mind racing with a million things to be done ASAP. I keep a pad and pencil beside my bed. When I wake up, I jot down the problem (and perhaps a solution) so that I don't feel I have to remember it for morning. With experience, I'm getting better at prioritizing tasks, plans, and resources.

It can be incredibly lonely being the only female administrator at a small campus in a small town. I'm still thinking about a solution.

Make room in your life for something other than your job. Although I had been warned about this, I'm still negotiating with myself. I love my new job so much that it could easily consume every waking hour. To avoid that temptation, I rarely take work home. I may stay in the office longer or come in on a weekend, but my home is a refuge where I go to renew myself. I now block three things in my office appointment book. One is in-office work time, for uninterrupted tasks. The second is minivacations to visit my children around the country. Third, I schedule lunch or dinner dates with friends and keep them as I would any other, no matter what else comes up.

If you're not having fun then you're in the wrong job advised my administrative fellowship mentor.

Wild and Weird Realities of Actual Administration

Your official job description has little to do with your everyday life. Quickly you learn that an administrator's office functions less like a well-oiled machine and more like a triage unit. I learned many people other than educators reported to me only after a stack of colored cardboard forms (time cards) appeared.

Take a good look at the top of your bare desk the day you move in as you won't see it again until you move out. You may aim for a clean or at least organized desk, but don't worry if it doesn't happen.

A strange thing about moving from faculty to administration: administrators see you as faculty and faculty see you as administration. This especially troubles the faculty. When I interviewed for my present job, a faculty member with whom I had worked on several projects was asked to get me to the next session. I noticed he said very little—unusual for this man who always bubbles with talk. Finally, he blurted out in a choked voice, "Claudia, how could you do this?" "Do what?" I asked. "Become one of them," he shuddered. I didn't know what to say. Later, I e-mailed him, asking whether he'd prefer to have someone in charge of his fortune who knew what faculty life was like or some-one who hadn't a clue. He agreed to preferring someone who actually knew the difficulties he faced.

It will be assumed that you have spent great sums of money on re-decorating your office probably out of the faculty travel budget. Early on, a faculty member casually said, "Well, redecorating this office must have cost the campus a bundle." I was glad to be able to say that I had rearranged and scrubbed things without spending a penny of campus money.

Motherhood is perhaps the best training I could ever have re-ceived to be an administrator. I can tell when someone is telling me something less than the whole truth, and I know exactly how to convey that message to them in a look, without saying a single word. Also, having been a mother has provided me with some valuable experiences (and a sense of humor) that I can apply to present situations.

For example, two faculty members sharing an office were having difficulties. One came to complain that the other was messy and taking over more and more office space. As the faculty member spoke, I had a sudden mommy flashback. Be-fore I could stop myself, I started laughing and said, "This reminds me of when my first two sons were about eight and ten and shared a bedroom. I put a strip of masking tape down the middle of the floor to settle their argument over space." I stopped, horrified that I had said something like this but, to my amazement, the faculty member started laughing too. "Don't look for your roll of masking tape," the person said. "I think we can handle this."

It's OK not to be perfect. In fact, a certain level of vagueness may endear you to your faculty. When our fall semester began, I was still very new and was supposed to introduce all faculty by name at the freshman orientation. But I had seen only a few! The seating chart from my staff assistants should have worked perfectly. In reality, several faculty who had other plans decided to show up. At the end of the introductions, I happily asked, "Well, have I introduced you all?" A dead silence prevailed until the rest stood and introduced themselves.

The virtues that one's faculty value in an academic officer differ greatly from what one might assume. At my campus, faculty seem to ap-preciate three things: family connections, speed, and tenacity. At my first inter-view, the engineering faculty weren't sure they wanted an English faculty member as chief academic officer. But when they learned all three of my sons are engi-neers, they asked the CEO to hire me. Later, the faculty kept telling my CEO they were impressed at how quickly I did things, especially answering e-mail and signing purchase requisition forms. Finally, they seem to admire my tenacity. As one said recently, "No offense, Claudia, but once you are hot on a project, you're just like a rottweiler on a soup bone."

Always carry a plastic bag with you. I got this rule from a wildlife technology faculty member who learned I routinely take long walks for exercise. Why? "You can pick up any roadkill you find, and our students can use them in the labs and then stuff them for display purposes." I later wondered what would happen if I happened to drop dead on one of my walks.

You must project a certain level of dignity because you're representing your school. I was sorely tried twice. I had counted myself as very fortunate to find a nice apartment on the first floor of a turn-of-the-century house in downtown DuBois. About a week into the job after a stormy night, I saw a tricycle float by, followed by miscellaneous planters and yard ornaments. That's when I realized my lovely apartment was in the middle of a flood plain.

My landlord offered to convey me to my office by canoe for a very important conference call that morning. Dressed in my suit, clutching my briefcase, holding my black umbrella over my head, and looking like Katharine Hepburn in *The African Queen*, I boarded the canoe. Then, doing what my daughter calls my Queen Mum wave, I was paddled to higher ground, the neighbors on their front porches cheering me as I passed.

The other occasion was less dramatic. Taking a family on a campus tour to recruit their son, I pointed to a building, when a little brown bat suddenly flew up under my armpit. I froze, arm rigidly extended, all eyes riveted to my armpit. What could I do and still maintain Penn State dignity? Luckily, the prospective student calmly plucked the bat off me, gently stuck him back under his ledge and we proceeded on our tour.

One will be called on to participate in a variety of extracurricular activities also not listed in the job description. Recently, the wildlife technology faculty told me their two-foot-long iguana was missing, but he would be much easier to find than their missing snakes that probably were still living somewhere in the ductwork. Would I keep an eye out for the iguana?

I've completed my first six months as an administrator. Have I been successful? Looking out my window, I don't see my effigy hanging in the trees. At a recent meeting, I asked a faculty group how they'd feel about something that I was considering doing. There was a silence, until one spoke: "You shouldn't worry about it, Claudia. It doesn't really matter what you decide to do, because in a year we won't like you anyway."

I have six more months to go.

Survival Strategies for New Women Administrators

September 1995
Linda Hartsock and Martha Burns
Principals, Integrated Options Inc., Virginia

"I am the only female administrator. I'm new, and all of the others are men who have been employed at this institution for ten or more years. I need survival tactics!"

As more women move up in administration, they face new terrain and new challenges. Coming either from faculty positions to the post of assistant dean or from staff positions on the nonacademic side to assistant director–coordinator, they suddenly assume administrative roles. Beyond being handed a job description or being asked to create one for themselves, they rarely receive adequate training for the real world of administration from their boss or institution.

They are expected to sink or swim, often unconsciously set up for failure by a system full of people who are too busy with their own issues. Here is a baker's dozen of practical tips that you won't see in any textbook but will help assure your successful transition to the other side of the fence.

Recognize that age is all in your head. If you're twenty-three and act like a late adolescent, you'll be treated like one. Conversely, if you're fifty-five and have moved from faculty to administration with a chip on your shoulder or wearing blinders, you'll be treated like a fossil.

Get the lay of the land before you plant your garden. Realize that real power may have nothing to do with positions or titles. A secretary or janitor may know more about what's really going on in your unit and who will succeed. Or your boss's significant other may be the way to get her or his ear. Cultivate their support.

Act like a leader not just a coordinator or an organizer. Assume that you have been chosen as an administrator because of your vision and ideas, which you must learn to present and sell.

Be careful with offhand remarks and sarcasm. Because of your position, you are now taken literally, and your authority is behind your words. One new administrator asked a faculty member to "represent us" at a meeting; the faculty member took this to mean that she had full authority to commit funds and personnel to the matter being discussed at the meeting.

Be a good listener. Identify key words and phrases from others. Your responses should feed their own words back to them, only with your own spin, to redirect, reframe, redefine their ideas to the way you, as their leader, think they should be.

Learn to run meetings. There's a big difference between convening and running a meeting. Move it along. Time is a valuable resource on campus, so set the agenda, goals, roles, and time frame. Successful meetings don't just happen.

Separate problem solving and decision making in your mind. Problem solving may be a group activity, identifying alternatives and preferences. Making the hard decision is the administrator's individual responsibility.

Make decisions objectively on merit not on friendships. Your job as an administrator is to have no friends but to be knowledgeable, capable, and fair. In fact, friends in the workplace can cause you real problems. This is especially true when you may be perceived as passing out favors in the form of budgets or travel money. Don't be paranoid, but watch out for those who would immediately become your buddy, guiding you through the minefield, only to later betray you or ask for special favors. It happens every day.

Learn to say no. Saying yes is fun and gives warm fuzzies, but it's more important to know when and how to say no effectively.

Add your own twist to tasks. When asked to do reports or present data, be sure to include your own insights and recommendations about what should be done. That's why you are there!

Recognize that not all change is progress. Resist the urge to make change for change's sake, especially in your first several months.

Do your homework. Look back at least five years in minutes, reports, and informal conversations to see what was suggested, by whom, and how it worked. You don't want to go off half-cocked, making recommendations that have already been tried and failed, or were the hobbyhorse of someone who wasn't respected.

Find a colleague from outside. A friendly ear from outside your office and organization, who is at your level and can maintain confidences, can provide another perspective. (In psychiatry, every therapist has another therapist outside the practice to discuss cases and share problems, worries, and successes.) Good administrators do the same, making very sure that their choice is outside the organization and can be trusted to remain silent.

Navigating Your First Year in Academic Administration

January 1997
Marlene I. Strathe
Vice President of Academic Affairs and Provost, University of North Dakota
Sharon Siverts
Vice President of Academic Affairs and Provost, Metropolitan State College, Denver

You've been named to a major academic leadership position—a vice presidency, a deanship. You've spent your career as a teacher, a scholar, a service provider. You know well faculty roles, protocols, and responsibilities; you've successfully demonstrated your career path as an academic. And you've learned what to do and what to avoid along the way. Now, however, the roles are new; the responsibilities are different; the context in which you work is broader; the relationships around you are changed. Most likely, you were selected by one individual, your superior, and the review and selection process may well have attended more to your weaknesses and areas of inexperience than your strengths.

How you navigate the first year of your new administrative role will be critical not only to your institution but to your professional future as well. Advancing a change agenda even in the best of times is difficult. You don't have time to make many mistakes. Here are some tips to help you succeed.

Attend to your professional staff. Learn their current roles and responsibilities, assess their strengths and weaknesses, not in relation to their current work but to your organizational vision, your needs, and your own work style. It's important to take the time to meet with your staff, solicit their input on office organization, and communicate your expectations. Do this often in the beginning and then on a regular basis.

Staff may have developed habits and work patterns that will not be of benefit to you and your office; you need to be clear what's acceptable and what isn't, and deal with troublesome personnel issues early. Outlining expectations, reviewing accomplishments, documenting progress or lack thereof, and working with the campus personnel director are critical to addressing personnel issues.

Attend early to the budgetary and human resource management policies and practices of your school. Early in your tenure, spend time with your budget officer, understanding not only your own budget but the institutional budget. When you understand the budget situation you inherited and the resources at your disposal, you're better able to think strategically about how to match budget to program. Ask about the financial obligations you've inherited, personnel as well as other unfunded commitments for which you're responsible. Clarify the flexibility you have in managing your resources.

Clearly articulate your administrative and leadership expectations for academic administrators reporting to you. Empower them to do their work, and hold them accountable for leadership in their units. People who report to you will either work with the attitude that you are their leader or they'll try to challenge you and work around you. Early on, it's important to help those who report to you to understand your style, expectations, and goals, and how you review and evaluate accomplishments. Although in any new environment, it takes time to ask, listen, test ideas, and then formulate a plan and vision, it's important to do it expeditiously.

Seek input on draft documents and, once they are approved, share them widely and refer to them often. Unit goals and objectives must be strategic, focused, achievable, and measurable. Although you may meet weekly with people reporting to you for routine issues, you might consider meeting quarterly to review progress toward the larger goals and determine what you can do to assist in their accomplishment.

Build a personal and professional support base outside your school. Recognize that within your school, you may have few, if any, peers. You no longer belong to the faculty, regardless of whether you retain faculty tenure or rank. In most schools, there's an us-versus-them syndrome. Building the *us* is the challenge. Recognize and accept that you'll receive few compliments and accolades on your own campus. Rather, take time to develop a support base outside your school. Get involved in your community in an area where you have interest and feel you can contribute. Go to regional and national meetings and become acquainted with colleagues with whom you can share issues, successes, and failures in a safe environment.

Communicate broadly and repeatedly but limit the flow of confidential information until you understand your school's communication culture. Although it is important to take time to meet and greet, to listen and follow up, it's just as important that you think before you speak. Give consistent messages, both verbally and in follow-up actions.

Be accessible and visible all the while protecting time for yourself to accomplish your work. Enlist your staff in helping to manage your schedule and time. Use technology to maximize your efficiency. In trying to be an open and accessible administrator, you will easily find yourself overscheduled. With the help of others, determine what events are most important for you to attend, calendar them, and then be there. The school benefits if you can focus your attention on your role as academic leader. Recognize crises about to occur, and plan extra time in your schedule to handle them without having to always cancel appointments.

Prioritize your agenda. Establish two or three themes for the academic division, and use those themes to direct personnel, resource, and curricular decision making. Avoid undertaking too many new initiatives too early and becoming scattered in those efforts. It often seems that everything in academia is significant or a crisis. Undertaking a number of initiatives creates a tremendous burden on you to accomplish everything the first year.

Recognize this trap, and with the help of your superior and staff, identify a few that will become your focus. At the same time, recognize that other agendas can become priorities at any time, such as a new mandate from one's board or another request from the legislature. Given these unexpected events, it's even more important to limit your own agenda.

Establish team relationships with other vice presidents or deans. Don't establish your division as a competitor to others. Although you have an agenda and a constituency, it's just as important that you take time to get to know your colleagues. Find out their responsibilities and priorities; talk about common agendas; find ways to partner and collaborate. Give support when jobs are difficult; attend to the care and feeding of your colleagues. Meeting as a group outside the normal working day can be an effective way to develop relationships and become better acquainted.

If you find you must do something that can affect another unit, take the time to talk to the appropriate administrator beforehand and seek his or her perspective. Modify your position as appropriate to collaborate and build your units and the school.

Assess early the expectations of your superior. Although faculty, staff, and other administrators will all hold expectations for you, your superior's expectations are the most important in the early months of your new job. Often, one's supervisor has the view that because you were hired, you know what to do. It's critical that you take the initiative to discuss and agree on initial expectations. Once you both identify them, keep your supervisor informed of progress.

It's also critical to know the style of the person you work for. Some want to be involved in generating ideas, some in information analysis. Some want to be involved in decision making, whereas others want you to come up with the solution. Once you know the style of your supervisor, you can find a way to work within that framework.

Understand the school's culture. Know where the real power resides, both formal and informal, and use it to your advantage. Gain multiple perspectives on the school, its past and present. Listen more than you speak. New administrators often think they must be the experts; they must talk and give the answers. In truth, it's the administrator who listens that has the greatest chance of success. Listen closely, summarize what you heard, and identify what needs to be done. Even if you can't act on all the ideas, the fact that you *heard* what others thought is vitally important to your success. Understand that the formal channels of the institution are important for getting process and procedures moving, but at the same time, ask and listen to more than those who are in identified leadership positions.

Know yourself well. Be grounded in principles, have integrity, and understand your values as guides in difficult and politically sensitive situations. No administrative position is easy. Pressures come from all directions. Without a firm internal belief system to guide your actions, you'll find yourself acting inconsistently. The various campus advocacy groups will see this quickly and use it to their advantage to move discussion and projected actions in directions that serve the advocacy group's purposes rather than the institution's. Politics enters academia, and decisions are frequently made on that basis. You'll be better able to defend any actions when you can articulate strong human and academic values.

Take care of yourself. Attend to your health, create leisure time, take time away from your school, and laugh often. It's easy to become so consumed by the job that you have no other life. Make a commitment to create time for yourself. Find a way to get some regular exercise, whatever it might be.

Create an environment where you enjoy coming to work each day as do those with whom you work. Don't lose yourself to your job. This is your life, not a dress rehearsal.

Special Caveats for New Women Presidents

September 1995
Thomas McDaniel
Vice President for Academic Affairs and Provost, Converse College, South Carolina
Increasingly, capable women leaders are becoming college presidents. It is not too
soon. Not only are women presidents excellent role models for female students
(who now make up more than half of all undergraduate students in the United
States), their leadership styles tend to promote more democratic, participatory
practices.

From total quality management to theory z, new research on women's ways
of leading tells us that women can expect to be successful in college presidencies
in the 1990s. But they should be aware of the danger of high office, especially if
they are serving colleges where women leaders are rarities.

My recent experience as interim president of an independent liberal arts
college gave me the unusual opportunity to gain insights about what new presidents should and should not do. Some of the mistakes described below I made
myself; some I saw in presidents at other colleges; some I observed in the two
women presidents on either side of my thirteen-month tenure. Here are a few
common pitfalls of presidential power and tips on how to avoid them.

Failing to Listen

Listening requires hearing, understanding, and remembering. It can be difficult
to hear good advice clearly when confronted with so many obligations and opportunities in a new position. But if you don't listen well now, you can be sure
there'll be major difficulties later. Most problems that get as far as the president's
office are complex and controversial. If they were easy to solve, a dean or vice
president already would have done so. Listen carefully with a "third ear" to the
nuances of values in conflict beneath the surface. The ability to hear well is a special strength that many women bring to leadership positions.

Gullibility

People who can talk easily and frequently with presidents almost always are be-
lievable because of their passion and sincerity, their knowledge and powers of persuasion. To prevent being beguiled, exercise careful listening, good judgment, and
caution. Make an occasional reality check, such as relying on disinterested sources
for additional information. Most crucial decisions should simmer in the saucepan
of reflection—not an easy course for new presidents who like to be seen as deci-

sive, action-oriented leaders. Some women presidents may feel a need to prove they have a command presence and a take-charge personality. That need can make you vulnerable to staff manipulation, so watch out.

Isolation

Don't get trapped in the trappings of your office. Make a special effort to visit as many people and places on campus as possible. Casual conversations in the offices of faculty members or other administrators have a different tone than those carried out in the inner sanctum—they are more likely to be open and direct. So sit in on a coffee break in the maintenance office, the print shop, or a faculty lounge. If there's a male domain on campus—a certain coffee shop, the mechanical engineering department—arrange strategic visits to break down barriers.

Micromanaging

Of all the skills of leadership, knowing how to delegate is the most difficult one to master. Even the best-intentioned micromanagers do more harm than good, undermining competent people's independence and confidence. Set goals and agendas for your subordinates, but don't tell them how to accomplish the assignments. Encourage them to assume greater responsibility for their jobs. If they are unable or unwilling to accept responsibility, change the personnel.

Failing to Support

Lack of presidential support for a person or project carries extraordinary weight in a college community. Presidents speak with great authority, and faculty and staff are quick to hear disparagement, faint praise, and disapproval. They can infer criticism whether or not it is intended. Even silence isn't safe; people assume the worst in the absence of your clear agreement. Public comments should focus on what is praiseworthy, commendable, and effective. Reprimands, disagreements, and criticisms are best handled privately. In colleges, success usually springs from success—recognized and nurtured by supportive leaders. Absorb the blame for what goes wrong, and credit others for what goes right. Women often have superior support skills; use them to build teamwork and community pride.

Seeking Instant Reform

Don't move too fast. Although you may have been hired for your can-do spirit and creativity, keep in mind that most campuses greet new presidents with some skepticism, anxiety, and fear. Followers grant leadership to presidents who have proved their credibility. Don't raise false hopes; don't raise hackles. Go slowly, and earn your presidential power. Unfortunately, women presidents are still more suspect than their male counterparts.

Failing to Lead

The above points warn presidents to take care before they take action. But it's equally important to establish yourself as a leader in the short honeymoon period you have. First impressions are lasting—everyone is paying special attention to what you say and do. Take advantage of this attention to prove that you are a person of vision, energy, and style. Because women leaders often must endure undue attention to their dress and appearance, this is another area for caution.

Presidents are hired to lead. They must lead boards, providing trustees with a clear sense of mission and a commitment to make the college better in discernible ways. Attend to board education and cultivation, and help the board fulfill its role in policy making. But claim for the administration the role of putting policy into action. This doesn't require sweeping action so much as it requires decisiveness: by word and deed, you can raise standards and communicate positive expectations. Others will see leadership skills when the president listens well, decides wisely, visits frequently, delegates prudently, supports consistently, and reforms systematically.

Mishandling Stress

Serving as a new president is *extremely* stressful. A new president's grace period to move in, learn about the campus, and meet and remember scores of faculty, staff, and supporters is brief, at best. At worst, pressures quickly mount, and it's even briefer. An assault on campus, a surprise budget shortfall, a key administrator's resignation, an enrollment downturn—the stress possibilities seem endless.

And because 80 percent of men presidents but only 20 percent of women presidents are married, you are less likely to have a sympathetic spouse at home. The pressures of office may tempt you to overwork, overworry, and overindulge, none of which help de-stress situations or people. Stress remedies include proper rest, reasonable work hours, physical exercise, time for family life and hobbies, and a healthy diet.

This list covers the key points, but I learned many other things about presidential leadership. I should have spent more time thanking those who helped me in my work and celebrating with them the successes we enjoyed together. I also should have worked harder to head off end runs by faculty and staff who take issues to the top before consulting their direct supervisors.

I'm glad to return to academic administration, where my interests and talents lie. I also look forward to helping our new president succeed. I'll be much more tolerant of her mistakes. (After all, I've made more than my share.) I know that she'll receive more criticism and scrutiny than she deserves. But like many new women presidents, she can prove equal to the challenge.

What I Learned as a New College President

November 1997
Sandra Featherman
President, University of New England, Maine

Now's a hard time to be a college president. Our institutions are in a state of flux. Technology is forcing many changes. Government regulations are weighing us down. We are criticized for rising tuition and held accountable for not solving society's toughest problems. New presidents face many challenges, including having to learn about their schools very quickly. I consider every challenge an opportunity to test or display leadership. It helps to ask many questions and listen to a lot of advice.

During my first two years as a president, I had to lead a major fund-raising drive, increase enrollment, merge two colleges, and lead the effort to integrate faculties, staff, student bodies, and alumni organizations. In the course of these activities, I developed some guidelines for decision making and action, most of which apply to any senior administrator. These guidelines work well, reduce problems, and let you sleep at night.

Respect lines of authority. In making decisions, don't go it alone. Always get a recommendation from the line officer responsible for the area. Don't make commitments for your administrators without discussing it with the individuals concerned.

Don't do everything yourself. Hire a good team of administrators, and rely on them to make recommendations.

Don't take everything personally. Learn to separate criticism of your role from criticism of you as a person, recognizing that people can be against your proposal without being against you. Senior administrators are frequent targets for complaints that could be termed *noise*. Accept a certain amount of this noise as inevitable, and keep your antennae attuned for substantive criticisms.

Announce your criteria for decision making. A president's actions need to be reasonably predictable. My own decision-making criteria are very Kantian and equity-oriented. Treat similar situations in like manner. When faced with sticky issues, ask "What if everyone wanted the same thing?" and "What if we did this all the time?" The answers guide me in making decisions.

Explore the parameters of a problem. I'm frequently asked to make yes-or-no decisions as if these were the only two choices. I've learned there's a range of possible solutions for almost any issue, along what could be thought of as a plane in three-dimensional, decision-making space. Where there are conflicts, we need to find compromises somewhere along these decision planes. Another way of exploring parameters is to consider what would happen in best-case and worst-case scenarios, to assess potential risks before we decide.

Be active not passive. With higher education changing so rapidly, you can't get much done sitting around waiting for things to happen.

Respect and listen to your faculty and staff. They have a lot more information than you do in many areas. Respect your students, and spend a lot of time with them so that you can be sure you're meeting their needs.

Be honest and open. The trust of constituents is our most valuable asset. By sharing information and concerns, we enlist the support of all members of the institution.

Don't be afraid to apologize. We all can make mistakes. When we do, it's better to admit that we have and fix the problem than to proceed with a flawed policy or decision.

Err on the side of humaneness. If unsure in a tough case involving a student or personnel issue, choose the most humane decision. Not only will the individual involved feel better but so will you.

Minimize hurt. Where possible, disrupt or inconvenience the fewest possible offices, programs, and people.

Watch the bottom line. Keep budget impact in the forefront of all decision making. Managing a budget is the sine qua non for all administrators.

Do your homework. Preparation is essential before every major presentation, key meeting, or critical decision. Be sure you're well briefed by the area's administrator. Never go into a board of trustees meeting or other major campus meeting without preparation.

Learn to listen. Many senior administrators are good speakers, but it's essential to be a good listener. People may not tell us all we need to hear, unless we learn to listen patiently and draw out observations and information. I was slow to learn this. Eager to solve problems, I'd jump in to resolve an issue, even before the narrator completed the story and made all the necessary points.

Communicate. Share as much information as you can, as broadly as you can, with both internal and external audiences. After you let people know what you're doing, tell them again. And again. You can't share information too much.

Give a helping hand to others. We lead institutions full of talented people. Part of our responsibility as leaders is to help others move up and sometimes move out to better opportunities. We're learning organizations for both students and our colleagues, so we should be generous as mentors and as references.

Be good to yourself. All senior administrators, including presidents, need to learn ways to remain energetic and healthy. A few tips are listed here. None of us in key positions can do all of them at any one time, but it is essential to do some at any given time.

- Make time for yourself. Set aside time for family, quiet, writing, or whatever refreshes you.
- Learn how to say no. It's okay to send a staff person in your place and to say you're overextended.
- Don't do everything yourself. Delegate. You can't do it all and you certainly can't do it all as well as good staff can.
- Use technology as a time-saver. Tape record memos, letters, thoughts you want to retain, sudden inspirations. Use a car phone to get information and put travel time to the best possible use. Use the Internet to ask colleagues for help, advice, and data.

Finally have vision. Keep the big picture in mind. You weren't hired to chair meetings, supervise employees, or balance accounting ledgers. You were hired to provide vision and leadership. Stay abreast of the trends, keep faith with your institutional mission, and propel your college forward.

CHAPTER FOUR

READING THE MAP OF YOUR CAREER 101

Careers of women who work on campus often take a different route from those of men. In administration, more men aspire and plan to be administrators than do women, for many reasons.

Women's careers are more likely to be circular than linear, opportunistic rather than intentional, a result of going with the flow rather than fixing on an objective and steadily working toward it.

Social conditioning causes many women to want to work with people rather than numbers and to resist roles that might involve conflicts, such as administration.

Women are more likely to fill acting and interim posts, considering them as opportunities for no-strings-attached trial runs, in which both parties reserve the right to end the experiment if the fit isn't good. Men are more likely to see them as giving away a free sample. Why give it away when you can sell it? And there's the factor of ego involvement, usually far less important to women than to men.

Seizing control of her career can help a woman make positive career choices. As career experts say, "If you don't know where you're going, any road will take you there." After mapping where they've been in careers, women can plot where they want to go, examining the options along the way to check whether they fit into the long-range goal and remaining open to opportunities that may present themselves.

Some resist the idea of planning a career because it means being intentional and serious about their work; others fear that their plans may change or that they somehow will be held accountable if they don't reach the goal.

Getting the job interview can be especially difficult for women because it often involves interactions in an alien environment. Unless the search committee is enlightened and sensitive to gender issues, women may have more challenges in the interview itself. Even having been offered the job, women are again at risk in negotiating a fair compensation package, but wise women are becoming less reluctant to make demands in new areas such as job flexibility, pensions, support, and family considerations.

This chapter helps women map their careers and follow the map.

Strategies to Move Up in Campus Leadership

May 1996
Linda Hartsock and Martha Burns
Principals, Integrated Options Inc., Virginia

When you find yourself magnetically attracted to job ads for no particular reason, it's time to take a hard look at where your campus career is going.

If you decide you want to join or move up in administration, a preliminary step is defining how you characterize the change. More salary? Larger staff? More authority? More perks, like credit cards or a school car? More visibility on campus? More status or a more desirable status? More travel?

For some, it's a step up the hierarchy. For others, it's moving from nonacademic to academic administration or vice versa. Or moving from one vice presidential spot to another. Or leading the faculty senate, with more visibility but seldom lots more salary.

But first, you need to determine whether your best bet is to move up where you are now or move out of your present department, division, or job. Making the determination is tough, but it will be easier if you consider these factors.

What ties you to the present site? Consider kids in school, husband's job in the same school or area, close relationships with colleagues, important commitments in the community, relatives nearby, and whatever else is important to you.

What conditions in your present job keep you from moving up? For example, if you were a grad student or support staff at your school, this image is difficult to shed, and you may always be seen in that role, no matter what.

What benefits can you gain by leaving the site? Perhaps it's extrication from a situation in which people knew you when you were less motivated or qualified for an administrative role. Or a separation from people who add stress to your life, such as a former husband or a difficult colleague. The opportunity to meet new people and enjoy new surroundings also can be benefits.

What are the liabilities of your deciding where you really want to be before such a position is available? The question may seem obvious, but women have languished and delayed their own administrative progress for years because they just had to be at a particular school or in a particular geographical area. Another option is to go for a lateral move to make your way in and then use internal promotion options to get where you want to be.

Once you've decided where to go, this toolbox of strategies can help.

Socially Integrate with the Group in Control

You can't move up until you are in the network, the group, or social set that controls the game.

There are only two entry routes, self-deprecation and service. Too much self-deprecation makes you appear unattractive to the group. Too much service steals the limelight and can also lower your attractiveness. By being aware of the extremes, you can avoid them.

Recognize the Difference Between Power and Authority

One can wield power with little authority or have authority but little power. Think of power as an exchange relationship.

For example, your boss wants greater national visibility. As a member of the program committee for a national conference, you get your boss on as a keynote speaker. You've earned some power chits. Be sure you recognize that you have them, and play them at the strategically advantageous moment.

If power is truly an exchange relationship, then only one who has something you want or need has power over you. When you tire of someone else wielding that power, ask yourself what that person has that you need. If you can do without it or get it elsewhere, you may decide to change jobs rather than tough it out where you are.

Learn to Negotiate

Develop skill in negotiation, a science rather than an art. Women rarely are well skilled in negotiating and often fail to realize that it should produce win-win situations. Here are a few quick tips:

- Never assume that what you want is what others want. Find out precisely what the other wants, and build it into your plan.

- Ask for more than you want or expect, and settle for what you really wanted, in FTEs, budget, or space.
- Never try to negotiate over the phone because negotiating face-to-face provides so many more clues.
- Never jump at a first offer, no matter how attractive.
- Refer to a higher authority to buy time and reaffirm your position: "I'd like to do business with you, but what my budget committee has allocated just doesn't agree with the prices you are quoting."

Volunteer

Volunteer for assignments to get experience and to develop the skills you'll need in a future position. Help out in another office; serve on a nonprofit's committee; seek an appointment on a state or national task force or association; or find a colleague who does what you'd like to do, and offer to take on a special project.

Volunteering helps you by letting you test whether you have the aptitude or skills needed to do a job, helping you prove yourself to someone who can serve as a reference, giving you a new line on your résumé that speaks directly to the area in which you want to emphasize and establish credibility, and separating you from the crowd as one who is committed, well organized, and self-motivated.

Think Outside the Box

New problems, situations, and issues demand creative new solutions. Instead of going with your first thought, try something new. Here are some techniques.

Brainstorm with yourself, colleagues, or friends what could be done if there were no constraints on human or financial resources. Then try to think of ways to get there on what you have or can get.

Read new books or listen to audiotapes to get new ideas on organizational behavior, personnel issues, or other management topics. But don't ignore novels, magazines, TV, or the news as sources of ideas you can recycle as potential solutions.

Play out what-if scenarios, the more offbeat the better. Play them through several times to ascertain who the cast of characters would have to be and how they would have to play their roles for your solution to work. Does it have a chance?

Put the best to the test. When you've developed what you consider a viable idea, don't spit it out all at once. Talk to your cast of characters about their roles, planting the seeds for acceptance of your plan. Entice others to buy into it and make it their own. Then you can present your idea, knowing your supporters will endorse it.

Build Idiosyncrasy Credits and Use Them Wisely

If you are a person who typically follows the rules, coming to meetings on time and generally cooperating and complying with direct requests for participating in campus events, you are banking idiosyncrasy credits as you go. From time to time, you can cash in these credits and use them to your advantage.

For example, if you want to move up in an organization, you may want to take an unpopular but notably principled stand on an issue. Because this would be contrary to your typical behavior, you'd be spending idiosyncrasy credits to do so, but you would be gaining stature as a person of integrity who has the courage to not just go along with the crowd.

You can spend these credits only on rare occasions as they take years to accumulate and only a few minutes to spend. If you try to overspend them, you'll soon be labeled a malcontent or a crackpot. Carefully spent, idiosyncrasy credits can be a singularly valuable asset that money can't buy.

Create an SLR System for Yourself

Borrowed from counseling language referring to a support-listen-respond (SLR) model, this strategy uses another person to help you think through options.

A friend or colleague can be a devil's advocate to challenge your unspoken assumptions, assess your skills and deficiencies objectively, and consider alternative ways to handle situations. This person need not always agree with you but must be a supportive "I'm on your side" person. You'll need to trust this person implicitly and value her or his ability to critically but not judgmentally assess you and your skills.

By using an SLR system, you control your moves and build your confidence and skills while choosing the openings that seem right for you, all in a supportive relationship seasoned with constructive criticism and feedback. In turn, you can do the same for another colleague, creating yet another win-win situation.

Trust: The Key Element in Your Career Advancement

May 1995

You can be smart, you can be effective, you can build new programs and new buildings—but if you can't be trusted, your career is dead in the water.

Although trust has a lot to do with shared values, shared goals, and shared perceptions, the bottom line is a confidence in another person's honesty, integrity, and reliability. It's also a matter of predictability, having faith that another will speak and act as you expect.

Leadership development doesn't often mention trust because trust is easier to define in its absence than in its presence. And it's easy to destroy and virtually impossible to rebuild once it's gone.

Linda A. Hill, associate professor at Harvard Business School, says that trust is a function of how an individual perceives a manager in three areas:

Competence: Does she know the right thing to do?

Character: Does she want to do the right thing?

Influence: Can she get it done?

Hill says that the more people trust you, the less often they'll require you to prove that you'll actually deliver what you've promised.

On the other hand, psychological studies repeatedly show that intermittent reinforcement is the most difficult response to extinguish. A little reinforcement now and then makes it difficult to entirely close the door on trusting someone.

For example, some might describe a colleague in administrative services as a flake. Meet at lunch, and her wisdom and understanding of sensitive situations are apparent. She's fun, a great person to bounce ideas off, get another viewpoint from, and reinforce that your perceptions can't be far from reality.

All of those attributes make you really want to trust her, but you've been burned too many times by broken promises, missed deadlines, incomplete reports, and innuendos to make that mistake again.

Say there's a movement afoot on campus to combine the offices of registration and financial aid. The heads of both offices are competent, well liked, experienced, and likely to do a good job heading a combined office.

Whom to choose?

Chances are, trust will be one of the unspoken variables in the decision.

How to Win Trust

The following suggestions are loosely adapted from the *Communications Briefings* newsletter, November 1993 issue.

- *Represent others' interests as well as your own.* People expect you, as a leader, to have your own wants, but they need to know how your agenda meshes with that of the group. If you are in a position of power and you constantly deny doing things that would achieve your own wants, you become a servant to the whims of others instead of a leader.

- *Gather information from others before making decisions.* Demonstrate that you are soliciting and considering their input and weighing the various options with sensitivity and logic. You don't have to do what they want, just consider it carefully, and be ready to justify your decision in your own mind.
- *Focus on the issues and ignore the egos.* Sometimes it hurts to make a decision that you know will benefit a smug competitor who will declare victory. Think about the long-term benefits to the campus rather than who will win.
- *Support others' decisions.* When they make a mistake, quick and clear follow-up can create a learning situation rather than an embarrassment.
- *Share information that can improve your unit's performance,* rather than hiding it to make yourself indispensable.
- *Admit your weaknesses.* Chances are, they already know them.
- *Communicate your fears and concerns* to head off problems and look for innovative solutions.
- *When you disagree with people, say so,* rather than stabbing them in the back later on.
- *Communicate bad news that affects others before the grapevine beats you to it* and erodes your credibility.
- *When you make a mistake, fess up, and move on.* Don't dwell on it, but accept blame and learn from it. It's more acceptable to be a human who occasionally makes mistakes than a know-it-all who has to be right all the time.

Trust is much more than not getting caught with your hand in the cookie jar. It's conducting yourself so that nobody would believe you ever had your hand there to begin with.

Mary Dee Wenniger

How to Get Where You Want to Go

January 1999

Why would a comfortable California consultant move to Washington, D.C., to identify and train women for the top academic positions of dean or above? The new director of the Office of Women in Higher Education at the American Council on Education (ACE) explained, "I feel like I'm doing the Goddess's work."

Having been the president of two colleges, adviser to search committees, and coach to top executives, Judith Sturnick knows the keys to professional advancement from all sides. She knows what the schools and search firms are looking for and how women who aspire to top jobs can best prepare.

In October, she led a workshop for Wisconsin Women in Higher Education Leadership, one of fifty state groups connected to her office. She's investing much of her first months at ACE in revitalizing the statewide networks for leadership development programs.

What Search Committees Look For

Search committees look for candidates who are intellectually alive, she said. Such candidates take committee leadership roles on campus or participate in a HERS leadership development program. They're extremely competent and seek out formal and informal professional development to acquire new skills.

They have the coping skills to deal with conflict and manage their own anger constructively. Emotionally resilient, they roll with the punches. They control their time, and they balance their work with other aspects of their lives.

A promising candidate plans her career and assesses herself realistically. She finds and works with a good mentor, who can help her determine when she's ready to be a dean or whether she belongs in administration at all.

Women can learn these skills. "You have more power and control over your life and career advancement than you may think you have. This is part of what we need to be teaching each other," Sturnick said.

Visibility on Campus

"Some of the most competent women are not in top spots because they're invisible," she said. As you train yourself for broader responsibilities, make yourself known beyond your own corner of campus.

- *Participate actively in daily interactions,* like informal contacts, meetings, and task forces.
- *Have a high profile on campus.* Be well prepared, and speak up with appropriate comments in meetings.
- *Practice persistence* to make sure you are heard. When others ignore your comments, repeat yourself as often as it takes.
- *Claim appropriate credit* for your ideas and suggestions. Firmly and politely stop others from running away with your input. Set up a buddy system with a colleague to speak up for you.
- *Work on interdepartmental projects.* Build experience and personal contacts beyond your department, office, or program.
- *Participate in a mixed-sex network.* You need not only women because they understand you but also men because the power structure is male.

- *Give others a chance to assess you.* Only by letting yourself be known do you let others evaluate your skills.

The most important thing has come to be relationships, Sturnick said. She's revitalized ACE's national forums to bring women who are qualified for senior-level positions together with women presidents who may choose to mentor and nominate them for appropriate positions. For two structured days, up to twenty-five women showcase their skills before a panel of established leaders who can make a critical difference in their careers.

Appropriate Risk-Taking

"The world is not going to come to us," she warned. Without risks you get nowhere, but think before acting.

- *Calculate the probable outcomes.* Be thoughtful and rational as you go in ways you never thought of before.
- *Consider the best- and worst-case scenarios.* Could you live with the worst case? Does the best case justify the risk?
- *Seek wise counsel.* Get input from a few whose judgment you trust.
- *Assess your inner self* to evaluate whether the potential political gain is worth the risk: How much emotional stress can you handle? How long can you endure uncertainties? What are your competencies and incompetencies? What's your level of resilience? If your scheme fails, will you bounce back?

Political Judgment

Some of women's problems result from misunderstanding the political culture. "We don't read the politics fast enough or thoroughly enough," she said. We aren't trained for it, we lack the right networks, and there aren't enough of us to test our realities on each other.

One factor is a difference in gender style. Men are always checking to see what their niche is in the organization. This means they're attuned to organizational politics from early in their careers, whereas women think more about inclusiveness, networks, and sharing information.

Power leads to more power. Women need to understand their school and know where the sources of formal and informal power lie. They need to acquire and use power tools like information, resources, and support systems.

Sturnick plans to develop a workshop on organizational politics that can be offered many times at both state and national levels. The more a woman understands political systems and masters the tools of power, the better she can deal with obstacles to advancement, for example:

- *The sticky floor.* Being irreplaceable in a boring job can block your promotion to something more interesting. Response: Train a successor or restructure the work so that it's easier to learn.
- *Rewards for obsessive behavior.* Some institutional cultures reward workaholism, praising a chancellor who lives in the dorm and answers e-mail at 3:00 A.M., or a dean who never takes a vacation. Response: Get someone from off campus to point out what's unhealthy in the culture.
- *Stereotypical views of women.* Some men say women are too emotional or aren't dedicated enough to their work. Response: Confront this directly without blowing your stack. Ask "What has led you to that conclusion?" or "How do you know that?"
- *Other women's hostility.* Women get angry at the system, then vent their anger on other women. Peers criticize out of jealousy; queen bees use their own success to argue that women don't face barriers to achievement. Response: Confront other women's hostility on the spot, preferably in the presence of other women so you don't get picked off. You can do this without violence and mayhem. When a woman president insists women don't have a problem at her institution, assemble enough power to force her to appoint a commission to discover the facts.
- *Self-doubt.* Like self-effacement, risk aversion, and distrust of power, self-doubt is an internal barrier that reflects cultural expectations. Women's confidence in themselves is easily shaken. Response: "We have the right and power to challenge anything," she said. Recognize and use that power.

Helping Women Succeed

"One of our concerns is staying power for women once they get into positions," Sturnick said. In her first six months at ACE, she worked with four women who were fired overnight; they either didn't see it coming or didn't have any strategy to deal with it. Although the number of women presidents in higher education has risen from 148 in 1975 to about 480 in 1998, on average they survive in office 2.2 years fewer than men. ACE is holding a series of roundtables for women presidents to compare notes on that phenomenon.

One told her that unhappy boards of trustees or regents send a message to men much earlier than they send it to women, and they send it in a male political code. A male board chair words a note in a way that lets a male president know he's in trouble. The same male board chair may delay writing to a woman president because he's not sure how to deal with a woman, or he may send a note in male code that she can't decipher.

Sturnick has seen this contrast repeatedly. In her previous coaching role, she got a call from a male president who had learned he was in trouble. He quickly phoned influential friends for support and was able to save his job. A few days later, she got a call from a woman president who had suspected she was in trouble but, hearing nothing explicit, went on about her business. By the time she was asked to resign, it was too late to do anything but negotiate the exit package.

Through workshops, forums, and roundtables, Sturnick helps women learn what they need to know to reach high positions and hold on to them once they're there. "We can achieve incredible things, and we can do it without being ruthless in the way men are sometimes ruthless. We can do it keeping our integrity and our values intact."

As part of her discussion, Judith Sturnick offered a guide to help women write out their thoughts on their careers.

Guide to Mapping Your Career

1. What are the title, job responsibilities, and salaries I desire within one year, two or three years, and five years?
2. List three obstacles to my mobility at my current school.
3. What is my history at the school, especially in the last three years?
4. What are three indicators of success in my current school, and how can I use them if I decide to stay there?
5. How would I characterize my current state of professional self-esteem?
6. How would I characterize my current state of personal self-esteem?
7. Am I limited by geographical location? If so, how much and why?
8. Am I limited by family responsibilities? If so, what are they, and will they change in the next three years?
9. What is the state of my health, including fatigue and burnout?
10. What do I want from my work and workplace, in terms of culture, values, work styles, teamwork, and reward system?
11. How would I describe my current professional image? Am I satisfied with it?
12. What skills do I currently lack for the job I want?
13. What are three strategies for gaining those skills?
14. Why do I want that job? List three reasons.
15. What could be one or two alternative career-life scenarios?
16. Who are eight people currently in my active network?

17. What specific help can I get from each of them?
18. Here are three concrete steps I can take to get my next jobs.
19. Do I expect to work, regardless of what else I might do?
20. What do I expect to happen politically, socially, economically, and techno-logically in the United States that will affect my life and career during the next five years?
21. What will be the most important campus issues during the next five years?
22. How do I feel about dealing with those issues?
23. What is my plan for self-care during the next six months, in terms of sleep, nutrition, exercise, support networks outside family, family support, time for reflection, journaling, recreation, vacations, calendar control, visualizations, affirmations, reading, and other?
24. At the end of my career, what legacies do I want to leave at my school?
25. What summary comments or observations have these questions evoked?

Sarah Gibbard Cook

How to Get That Job Interview

April 1999

The whole point of a résumé and cover letter is simply to get you an interview, so make them show you're the right woman for the job. Vice President Kate John-son of the Spelman and Johnson Group, a higher education search and consult-ing firm, reviews five hundred to one thousand résumés a year for client colleges and universities. "We find people spend hours and hours doing their résumé and cover letter, then they use exactly the same résumé for five different jobs," she said at the NAWE meeting in February, where she and Ellen Heffernan described the realities of today's job market.

Start by studying the ad to learn what the school really wants. What phrases come up again and again? What assumptions does the ad imply? What's the back-ground of the school and the position? Do they want a self-starter or a yes-per-son, someone to lead in new directions or to follow in the founder's footsteps? Try to crack their code.

A university advertised for "a Vice President for Academic Affairs/Dean of the Faculty who can assist its new President in actively developing the University's strategic intent to become the nation's leading 'New American College'—a truly integrated model of the traditional liberal arts and professional/pre-professional studies."

The ad described the university's "teaching resources at the cutting edge of technology" and its award-winning information technology center. Other key words besides technology included delegate, innovation, teaching, and scholarship. The woman they hired had been an American Council on Education Fellow at a top New American College, just the type of school the university aspired to become. "Don't try to reinvent yourself," Johnson said. Don't mislead, but be selective. Which of your many traits, skills, and experiences make you a great fit for this job?

It Ain't Necessarily So

Myths about résumés abound. For example:

- Myth: *Fancy paper makes the best impression.* It's tough to fax and impossible to scan. Stick with good quality bond.
- Myth: *A résumé should never exceed one page.* A second or third page is fine if it's all relevant to the search.
- Myth: *Educational background always comes first.* Sometimes it does, and sometimes it doesn't, depending how much it strengthens your case. Start your résumé with whatever is most important.
- Myth: *A spellchecker will catch all your errors.* Don't putt two much trussed inn it too dew yore proofreading four yew.
- Myth: *E-mail experience counts as computer competency.* Ha!

Instead of a set formula, arrange the résumé to highlight whatever the school is looking for. Be creative; put the pieces in an order that makes sense, emphasizes functions, and connects you to the position description. Keep it simple and easy to read; attention wanders after page one. Give context for your experiences: "Smith, a small private college." Give scope and perspective: "I started a new program on X that attracted Y students." Johnson and Heffernan's firm doesn't look further back than ten or fifteen years; if your publications go back forever, say that you've published eighty-four papers and will provide citations on request.

The cover letter has the same goal as the résumé, to get you as far as the interview. It should run about one or two pages and use bullets for easy reading. Use it to repeat points on your résumé that link you to the ad; explain any gaps, like the year you spent touring Europe; show you know something about the position and have bothered to learn about the school; and make the case for why you're a good match to the job.

References

Choose carefully who can speak to your talents and achievements: professional and academic colleagues, supervisors, alumni, or even students. One committee seeking a vice president for student affairs insisted on a student reference. If you and your supervisor don't get along, tell the search committee up front: "Our styles don't match; that's one reason I want to leave." Sooner or later, they'll talk to him anyway, but you'll have paved the way.

Call your references and tell them what you're doing. You don't want them telling the search committee, "Oh, sure, I remember her. I haven't talked to her in years! What's she up to these days?" Double-check their phone numbers, addresses, and job titles. Can they be reached by e-mail? Do they mind being called at home? Send your references the ad and your résumé, and explain why you'd be a good fit for the job. Prepare your references to speak on your behalf. Later, you can go back and ask them what they were asked. Keep them up to date, and don't forget to say thanks.

Getting Set for the Interview

Do your homework. "You're interviewing the school as much as they're interviewing you," Heffernan said. Get some historical information, and ask your colleagues about the culture. What are the offices like? Where are the tensions? Make a list of questions you want answered. Use a campus visit to learn the institution's expectations for itself and for you. "It's becoming wild and woolly out there in higher education," Johnson said. Contracts today specify numerical goals for students, dollars, or the like. The school may envision rapid change or deep-rooted tradition. Make sure it fits not only your qualifications but also your beliefs and values.

Then walk into the interview with three reasons you want them, three reasons for them to want you, and three good questions you plan to ask. Good luck!

Sarah Gibbard Cook

Negotiating a Win-Win Job: Practical Tips from the Hot Seat in Dreaded Job Interviews

August 1996
Donna Clevinger
On the road to another interview for associate dean
Just as the turn-of-the-century melodrama often had two titles, such as *Pure as the Driven Snow,* or *A Working Girl's Secret,* so does the job interview: theirs and yours.

These practical tips come from your side, based on about twenty-five recent interviews by my colleagues and me.

Before the Interview

Do Your Homework. Find out all you can about the job and school. Ask the search committee for an information packet on the school and surrounding area. Check the student newspaper. Find out about the faculty, staff, and administrators you would be working with regularly.

While researching one small college, a colleague noticed two-thirds of the teaching faculty had at least one degree from the same state school. Having failed the phone interview, she later learned the school had hired the interim who, not surprisingly, had also graduated from that same state school.

Check Out the Environment. Realistically, could you live there? Would it serve your professional and personal needs and goals? This might seem insignificant now, but it could be vital to your future comfort.

To get in the mood, try those books on how to interview. Current materials such as the *New York Times,* journals in your own field, your resume, and, of course, *Women in Higher Education* will come in handy as well. Be sure to buy a local newspaper once you arrive. You might also want to write down your name; I forgot mine briefly once during introductions.

Prepare for the Phone Interview. Before deciding whom to invite to campus, many search committees interview a short list of candidates by phone. Some calls can be very pleasant and positive, whereas others can be confusing and intimidating. Whether formal or informal, the phone interview deserves your serious preparation.

At the beginning, make sure you're introduced to all those who are listening to or participating in the call, to help you decide how to answer their questions. Candidates who survive phone interviews share these traits: enthusiasm, conversational approach, truthfulness, confidence, positive attitude, sense of humor, and being oneself.

If you make this short list, stick to your game plan. There's information you want to share, so make sure to find a way. After I bombed in one phone interview, I found it helpful to rehearse aloud with a friend. During that unsuccessful interview, I became frustrated while shuffling through my notes and changed my style and answers to fit what I thought the interviewer wanted. Asking for clarification on some questions, I got the curt response, "However you want to interpret it."

Stick to a pace you feel comfortable with, even if the interviewer seems to be pressing for a speedy response, trying to keep that day's phone interviews on schedule. Express your personality through your answers, and stay in control of the situation. Try to say something distinctive that the search committee will remember, to help you stand out from other candidates in a positive way.

Above all, be honest when answering questions. Use concise phrasing, don't stumble over words, watch long silences while responding to a question, and sound professional, like you know what you're talking about. They can hear many things through the phone, so watch the deep breaths, background noises, chomping on a pencil or ice, and shuffling papers.

Sometimes the interviewer is difficult to understand due to a regional dialect or to the speakerphone itself. Don't hesitate to ask for a repeat of the question. This is your last shot at getting an on-campus visit, so make sure you understand what they are asking of you.

Finally, don't forget to take the chance to ask questions, even though the interviewers may say the time is almost up. This is your interview too, even on their quarter.

The On-Campus Interview

Take Phone Numbers. Before leaving for an interview, make sure you get an itinerary, including travel schedule, meetings, meals, hotel, and office and home phone numbers of contacts in case plans change. A friend was scheduled to fly in Sunday evening and be driven to the hotel by members of the search committee. When no one met her at the gate or responded to paging, she decided to call the chair of the search committee, discovering that she had only his office number and the home number was unlisted. Luckily she remembered the hotel name.

Bring Only What Is Necessary. Even for a two-day interview, don't be bogged down with luggage. When two men from a search committee met a colleague at an airport, they were shocked and delighted that she brought only one carry-on suitcase. They said the last candidate brought "enough suitcases for a fashion show" and spent more time "fixing herself up" between meetings than attending meetings.

Bring just what you need based on the itinerary and one extra outfit. Good hotels have irons. For air travel, carry on your bags. Traveling light makes it easier for all and could make a good impression. And you have only one chance to make that good first impression.

Books on interviewing warn of using fragrances and extreme hairstyles. They also suggest going for a natural appearance, dressing comfortably and conservatively, and bringing a briefcase instead of a purse.

Have interview materials like pad, pens, and résumé easily accessible in the briefcase. Once I missed the first two questions of an interview with my head stuck in my purse, searching for a pen. This was not a great beginning.

Bring Medications. Travel changes your stress level, sleep patterns, and diet, and could cause discomforts such as an upset stomach, nausea, or headaches. So bring the vitamins and medications you take each day, as well as medications for just in case. Don't rely on hotel gift shops or all-night pharmacies. Sticking to foods you are accustomed to, along with your usual sleep time, will help the body and soul handle brief setbacks. As they say on TV, "Don't let them see you sweat," even if you're not feeling your best. Knowledge eases the stress level.

Bring Food. Maria Perez, who heads a New York city search firm serving colleges, advises bringing emergency food to refuel. A peanut butter sandwich once saved me.

The search committee's first meeting was a buffet breakfast. Everyone was eating while my meal sat before me, as committee members took turns asking me questions. Eating was impossible for me, for fear of food being fired out of my mouth or nose during a response or, worse yet, choking! So I held out for lunch, thinking I might be able to cram down a sandwich. But no way! The lunch was yet another gathering of different administrators and faculty members. Once again, my food sat. So before the afternoon meetings, off to the rest room I went to scarf down my peanut butter sandwich. It was my best meal of the day!

Take Attendance. After several days of preparing for an interview and then traveling more than five hundred miles with two plane changes and an overnight weather delay, a friend arrived at the interview site only to find that the dean had chosen that time for elective surgery. She was told that the search committee, after interviewing the five candidates invited to campus, would make three recommendations to the dean, who would then follow up with phone interviews. None of the five candidates was ever contacted by phone, she learned from the dean's secretary, and the interim got the permanent job.

After hearing this and similar tales, I now ask the search committee before I go whether I will get to meet and talk with all those involved in the hiring process. I also ask if an inside candidate is being considered. Of the sixteen schools with inside candidates for the positions I applied for, only three hired an outside candidate. In reading the *Chronicle of Higher Education,* I noticed that vacant positions are often filled by the interim candidate. It's difficult to dethrone one who has already tried out for the job, so consider this in deciding whether to interview.

Assume Nothing. Even if the interview goes extremely well, don't assume you'll be offered the position. You usually have no idea who is your competition or what went on in other interviews. I felt great after one two-and-a-half-day interview: committee members were all smiles; I received compliments on the way I handled the tough questions, numerous pats on the back, and even a hug from the dean. But I never received the congratulatory phone call. My "You're fantastic but. . . ." rejection letter came ten days later. Besides being hurt, I wondered what had happened. Now I make it a point to follow up on all interviews.

Follow Up. Before I leave an interview, I ask when they expect to reach a decision. I follow up by asking if I could contact her or him if the decision is not made in my favor. But be careful here, as this is not the time to undercut the great impression you've established. If you do ask, do so in a positive, upbeat manner. Personally, I want feedback for self-improvement, learning what my competition had that I lacked, and developing my job search skills.

Those Special Interview Questions

Illegal questions. Watch out for illegal questions that may sneak in at any time: during a one-on-one meal, a reception, a social gathering, or a stress-filled meeting. A faculty member, administrator, or even a spouse may discuss his personal life, marital status, age, children, religious beliefs, or native traditions and expect some kind of response. He may ask questions he does not realize are illegal or would not ask in a different setting. So before you get caught up, decide ahead of time how you'll answer those intentional or unintentional questions. Whatever your choice, be positive and tactful, ask for clarification or relevancy, and always use good eye contact.

What-if questions. Designed to find out how you would handle certain situations or individuals, or to reveal your character, these questions can offer you a chance to present winning examples from your own work history.

Questions they are most likely to ask. What can you tell us about yourself? Why do you want this job? What can you do for us that no one else can? What are your greatest strengths? What are your greatest weaknesses? Why do you want to leave your present or last job? What do you see yourself doing in the next five or ten years?

Questions you should ask. What can you tell me about your department, college, or school? Apart from the job description, what attributes would your ideal person have for the position? What are your department, college, school's greatest strengths? Greatest weaknesses? Why is this job vacant? What does the department, college, school see itself doing in the next five or ten years? What is the salary and benefits package?

Weird questions I've been asked. Who would you least like us to contact as a reference and why? Can you name three people who have affected your professional life for the better and for the worst, and explain why? What color is your lipstick? How short are you? And the one that gets the prize: Would you write something for us so we could analyze your handwriting?

After the Interview

Back home, you should feel confident you did all you could do to match with the position. This is the time of reflection, deciding if you would accept the job if offered, weighing its advantages and disadvantages.

Talking to trusted friends, colleagues, and family members is important, but the ultimate decision is yours. After much encouragement from friends, a colleague turned down two separate job offers after realizing that the schools could not meet her professional goals and the environments were not suitable for her family.

Write thank-you notes to the search committee and others at the interview. You never know what the future may bring, so leave a positive lasting impression no matter what the outcome.

If the search committee plans to telephone the candidate of choice within a certain time period, don't be a slave to the home or office. Take time to reward yourself. After all, a single position could have hundreds of applicants, so your making it into the final four is a great accomplishment in itself.

Even if either party decides against the match, believe me, the next interview will be a lot easier!

Negotiating a Win-Win Job as a Campus Administrator

December 1996

When the big job is almost in your pocket, it's tempting to overlook pesky little details like salary and benefits. But unless you do pay close attention to them, don't expect to get what you're worth. That's the view of Janet Wright, a Toronto-based search consultant with extensive experience in the university environment. Wright discussed the art of negotiation in the September 1996 issue of the *SWAAC Newsletter* (Senior Women Academic Administrators of Canada).

Negotiating a contract for a senior position in academic administration is a "delicate, and to many people, a distasteful task," she notes. Unless you do it carefully, chances are very high that you won't be fairly compensated for the hard work you do. Some women administrators are unskilled in and disinclined to negotiate. One way to look at negotiation is to compare it to lovemaking. Both parties want to please each other, and they want the union to be long and mutually satisfying. But unless they each ask for what they want and need, chances are that neither will be entirely satisfied.

When to Negotiate

Depending on circumstances leading to your candidacy, you may need to set ground rules even before becoming a candidate: "Nobody wants to have their search committee fall in love with someone they can't afford," says Wright, "or somebody who has preconditions that are going to be problematic when it comes time for appointment." If you're approached by someone on behalf of an institution, you owe it to the recruiter to outline your conditions early on.

However, if you are applying directly for a position, she suggests waiting until there's some expression of interest from the school before stating your needs. "You don't want to be seen as a prima donna who has unrealistic expectations, before you even know if the committee is interested." Once you're short-listed, it's a different ball game. Ask the person handling the recruitment when terms and conditions will be discussed. Ask when the selection committee expects to make a decision about the appointment.

Evaluating the Offer

When the offer comes, how do you know what to ask for? Wright says it's important to consult with colleagues in comparable situations. "I think women are not particularly good at getting advice from their colleagues. Men will ask questions and share information among themselves, but women sometimes assume they're out there on their own."

For salary information, consider talking to someone in the same geographic region and at the same size and type of school. Before presenting your needs, she also recommends asking the recruiter about the incumbent's salary and perks, and the salary range the institution has in mind for you. You may be able to figure out what the norm is and has been. Beyond salary, what do you include in your contract? Although it depends on the kind of position, SWAAC members suggest considering a variety of terms.

In the final stages of negotiation, professional advisers can be helpful. An accountant or financial planner can help you calculate your after-tax income and other financial implications, and a lawyer should review the contract before you sign it.

What About a Search Committee?

What role does the search consultant play? Wright emphasizes that although a third party is hired by the recruiting school, her job is to be an honest broker between candidate and school. "Our role is to help our clients find the best and the brightest candidates for the position and to help candidates determine whether this is the right fit for them, and then to make the match," she says.

It may be easier to discuss salary and contract issues with a consultant than with a future colleague or boss, and you can reasonably ask the consultant to keep some of your concerns confidential. If you have serious reservations about the position for any reason, the consultant should be aware of them and may be able to help resolve them.

Contract Considerations

Keep in mind the phrase "Everything is negotiable" as you consider what would make you most happy, effective, and likely to succeed in your new administrative campus job. Remember, what you may find most important may be no big deal to another and vice versa. Consider length of term; when and how to determine reappointment; phase-out or termination provisions; provisions for annual goal setting and performance review; relocation allowance, including packing and return move if needed; determination of salary increments; pension provisions; conditions of disability insurance; tenure conditions; administrative or academic leave; expectations about teaching and research; travel expenses; expectations for gifts, donations, and entertainment; administrative support; salary and rank upon return to faculty position; other perks, such as child care, club memberships, car, free tuition for children, and housing allowances; research funds; discretionary funds; and legal fees.

Dianne Jenkins

How to Get Paid What You're Worth in Your New Job

April 1998

You'll never have a better chance to negotiate the best compensation package for yourself than when you first come on board. Women realize there's more to compensation than meets the eye, considering other benefits besides salary, especially in the higher administrative levels.

The tangible payoff for your hard work at personal career development depends on your own willingness to work equally hard to get the best package possible for *you*. Five rules apply to female academics as well as corporate executives.

Rule 1: Know Your Market Value

Every spring, the College and University Personnel Association releases a report covering more than 150 administrative positions in doctoral, comprehensive, baccalaureate, and two-year schools. Check it out, then use your networks to learn regional variations, the norms for nonsalary elements of compensation and the salary differences between public and private schools.

Many public schools have an inflexible salary range for each position. That range is public information although it's bad form to ask the search committee any financial questions before you're under serious consideration. But it's fine to ask the search consultant if the institution is using one, says Maria Perez, head of Perez-Arton Consultants in Ossining, New York. Consultants are most often involved in recruiting candidates for jobs at the dean's level and above.

Rule 2: Be Reasonable

Bizarre, premature, or constantly changing demands can make a committee regret it ever met you. Ask about compensation policy details before signing a contract, but don't expect a waiver of every policy you dislike. Again, private schools can be more flexible than public ones. You have the most negotiating power if you're a rare very hot property as a faculty member or a candidate for dean, vice president, or president.

Some top-level women administrators negotiate compensation packages that provide flexibility and personal time, especially if they're working on doctorates. Two examples are Mary Fox, vice president for university relations at St. Mary's University, Minnesota, and Lynn Gangone, executive director of the National Association for Women in Education (NAWE). Both negotiated for reduced time on the job so they could attend classes and work on dissertations.

In some circumstances, it's reasonable to ask the school to update its policy. As a president, you're expected to entertain. What if all your predecessors had wives to play hostess? "They think you can do it all. After all, you're Superwoman!" Perez said. One presidential candidate negotiated full-time household help and the right to change her staff. A mother with three children needs to be free to make adjustments if the housekeeper hates kids.

Plan to keep any redecorating well within the decorating budget and institutional and community norms. Presidents have gotten into trouble for redecoration that was extravagant by local standards. If the house or office is in nice condition but doesn't suit your taste, you can ask about redecoration, but don't take it for granted. A no for reasons of cost might be open to discussion, but in a historic building you may have to live with the Victorian wallpaper.

Rule 3: Know Exactly What You Want

Make a wish list and then sort out the musts from the things you can live without. If you plan to insist on some items outside the school's traditions, you'd better be ready to compromise on others.

An administrative relocation can make you give up a lot: job security, professional development opportunities, retirement plans, and even home equity if the school provides your housing. Check it out.

Not every administrative position automatically carries faculty rank and tenure. Many prohibit both at the dean's level and above. Some permit faculty rank but not tenure, and others allow tenure but only after a waiting period of up to five years. Decide how much you care even before you ask.

How important to you is your own professional development? The university probably has institutional memberships in associations like ACE, AAHE, AACC, or AACU; does it also buy you an individual membership, or will you have to pay for it yourself? Will the school pay your way to appropriate leadership institutes like those at NILD, HERS, or NAWE, or the New Presidents' Institute at Harvard?

What happens to you if things don't work out? Institutional policy may or may not permit severance agreements. A $100,000-a-year vice president who drops to faculty rank at $50,000 takes a 50 percent pay cut. One who's not allowed to switch to teaching is out in the cold. Here's where tenure comes in handy. Position yourself so that you won't lose health benefits, life insurance, or unused vacation time.

Rule 4: Don't Overemphasize Salary

If the college or university can't meet your salary goals, look at the rest of the package before you say no—and if the salary looks good, be sure you know what job-related expenses it's expected to cover. The higher your level, the more financial elements a package involves in addition to salary.

Retirement. "Some thirty- or forty-year-old candidates may say they don't need to worry about retirement yet. They do," Perez said. What's the retirement package? Is it portable? Plans are changing rapidly, with greater employee contributions and changing federal laws.

Most private schools are in the TIAA program, which vests reasonably quickly, but some state systems take ten years to vest. That means if you leave after nine years, you take out only what you put in. Ask if you can switch to an alternate plan like TIAA or Fidelity. "People need to crunch the numbers on retirement. Women are getting more sophisticated about this," she said.

Travel. Don't take anything for granted. Some community colleges don't reimburse candidates for travel expenses. Many schools won't pay for your family or significant other to visit the community. A few don't pay relocation expenses, and some pay a fixed amount for relocation, regardless of actual cost.

Get a clear definition of appropriate use for any car the school provides and plan to keep scrupulous records. You never know who may demand them: the regents, the legislature, or the IRS.

More and more colleges and universities have relationships with schools overseas. Learn the policy on overseas travel on behalf of the school. It may vary according to your position level. If you want your spouse or significant other to come along, that's your business and usually your own expense.

Entertaining. At the dean's level and above, ask what entertaining you're expected to do. Dinners for students, faculty, alumni, and community notables? Then you'll need an allowance with very clear guidelines for uses and accounting. What will the university provide, what comes out of your entertainment allowance, and what's your own financial responsibility?

To avoid issues later, keep a sharp distinction between personal and school property. "That can be one of the uglier ones," she said. One presidential couple used their own silverware, china, and linens when they entertained for the university. Their associates assumed that all were university property. When the couple moved on, they were unjustly accused of absconding with university property.

Housing. Many schools provide housing for the president; a few private ones also house vice presidents and deans. Ask if you have to live there and whether there's a housing allowance. Request a professional inspection, and have the school do all necessary repairs before you move in.

Get a clear definition of the line between public and private areas of the house; its appropriate and expected uses; and the financial responsibility for heat, light, phone, and meals. Learn the IRS rules before you calculate expenses; housing isn't free if it's taxed as compensation.

Rule 5: Be Willing to Walk Away

Only you can define your bottom line. Tenure and generous severance and retirement provisions? The right to choose your home in the best school district for your children? Health benefits for a domestic partner? Time to finish your dissertation? Knowing your walk-away point helps you negotiate with confidence and protects you from accepting a job that you know in your heart can't meet your needs.

Perez's basic advice: "You ask, you ask, and you ask for it in writing." Crunch the numbers. Involve your attorney and accountant. "This is your life. Pay attention to the details."

Sarah Gibbard Cook

A Practical Guide to When It's Time to Be Movin' On

December 1999
From the October 1999 conference of the Organization for the Study of Communication, Language, and Gender, Wichita

When to Make a Change

Caryn Medved, visiting assistant professor at Ohio University's School of Interpersonal Communication, spoke at the OSCLG annual conference. She suggested:

Look at your personal life. Personally, I couldn't see myself explaining to my husband, who had moved twice for me, why I couldn't relocate to accommodate him.

Check for compatible goals. If your goals are not those of your department or your school, it's time to go.

Expand your vistas. You need not stay in academe, when there are opportunities in business and elsewhere.

Forget about being indispensable. We all want to think we're impossible to replace; I recently saw my former grad students, who are doing fine with their new advisers.

Gain new experience elsewhere. If what you need to reach your long-term goals is elsewhere, go after it.

Consider refocusing your own job. Following new interests within the framework of your current job, such as a new research focus, is still moving on.

Compare the differences between organizational and professional loyalty. I think of my job as portable; I could work anywhere. I'm tied to my profession but not to the organization as a tenured faculty would be. Having moved six times in seven years, twelve times in my lifetime, I believe leaving is a good thing if you do it in a way that's true to yourself. I enjoy the change!

Top Ten Tips on When to Move On

Lois S. Self, who chairs the Department of Communications at Northern Illinois University, offered some thoughts as well:

At my university a story is ritualistically told to new department chairs by experienced chairs.

> "Have you found the three envelopes in your desk drawer from your predecessor? They're numbered and to be opened in sequence when you hit major crises."
>
> The initiate proceeds happily until a major conflict surfaces, and then she opens envelope number one. The message is "Blame it on your predecessor." This strategy gets her by.
>
> But another crisis soon descends. The message in envelope number two is "Blame it on the dean." This seems to get the chair off the hook, and things proceed smoothly for some time.
>
> Then academic internecine war breaks out. With high hopes for relief, she opens envelope number three. The message is "Prepare three envelopes!"

This story represents an all-too-common but unhealthy pattern of how campus career decisions about moving on are often made: leave when there's no one left to blame for your failures and frustrations but yourself. Of course, there's a kernel of wisdom in taking personal responsibility for both career satisfaction and success.

Most of us want more out of our careers and organizations than playing blame games. Fortunately, there are other more positive and proactive ways to decide about career change, ones that are more conducive to sustaining both your ego and your reputation. Based on my own experience in a career now almost thirty years in the making, here's my top ten list for how and when to make a change.

- Move on when you're bored. This means you can't find engaging new challenges and interactions, and you're spinning your wheels and collecting dust.
- Move on when you feel too frustrated to be effective. If you're making yourself and most likely others angry and collecting bad memories, it's time.
- Move on when you aren't learning anything new. Having your job down to a tee is great, but if it gets to be a career-mental-spiritual dead end, it's time for a change.

- Move on when you can't seem to please anyone, especially yourself, and your life priorities seem out of balance. It isn't working; your time and energy are not sufficient for what you're trying or are simply not netting a good return on investment. Change is tapping you on the shoulder.
- Move on when you're getting paranoid, thinking even your best friends or family no longer understand or support you. Either they don't or you're too stressed out to be effective or both. Change is likely to help all concerned.
- Move on when those you mentor more often have to make you look good, instead of the other way around. Either you're not giving much or your ego needs have gotten too big or both.
- Move on when you feel you're making excellent cases for important priorities, but no one is listening. You probably aren't, and they aren't either.
- Move on when you hear the winds of change at your back, but you don't want to ride them. Maybe you'll see someone behind you who really does want to and will do it well, who will preserve and improve what you've accomplished. Don't be so sure your job is your baby; you can let the baby grow up and move on.
- Move on when you see how you can take with you experiences and knowledge, what I call "system savvy," that will help you make a bigger contribution and take on more rewarding challenges. Caution: don't assume it's all transferable and that you can walk into a new arena with all the answers.
- Move on when your inner spirit says it's time, when you could happily stay, but the open road beckons. Don't wear out your welcome. Move while they still want you to stay, when you know you've done your best but making a change really seems like more fun.

Remember, your career is all the productive stuff you do, not just this job. Your life is much more than that, and change is the only constant—which is what keeps it interesting.

Mary Dee Wenniger

Tips to Help You Survive a Midlife Career Transition

June 1999

Midlife women professionals no longer assume they'll keep the same career until they retire. Realities for the baby boom generation include the prospect of multiple career changes and work beyond any predetermined age. That's true for females in academia as well as any other sector, if not more so. But because change is common doesn't mean it's easy. At a workshop on career transitions for women in midlife, preceding the NAWE annual meeting in Denver in February 1999, Suzanne Forsyth described what to expect and how to get through the internal trauma of a big career transition.

She spoke from personal as well as professional experience. Formerly assistant director of personnel and associate dean of students at Georgetown University, she directed human resources for the American Council on Education (ACE) for more than twenty years. She left when she saw ACE building a hierarchical model after she'd spent her life advocating for and doing participatory management. In 1997, Forsyth joined the Kaludis Consulting Group in Washington, D.C., as a vice president.

Breaking from the Past

"Change can occur in a minute, but the transition can take years," she said. Transition, like grief, has predictable stages that are important to work through. It starts with the four Ds: disengagement, disidentification, disenchantment, and disorientation.

Disengagement. Before you're really ready for something new, you must leave the familiar behind. Take time to get away. Newlyweds take a honeymoon; adolescents go off to college. Go on retreat or find another way to break out of your old surroundings.

Disidentification. Self-image, self-definition, and social relationships all change when you leave a career. This is the inner side of disengagement. Unless you let go of your old professional identity, it's likely to get in the way. You may need to resign from professional organizations that can't help you network toward your new career.

Disenchantment. You probably started your last career with rosy optimism, but somewhere along the way something changed. It's not unusual to sense that your workplace betrayed your trust, like a child who feels betrayed by her parents when she learns there is no Santa Claus.

Disorientation. Whether or not you've already left the old job, breaking away emotionally can be disorienting. Past, present, and future don't flow the way you're used to; cause and effect don't follow their normal patterns. You're not sure which coincidences are meaningful and which just happen by accident. There's a gap in the continuity of your existence.

The uncomfortable neutral zone between your old and new identities will pass, but it's wise to spend some time there before you move on. "It feels terrible, but it is a critical stage," she said. "Look at your fears and gain courage and permission to feel lousy."

Fertile Emptiness

You can use that disconcerting gap between ordinary life and the future as a fertile emptiness to plant the seeds for your new life.

- *Take your time.* Living through transition is a long slow process. Don't try to bypass it by jumping at the first available job.
- *Arrange temporary structures.* A short-term position or project can help shape the interval between jobs or careers. ACE has frequently designated some people senior scholars to give them time and space between more permanent career moves.
- *Don't act for the sake of acting.* Resist taking the wrong job just to have a job. Allow space for personal growth and grieving.
- *Recognize why you are uncomfortable.* Even the most desirable change involves loss and confusion. "Distress is not the sign that something is wrong, just that something is changing," she said.
- *Take care of yourself in little ways.* Be kind to yourself. Cultivate a support system. Find times and places to be alone. Soak in a bubble bath.
- *Explore the other side of change.* Apply learned optimism to reframe your losses as opportunities.
- *Get someone to talk to.* Friends, allies, or counselors can ward off isolation, especially if they don't pretend to know the answers. "Beware of listeners who know exactly how to run your life."
- *Find out what is waiting in the wings of your life.* Our jobs can never use our entire selves. What potential interests or skills do you have that you haven't yet tapped?
- *Use the transition as an impetus to a new kind of learning.* This may be your opportunity to pick up computer skills or start your first-ever journal.
- *Recognize that transition has a characteristic shape.* It moves from the break with the past through the emptiness of the neutral zone into positive planning for the next phase of your life.

Looking Toward the Future

Just as children are trained to look both ways before crossing a street, in midlife we need to look at both our past and our potential before we can cross safely from one career to another. The fertile emptiness between careers is a time for introspection. Many guidebooks and workshops can help you clarify who you are, what you want, and what you have to offer.

During her transition from administration to consulting, Forsyth drew daily sustenance from the following poem by Marla Visser in *Images of Women in Transition:*

A New Day

The world is clean—
    Washed by the rain,
Fresh and new, smelling of
    damp earth, green grass and spring;
And I feel as if life were beginning
Again for me, that like the
    willows, I have renewed my bones
With fledging leaves. My face
    turned upward to welcome the rain;
And I, for all my years, am newly born,
Seeing the world with wondering eyes.

    Marla Visser

Principles of Change

Change creates fear
    but fear can be overcome.
Change is hard
    but it's doable.
The only person you can change is you
    and nobody else.
Expect change
    and enjoy it.
Change is action
    in the face of fear.
Change is really exchange
    so go for it.
Change is possible
    even if it doesn't feel like it.
Don't attempt major change alone;
    do it with an ally.
The answer may be acceptance
    and not action.
Change is a process
    and not an event.

    Suzanne Forsyth

Of Choices and Trade-Offs: Reflections on a Twisted Path

September 1998
Sarah Gibbard Cook
Independent historian

If I'd known as a graduate student in the 1960s and early 1970s what I learned later about academia and gender, I might have made some different decisions. But I'm not at all sure I'd be happier today as a result.

Perhaps I'd have smiled less and argued more in class. I might have decided against getting married or at least kept my original last name. I might have postponed having a child for a decade or so, though any timing brings its own challenges. If I'd understood how the informal residency requirements differ from the formal ones, I might have stayed at Harvard instead of joining my husband in Ethiopia. Becoming a familiar face on campus might have improved my academic prospects, and I never would have known what I was missing. It's all trade-offs. Whether we make them deliberately or by default, most women sooner or later shortchange some aspects of our potential for other aspects. Men too, I suspect, though the patterns are different.

Academic Upbringing

I grew up on university campuses; my vision of heaven was green rolling lawns, ivy-covered buildings, and endless books. My father was a sociology professor and academic administrator. My mother, limited by nepotism rules and geographical isolation, earned two master's degrees and taught French to engineering students who needed to pass a language requirement. To earn her Ph.D. would have required a three-hour commute. She was promoted from lecturer to assistant professor the year she retired.

Perhaps I was raised to fulfill my mother's dreams, though I didn't see it that way at the time. Certainly I was not raised to be a Cinderella. In the 1950s, when girls asked each other whether they wanted a family or a career, my parents told me there was no reason not to do both.

It was a good message for which I am grateful. I misinterpreted it in two ways: undervaluing my mother's choices and underestimating the challenges ahead. With youthful arrogance, I assumed the previous generation's failure to combine motherhood and profession gracefully was the sum of their individual failures. If you were good enough—my transcripts and test scores rated me very good indeed—nothing could bar your path.

Undergraduate Success

Four idyllic years at Oberlin College reinforced my ideals and illusions. It was not only possible but practically obligatory to aim for the academic heights, and in those boom years of the 1960s there was no doubt we'd achieve them without having to sacrifice a thing. Not that we actually had women professors with husbands and children to show us how it was done.

At a meeting for senior history majors entitled "After Graduation, What?" a faculty panel told how to choose your graduate school, how to apply, and what to expect in grad school and your college teaching career. They opened the floor to questions. A timid hand rose in the back of the room. "What about those of us who don't want to go to grad school and teach college history?" After an awkward silence, one professor took the bull by the horns. "You could do something else, I suppose. Next question?"

Harvard Grad School

Grad school at Harvard was culture shock: big, urban, formal, and impersonal. For the first time, I had to open my book bag at the library exit, an insult after Oberlin's honor system. I thoroughly enjoyed exploring Cambridge and Boston, and spending musty hours in the library basement using books that hadn't been checked out since 1893. My roommates and I cleaned the apartment to the sound of the Beatles, and my college-boyfriend-turned-soldier came for weekend visits by motorcycle. Two months into my second year, I got married.

My faculty adviser congratulated me, suggested a dissertation topic viable regardless of location, and promised me a job "wherever your husband might be." In fact, my husband planned to work wherever I got a teaching job, but my professors assumed the opposite. By the time my dissertation was written, my adviser had retired and the history job market had collapsed. Another professor remembered me only as "the one who went off and got married." The Harvard history faculty strove to place their "serious" graduates but took no responsibility for anyone geographically restricted by a husband. I wasn't, but it made a good excuse.

Not Just a Pretty Face

In a ritual now familiar to many, I studied job announcements, exchanged two hundred applications for letters of rejection, and flew off to interviews where I came away as first or second alternate. I knew it was my fault: I looked good on paper but lacked charisma. One year, I was the visiting assistant professor of British history at the University of Chicago, where one department member described my contribution as "decorative" and another praised my "ready smile." When they told me about the ideal man to be hired for the permanent position, they said if they hadn't found him, they'd have asked me to stay—for a second year, while they continued the search.

Life went on; it usually does. Half-a-dozen years out of grad school, I began to notice that some whose careers had started more propitiously than mine weren't getting tenure. Meanwhile, I'd done odds and ends, worked two years for a publishing house, then settled into a fascinating job managing not-for-profit international development programs. My sense of failure faded, as did my willingness to relocate in order to teach. I learned a lot about international development and did some good in the world.

Life didn't go on for my husband. After his death from cancer, I stayed five more years in international development but found myself yearning to get back into history. Eventually, I left my job for a vaguely defined intent to write. Thanks to contacts and referrals from my old life in publishing and not-for-profits, within a few years I had enough freelance assignments to keep me in groceries. In time, I met my new love over the Internet. Because my business was more portable than his, we agreed on his locale to start our life together.

Academics Doing Other Things

So here I am amid the cows and cornfields of rural Wisconsin, near enough to Madison to find an ethnic restaurant and far enough out to see hawks by day and stars by night. I'm here by the usual mixture of choice and dumb luck. There are a lot of us out here, women who trained for academic careers and wound up doing something quite different.

I don't advise others to follow my path. They couldn't if they tried. Besides, where I am now would not satisfy many measures of success. My annual earnings as a freelance writer are about half what I made managing international programs (though they may be higher than I'd have made as a part-time instructor). I don't have a lot of job security (though perhaps as much as a lecturer hired from semester to semester). I'm far from famous, and the things I do with the most obvious benefits to humanity, I do as a volunteer.

Trade-Offs Require Choice

It's all trade-offs. Acknowledging that we all make choices among limited options, we need to respect each other's decisions while we challenge the institutional barriers that force women to make trade-offs that shouldn't be necessary.

The trade-offs lead us places we may never have imagined. A student having second thoughts about her choice of grad school asked if I'd ever regretted a decision. I answered, "The decisions I regret are the little ones, like not carrying an umbrella on a rainy day. Big ones, no. It's too hard to tell what would have happened if I'd done something different. I don't second-guess the past. I take the present as given and try to figure out what to do next."

Meteorologist Ed Lorenz, a founder of chaos theory, showed why it's impossible to forecast weather meaningfully more than ten to fourteen days ahead. A butterfly flapping over China can affect the weather in New York City a few days later. Life is like that. All we can predict with reasonable confidence is that, whatever path we choose, life will be both difficult and filled with opportunities to learn, love, serve, and wonder.

This isn't an argument for fatalism. Like anything else we do, whether voting or singing a solo or running a marathon, the act of choosing calls us to do our best with what we know at the time. Then we live with the results and move on.

Here I am, happy where choice and circumstance have conspired to bring me. Perfectly satisfied? No, I still face choices between imperfect professional alternatives. Happier than I would have been had things gone differently? There's no way to know, and I don't give it much thought. "To live is so startling it leaves little time for anything else," Emily Dickinson wrote. I'm happy enough.

CHAPTER FIVE

ROADBLOCKS AND ROAD RAGE

Not everyone is delighted to see women making progress in higher education. The current national backlash to affirmative action reflects a fear that women are getting ahead at the expense of white males.

Sometimes the roadblocks that women experience are remnants of an institutional culture. Pervasive mind-sets of "It's always been done this way" and "If it ain't broke, don't fix it" are deterrents. Sometimes it's a man in a skirt, a queen-bee type of woman who has worked her way to an influential position by her bootstraps and believes that others should too, especially women.

Internal roadblocks are also at work. Women are less likely than men to apply for jobs unless they meet every single one of an idealized set of 106 criteria. They're less likely to puff up their credentials and references. Some women have less self-esteem, so they need to be told that they can do it and to be nominated rather than apply themselves. Women are more tied to their families and less willing to uproot them to take a job. And many women who could be administrators simply do not like the job, due to socialization that has taught them to behave and be quiet and be nice.

There's also the need for campus women to balance competition and collaboration, and individualism and collectivism, and to consider who will do the housework when both Martha and Mary are on the tenure track.

Feminist scholars, who might be expected to help ordinary women solve ordinary problems, have created their own language and theory to explain the realities they perceive. By doing so, many have so isolated themselves from reality that they might as well be on another planet.

This chapter offers both practical and theoretical help for women dealing with challenges of roadblocks and road rage on campus.

Maintaining Diversity Amid Threats to Affirmative Action

October 1996

With affirmative action being challenged in Texas, California, and other states, campus administrators are debating how to preserve the diversity that has given many women and minorities a seat at the table. The hot issue on campuses in every state will boil in November, when the California initiative to ban affirmative action comes to a statewide vote.

Georgia Lesh-Laurie, interim chancellor at the University of Colorado at Denver, says, "We believe that if a court case came in Colorado, the ruling would be similar to that in Texas," referring to the Hopwood case striking down preferential admissions processes at the University of Texas Law School. "It could have happened here," agrees Barbara Taliaferro, assistant to the president for human diversity at Kutztown University of Pennsylvania. The attitude is "Let's watch and see what happens in California." She says, "People are looking with caution and concern at what appears to be a mean-spirited phenomenon."

Administrator Confronts the Issue

Earlier this year, some faculty and emeriti ran a full-page ad in the Kutztown paper, claiming the white male model was being sacrificed for blacks and women at Kutztown University, Taliaferro says. "But we have many committed faculty and administrators—and the president—and will continue to move forward on diversity programs." Usually the attacks on affirmative action are more subtle, she points out, most often using the budget. "When they downsize, they look first to student affairs, where they often find the minority staff on white campuses," she says. Or a college will decide to close down a department with a majority of women students and faculty, like closing the Department of Dental Hygiene in the School of Dentistry at the University of Iowa.

Taliaferro and Lesh-Laurie, who identify themselves as affirmative action hires, remain committed to the goals of affirmative action. "Affirmative action may not have done everything everyone wanted it to do, but it's way ahead of whatever is in second place," Lesh-Laurie points out.

Solutions for Admissions, Scholarships

Despite the ad attacking affirmative action, "Most Kutztown programs are not race-based now," Taliaferro says. With no athletic teams at Denver to encourage race-based scholarships, "Our small numbers of scholarships that could even be considered race-based are mostly based on ethnicity," Lesh-Laurie notes. For example, most students who would qualify for a scholarship to a student of Greek ethnicity are white. Still, the University of Colorado system is taking the potential threat to affirmative action seriously and developing new, nonrace-based scholarship criteria, Lesh-Laurie says. "We hope these will be in place by spring 1997."

Colorado is exploring two strategies to support a diverse student body: (1) Where possible, place scholarships on a geographic basis, either for students from a particular area of the state or from certain high schools. The award winners would then more likely reflect whatever group the scholarship donor aimed to support. (2) Ask the donors of scholarship funds to select the scholarship winners. Some donors are reluctant to make the determination, Lesh-Laurie reports, but then the school can't accept the money. With private scholarships, "There are not really large dollars at risk here. But we don't want to lose the federal programs. The federal programs do represent large dollars."

Another strategy to support student diversity is giving preference to first-generation college students. "It's something we should run by our legal counsel," Lesh-Laurie says. "We run everything by legal counsel." Because most Kutztown students are already first-generation students, Taliaferro notes, the strategy would have little effect on its campus diversity. Kutztown is instead focusing on the personal approach to get and keep students, using accelerated and assisted programs, Taliaferro says.

"We meet prospective students at college fairs and work with them on completing their applications. We follow them through the application process and give them lots of support through the admissions process." And they ask young alumni to help. "If, for example, there's a young alumna of color in Philadelphia, where a prospective student lives, we contact her."

The assisted program, run through the president's office, focuses on retention, Taliaferro says. It includes a "retention action committee—not a study committee," she stresses, "to deal with financial, cultural, and other issues to meet students' needs." In addition, a university-wide mentoring program is available to every student at risk, where each is assigned a peer mentor. "Students at risk are identified by grades and by a number of other categories, but they are not color-coded," Taliaferro explains.

Supporting Diversity in Hiring

"We carefully review all positions when vacancies occur," Taliaferro says, as part of the continuous improvement movement at Kutztown. "We reexamine each job description." At Kutztown and elsewhere, "The biggest stumbling block is to get the candidates on the short list, the interview list," Taliaferro states. To get more women and minority candidates interviewed, "They can ask hiring committees, 'Have you contacted them? Have you courted them?'" In addition, "We can refer possible candidates we've met at conferences. And we can use faculty exchanges. If a faculty member works out well in a temporary position, we can suggest that she or he be moved into a tenured position."

Lesh-Laurie concurs. "When departments begin the interview process, we ensure the interviewees reflect the field. If a field has 25 percent women, one interviewee had better be a woman." But the real problem comes later. "The problem is retaining minorities after they've been hired," she says. "If they're successful, they become attractive to other institutions," and establishing a deeply supportive campus culture takes time. Lesh-Laurie acknowledges, "It's an uncertain time in higher education." But despite the challenges and uncertainty, "We still intend to meet our diversity goals and to remain within the law" in the process.

Taliaferro believes that regardless of what strategies institutions develop to maintain diversity, "Collaboration, not collusion, is key." The bottom line, she asserts, is "quality leadership and vision that tend to make the clock tick."

Assess Your Affirmative Action Program

Here's a checklist to help you rate your school.

- Does the school's commitment to a diverse student body remain valid as an educational policy?
- Has the school met goals on student and faculty diversity?
- Do legal risks shown by recent court decisions outweigh the educational benefits of affirmative action?
- Which programs to promote diversity are high risk and which are low risk?
- Is the school able to assess its diversity efforts, with the president close to legal counsel, senior staff, and deans?
- How should the school publicly explain its purpose in supporting student and faculty diversity?
- How can the school explain its position without appearing politically partisan?
- What are views of other educational leaders? Is there a consensus?
- How should the school respond to claims that affirmative action programs are unfair to white students, faculty, and others?

• How do the school's needs differ from those of peer schools?

Doris Green

Unstack the Deck: Strategies to Overcome Search Committee Bias

February 1994
Linda McCallister
Dean, College of Business and Economics, Christopher Newport University, Virginia
Although women receive more than half of all associate, baccalaureate, and master's degrees and one-third of all doctorates, they have been systematically denied campus leadership positions. Women are just 15 percent of university and college CEOs. In the dean's position, a stepping-stone to top jobs, women are also scarce. More than 50 percent of business students are women, but less than 3 percent of the American Assembly of Collegiate Schools of Business's members have women deans.

Role of Search Committees

As gatekeepers controlling access to leadership positions in higher education, search and screen committees help select tomorrow's leaders. But the ultimate hiring responsibility remains with the top administrators who make the appointments. Only their commitment to equality and meaningful change can override a search committee's often androcentric recommendations.

Charles Reed, Florida State University system chancellor, rejected the six male finalists presented to him for the provost's post at the University of Central Florida. He said, "For the provost's search committee to conclude that it can find no qualified women in America to present to the president for his consideration is simply unacceptable."

Strategies for Inequity

Committees often go through the motions of meeting affirmative action requirements but wind up with a final list of candidates void of qualified women and minorities. Here's what I've seen done.

Stacked search committee. Committees often are exclusively white or male, contain vulnerable women who are untenured or even graduate students, or contain a token woman whose lone voice is unheeded. Another tactic is to include women who are unassertive or known to be unsupportive of other women.

Benign disqualifiers. Search committees often eliminate women early through overly restrictive qualifications. If a candidate for dean must have been a department chair, many otherwise qualified women are eliminated because chairs are usually elected and male voters still outnumber females. Add "five years in the post" or "experience as dean at a large or comprehensive university," and the pool of women candidates is effectively zero.

Subjective requirements are "evidence of scholarly contributions suitable for appointment as a full professor" and "appropriate degree." I've seen both used repeatedly to eliminate qualified women. Additionally, male candidates totally lacking required credentials often apply and often do end up in the final pool, whereas women candidates are more likely to apply only for those jobs in which they meet every criterion to perfection.

Highball lowball rating forms. Biased search committee members can deliberately rate the top women candidates lowest so that only the least qualified women candidates will progress to the interview stage, where they inevitably lose out to the top men finalists. A variation on this technique involves using the grapevine or e-mail to actively solicit dirt as a way to blackball women candidates.

Disappearing files. When there is no centralized plan to log in and track every single application and nomination, files from women and minority candidates have a way of conveniently disappearing. Some are discarded, lost, placed in the "incomplete" file, or otherwise waylaid.

Search firm masquerade. Not being in the business of creating social change, search firms reflect the opinions of those who pay them. They can serve as expensive pawns to demonstrate that "We tried to find women, but there weren't any available." A recent dean search cost $30,000 and resulted in a pool without one woman.

Omnipotent closing dates. Qualified women candidates face elimination because they don't find out about the position in time or because their files lack one bit of information. Firm closing dates are more likely to discourage women than men. There's something fishy about an aggressive affirmative action search that lasts two weeks.

How to Do It Right

A courageous person at the top must be willing to take the heat from faculty members and search committee members opposed to women in power. Administrators must be willing to remove committee members and chairs when a problem is apparent. Top administrators must be held accountable for search outcomes, using rewards and penalties; affirmative action officers need real clout in the search.

To overcome stacked search committees, include an equal number of men and women for all dean, vice presidential, and presidential searches. A nonfaculty majority guarantees administrative accountability. Reshape requirements by looking at exactly what administrators need to do and then searching for people who have the skills to do it. Overcome rating inequities by dividing male and female candidates into separate pools and putting top people from each pool on the short list. To prevent disappearing files, use a central tracking system controlled by someone committed to real affirmative action, with the power to act.

Search firms should earn their fees only if their pool of qualified candidates includes women and minorities. They can be proactive by contacting associations and women leaders for nominations. Set flexible closing dates by stating, "Review of applications will begin on such and such a date and will remain open until the position is filled." Conducting a comprehensive search requires more than just going through the motions to appear equitable. It's amazing how many qualified women surface when search committee members know that you mean business.

Are Women Socialized Away from Administrative Roles?

December 1998
Patricia Matthews
Vice President for Academic Affairs, Marywood University, Pennsylvania
I've spent twenty years in higher ed administration, first as an undergrad dean for eight years and now beginning my thirteenth year as a vice president for academic affairs. Part of my agenda has been to advance women on my campus. In some areas, I've had success: improving the ratio of women to men in the associate and professor ranks, and mentoring and fostering the professional development of a female assistant vice president for academic affairs. But I don't always succeed. I've concluded that in addition to external barriers, there may be concerns deriving from women's socialization that may make it more difficult for women to handle the burdens and conflicts of administration.

Some Reject the New Role

One woman whom I encouraged into a deanship was very successful at the organizational demands of the work and well regarded by faculty. She stayed one term and then left, much to the surprise of many colleagues.

Why? A single woman, she had built her life largely around friendships with other women on campus. She found that being in administration disrupted these relationships. She was no longer one of the gang; she had information that made it impossible for her to sit around and speculate, a favorite indoor sport of the group. And she found it difficult to deal with these friends professionally.

Such is the hazard of moving from faculty to administration on the same campus. Some might sacrifice the relationships to join administration; this woman would not. As she explained to me, the work could never matter enough for her to be willing to jeopardize such important relationships.

In a similar case, a new dean learned that an old friend wasn't such a good teacher. A student had complained, and she started to look at our data evaluating teaching. I knew it was the beginning of the end. She resigned, saying, "I always liked the faculty. I don't really want to know this side of them."

A female administrator woman in our campus library resigned her better-paying management role to move out front to public access, which she finds more satisfying.

Women Value Relationships, Service

What am I suggesting? To most women, I believe relationships are very defining. And it *is* lonely at the top. At work we may strive to be friendly and caring. But as decision makers, resource allocators, and judges of conflict, we need to be for all: impartial and willing to hold all to the same standard. This can strain old relationships; for some, the price appears too high.

Another issue is women's propensity for direct service roles. We're attracted to jobs where we serve one-on-one, and we get satisfaction from the affirmation that comes from generous, pleasant service. These roles may lead to a promotion to management, where ironically we do little or no direct service to students or faculty. Rather, such jobs require planning, budgeting, and spending hours making things happen, which means writing memos, signing forms, and moving paper. The loss of direct contact—knowing students' names and stories, getting a smiling thanks—can be hard for those whose orientation and self-esteem are based on direct service. After women earn administrative jobs, they often need counseling about the value of administrative tasks as service and how to deal with this change in their work. Some compensate by finding a direct service role as community volunteers.

Conflicts in Move from Faculty to Administration

One of the most difficult moves is from faculty to administration. It's more than just going from a nine- to a twelve-month calendar. Faculty in universities have a great deal of independence about when they work and how they set priorities. They also have an inordinate amount of freedom to express their opinions, ask questions, and just plain speak out.

Your first administrative job can seem quite constraining. First, there are all the things you have to do just because they get done out of your office. Then, there are the priorities of your supervisor and the president. This leaves little room for your own agenda, especially in the beginning as you learn the ropes. In addition, you're expected to support the school's administrative decisions and practices. Even if you objected before a decision was made, you must publicly support the final decision. Continuing to object only undermines your own credibility. Some women found this all too constraining and compromising of their integrity. They did not stay long in administration.

Men: Better Administrators?

Although the above data is anecdotal, it has caused me to think about women's socialization and the assertion that senior administrative roles are better suited to men. As a feminist, I abhor such sentiments. This conflict is not about what is natural to us but rather about what we learn about how to live, what to value, what makes us comfortable—before we ever get to try our hands at these roles.

A few weeks ago, I had to terminate an employee. She is a good person who worked very hard for our school; she simply couldn't do what we needed. I probably waited too long to make the move. A male colleague told me just that, going so far as suggesting that I was letting my more feminine characteristics affect my judgment, with negative consequences. Of course, this is not always the case. Often, I know I do a better job because of all that I bring to my work as a woman. But our very strengths, if pushed too far, can become deterrents to our moving into senior positions. Let me assure you that I like what I do: resource allocation and creative reallocation, problem solving, and making the pieces fit together in a new way. I'd like to convince other women that they would, too.

Hiring 'Em and Hanging 'Em Out to Dry

May 1994

"Women and minorities are often hired to fail," a man remarked at the American Association of Affirmative Action conference in April. Laws, ethics, and political correctness may dictate gender equity in hiring and promotion, but the human factor can never be eliminated.

Each time a woman fails, most likely due to factors other than those within her, the failure is seen as damaging to others of her sex and perhaps her race. Either an individual or the institution as a whole fails to embrace the diversity she brings. "We tried hiring a woman, but she just didn't work out" is the usual explanation, given by both those who successfully sabotaged her career and the in-nocents who practiced benign neglect. The scenario can deter future hires of peo-ple sharing the same sex, race, age, ethnicity, or eye color. How can women administrators and academics avoid getting in a no-win situation or negotiate to create a supportive situation where none exists?

Individual Strategies

Check the Job. Sometimes a no-win situation results from the very nature of the job itself. Ask yourself: Can *anyone* be successful in that job? "If an institution wants you to fail, probably you're going to fail," predicts Marcia Boyles, president of Educational Consultant Services, which conducts gender-equity assessments on campuses. Situations that should set off warning bells include, for example, being the affirmative action officer in a school that has historically allowed racism and sexism or taking a job with inadequate resources.

Josephine Davis, president of York College in Jamaica, New York, recalls being hired elsewhere as a vice president of academic affairs. "I naively assumed I'd have the resources to do my job. All I had was money for coffee and doughnuts," she said. Or the job description may split a position between two or more supervisors who have conflicting goals and demands, or personal antagonism, where the new hire would be a pawn.

Check the Supervisor. Try to find out as much as possible about your future su-pervisor's reputation, clout, time availability, and long-term plans. Working with an ineffective or unsupportive or too-busy boss is a recipe for failure.

In conversations and interviews, try to assess hidden agendas and attitudes of potential peers and your supervisor. Beware of gender-stereotyped expectations, in which the men are visionary and assertive, whereas the women are meek and submissive. They'll affect your position at work. "Being kept out of the informa-tion loop is a very common and very powerful way to make you fail," Boyles notes.

Check the Organizational Climate. "Many women seeking to become adminis-trators are so excited about being given the chance that they don't take the time or make the opportunities to ask questions," Boyles explains. She suggests talking to powerful women administrators and faculty on campus to get their sense of the climate and looking at the composition of the governing boards and other groups you would be reporting to, directly or indirectly. "Keep in mind the issue of crit-ical mass," she says. "If you're the *only* one, ask why. How did it happen? There are places that are virtually impossible for women. You have to be realistic."

Negotiate for Success. If red flags signify a potential problem, head off future conflicts by negotiating with the hiring committee or supervisor. Spell out your specific concerns, and identify resources and strategies to resolve potential future conflicts. Oral agreements can be tenuous, so get it in writing if possible.

Institutional Strategies

As a campus leader, you can help your school develop strategies to recruit and retain women, to end the revolving door through which a healthy percentage of new female administrative and faculty hires leave after just a few years. Even among those who explain that they left because their husbands took other work, or other perfectly valid and blameless reasons, misrepresentation is rampant. They may imply that their own situations had absolutely no effect on their husbands' choosing to accept other jobs, when in fact spouses rarely change jobs in a vacuum.

Top administrators can hold directors, deans, and department heads responsible for creating and maintaining a climate of trust and support for women. Ongoing training for new hires should include orientation seminars, a handbook of information that is on-line and regularly updated, and regular meetings.

Supervisors should communicate clearly and regularly about job expectations, goals, and resources available, and provide regular feedback.

Leaders can prepare a plan, with specific goals and timetables, to hire women in leadership positions on campus.

Work to provide gender equity in salaries by requiring all leaders to justify or rectify especially low salaries for women, or those that are not commensurate with their achievements, as well as differences in nonsalary compensation.

Support networks of other women in the department or division or mentors on campus can help women dance through the minefields.

Regular, frequent reports by leaders on the number and percentage of women at all levels in units and departments can reinforce the goals of recruiting and retaining more women.

Openly stated zero tolerance for sexual harassment through education and sensitization of faculty and staff shows that you mean business.

When a woman fails in a job on campus, it's often a failure of the whole campus climate to adapt to the diverse values, styles, skills, and viewpoints that she offers. And a failure to add to the richness of the higher education community experience.

Mary Dee Wenniger

Balancing Competition and Collaboration on Campus

May 1997
Judy A. Mantle
Chair, Department of Specialized Programs, School of Education and Human Resources, National University, California

Campus life is rife with ethical questions. Who owns curriculum design and development? How should we evaluate personnel? Select new faculty? Equalize teaching loads? Identify the real author? Recognize professional achievements? As women on campus, we want to contribute to the solutions to these and other questions. Paradoxically, we must fit in the campus culture yet compete for scarce resources and rewards: promotions, tenure, merit pay, and advancement or transition to administrative careers. If collegiality on campus is the mantra, how do you know when to collaborate and when to compete, and what are the rules?

Over and over again, administrators and faculty must recall why collaboration is important in the first place, decide with whom to collaborate, exactly what to collaborate about, and where and when collaboration will occur. Ditto for competition. The climate can be quite amiable or emotionally volatile, and it can shift. New women faculty, especially, must adapt quickly to the requirements of this dynamic and complex culture, learning how to collaborate as well as how to compete in male-dominated academia. Good communication skills, flexibility, and political savvy can help.

Women administrators often find all eyes are on their every act and decision, especially when in the minority. With more women on campus, the potential for significant change is real, threatening many men who are being asked to share the power they have so long hoarded.

Potential Areas of Vulnerability

Success on campus requires being adept at both collaboration and competition. Upsetting the delicate balance between the two can result in confusion and dissonance. Behaviors and skills required for teamwork clearly differ from those required for competition. Shifting back and forth between the two paradigms can be intellectually and emotionally taxing.

In her book *The Secret Between Us: Competition Among Women* (1991), Laura Tracy discusses how women perceive competition at work. She reports that women feel that competition means loss and competition with other women feels like failure. Many perceive themselves as victims, based on their upbringing, having learned to face competition with each other with dread and anxiety. Some women actually can't even admit they compete against other women.

Ethics and Moral Responsibility

With more women entering the campus workforce as both administrators and faculty, we need a clear understanding of some key ethical factors that can influence women's effectiveness. Without it, women will have difficulty advancing as far and as fast as their male peers.

Understanding how to collaborate and how to compete according to formal or informal ethical guidelines is vital to success in the academy. This can be especially difficult when confusing organizational values and conflicting messages come from different directions. Women seek not only to demonstrate the highest levels of personal and professional ethics but also to model new ways of teaching, leading, managing, and administering that are both effective and exemplary.

How do you do that? For each of us, personal morals and ethics are fundamental points of reference guiding our behavior. Maintaining a conscious centeredness in sound morals and ethics is vital if we are to demonstrate high levels of integrity in the many types of collaborative and competitive activities that are integral to success.

Empowerment and Contribution

Academia clearly is a competitive arena, requiring a certain art to the style of competition. To succeed, we must empower ourselves with high self-esteem, eliminating both the thoughts of being a victim and fears of competition. Being self-assured and adaptable, using good judgment and personal integrity, can go a long way toward our success. We can bring models of behavior that integrate nurturing, creativity, and tenacity within the academy. Communications and human relations hold potential for our greatest success. Developing mentoring and support structures can help unite us for this paradigm shift.

Each of us is responsible for her own behavior in defining and acting in collaborative and competitive situations, and is accountable for her actions. Each of us must wrestle with her own conscience, applying her best decision-making skills and arriving at good solutions to problems, especially in conflict-ridden circumstances.

Nearly every initiative, whether collaborative, competitive, or mixed, poses a potential challenge as well as an opportunity for growth and learning in everyone involved. By our actions, each of us can contribute to the evolution of an academy that ultimately reflects more sophistication and maturity. It costs us nothing to engage in a personal assessment of our own behavior. It costs nothing for leadership to emerge and ignite the fire for productive discussions. But the price of lacking a clear understanding of professional ethics and personal integrity may be high: great emotional stress, loss of advancement opportunities and other rewards, professional embarrassment, and possibly even litigation.

In *All I Really Need to Know I Learned in Kindergarten* (1988), Robert Fulghum provides simple rules: share everything; play fair; don't hit people; don't take things that aren't yours; say you're sorry when you hurt somebody; when you go out into the world, watch out for traffic, hold hands, and stick together.

Individualism Versus Community in the Higher Education Culture

May 1995

Like the Western culture it is part of, higher education in North America values individualism over the collective culture that emphasizes harmony among people and typifies Eastern thought. On campus, it translates into a cultural model that stresses objectivity, separateness, competitiveness, and hierarchy. In contrast, women tend to work and learn better in an environment that emphasizes connection over separation, understanding and acceptance over assessment, collaboration over debate—in short, one exemplifying the collectivistic pattern of behavior.

The result is that women themselves are undervalued on campus, according to Georgia State University Professor Lawrence J. Rifkind, who in January addressed the University of Texas-El Paso conference on Women in Higher Education. "Women at every rank, in every field, and in every type of institution continue to earn less than their male counterparts in the 1990s," he said. As an example, he cited a school at which a man was given the permanent position of assistant vice president, whereas a female colleague of equal worth was given only an interim appointment.

The unit she entered was in disarray, so she must make unpopular decisions in order for it to survive, he said. She is disadvantaged by being kept out of the informal communications because she does not play racquetball, attend sporting events, or use the male rest rooms. And, should she be successful, she still must compete for the permanent position after a nationwide search, trials that the man escaped.

Communication Interprets Symbols

Rifkind suggested that the differences between the collective and the individual approach are feminine and masculine styles of communication. Communication is interpretive, in the sense that messages may not be sent purposefully, and transactional, with feedback going back and forth between the sender and the receiver. People create shared meanings, using symbols to communicate with others, who must interpret the message.

In addition, all communication occurs within a context, a frame of reference that enables one to decide what a specific action means, and is interpreted within the culture of one's environment. Because the culture so pervades the self, people are unaware that the foundations on which they base their values and their lives are constructs resulting from stereotyped views, which can be traced to their origins of cultural communication.

Individualism Versus Collectivism

In an individualistic culture, people are expected to look out for themselves and their immediate families only; the I takes precedence over the we, and initiative and achievement are prized. Individual goals are most important, relationships are adversarial and become win-lose conflicts, friendships are made for specific purposes, confrontational tactics are popular, and students are conditioned to speak out and question in the classroom.

In a collectivist culture, decisions reflect what is best for the group, which is one's most important social unit. The emphasis is on loyalty, belonging, and fitting in. Friendships are long-term, relationships are stable, and avoidance or third-party intermediaries are used to save face. In return for absolute loyalty to the group, an individual can expect to be taken care of. Rifkind illustrates the contrast between the two viewpoints by the individualistic (Euro-American) maxim "The squeaky wheel gets the grease" and the collectivistic (Japanese) maxim "The nail that sticks up gets pounded."

Winners and Losers

The competitive individual needs to excel over others and distinguish herself by seeing others fail. Despite supposedly equal opportunities, women often are perceived in the "other" or "loser" category, in support and less critical staff positions. Other consequences of the sometimes unconsciously stereotyped treatment of women are overemphasis on advancement, which requires stereotyped male behaviors; continuing behaviors that are essential to social and emotional health but detrimental to promotion; and the belief that if women haven't succeeded, it's their own fault, not that of the family or community failing to support them.

Exclusionary practices also limit women, when policies for advancement are vague so that women must compete with each other by male competitive comparisons, to enhance their own self-worth and exaggerate the negative qualities of others. Increasingly, women are challenging the traditional signs of success and reinforcing the cooperative nature of organization and society by valuing family, community, and entrepreneurial ventures above advancement.

Recommendations

Continue to question traditional ways of viewing society, promoting a collectivist style. Instead of representing the "other" as separate, excluded, inferior, and marginal, consider them as having an advantageous viewpoint. Reframing the question allows a critical assessment of the dominant individualistic culture.

Establish the value of a cooperative approach by making cooperation a more visible and salient alternative, changing the structures, work flow, and business transactions.

Recognize the value of women's life experiences to reframe social issues, knowledge, and relationships. Without assuming that all women share the same experiences, recognize the fluid nature of boundaries between personal and work lives.

Incorporate a cooperative work ethic into daily life. Modify individualistic tendencies by creating alternative ideologies and reaching out to the majority with more collectivist solutions to issues.

Learn to value relationships, accept the relativity of right or wrong depending on the situation, and accept the changing of personal identities that recognizes renewal and flexibility.

Mary Dee Wenniger

Why Women Don't Support Other Women

December 1993

You had done all your homework and legwork. You crunched numbers, and they looked excellent. One by one, you discussed your idea with everyone who counted in your unit on campus. You'd even endured old Hubert's phlegmy rasps and smoke-filled office as he drew on another Marlboro, and he seemed to think your idea was pure genius. At lunch Tuesday with Ruth, her eyes danced as your words spun visions of turning plans into action. Your presentation at the department meeting went smoothly. Heads nodded; mouths turned up in the corners. Only when your words stopped and Hubert's breathing was the only sound in the room—until your boss cleared his throat, thanked you, and dismissed the meeting—did you realize that it fell flat.

You'd been stiffed before, but this time you'd counted on support from Ruth, who had said such great things just three days ago. What happened? And why? Sometimes women are our worst enemies. Although women often anticipate their male adversaries, especially in a good-old-boys environment like higher education, antagonism or apathy from another woman may come as a surprise, bringing confusion and a sense of betrayal. Women may not realize that an attack, or a lack of expected support, is more likely to be political than personal. The real reason for it may be unarticulated or even subconscious.

For example, a nonsupporter may point out weaknesses in a woman candidate's résumé because, subconsciously, she's insecure about losing her status as the only woman vice president. Will another woman at her level invite comparisons? Will she be isolated with her, instead of still being considered one of the boys? Martha Burns and Linda Hartsock, former college administrators who operate Integrated Options Inc., a management consulting firm in Washington, D.C., point out that a woman nonsupporter may have legitimate professional concerns. She may think someone else is more qualified or that a job candidate lacks integrity or has a personal problem that could affect her work, such as alcoholism or a contentious personality.

Women and Biases

Alternatively, deeply ingrained social roles and expectations may be at work. Burns and Hartsock note that in higher education

- Women who have had only male role models may adopt their male values, believing that "A woman can't do that job on this campus."
- Women may fear being viewed as maternal, rather than strong and independent, if they support and mentor other women.
- Women have been socialized to compete as individuals rather than as team players.

One specific area in which women have been socialized to compete is physical attractiveness; high scorers may draw resentment from others.

The Bootstraps Mentality

Other motivations may be operating just barely at the conscious level. Although she won't say it aloud, a nonsupporter may be thinking (1) "I had to give 150 percent to get where I am; why should she have it any easier?"; (2) "If she's good enough, she can make it without my help"; or (3) "I'm not threatened by working with men. I don't need another woman to support my ideas."

Political motives are closely tied to the personality of the nonsupporter, sometimes in inverse correlation to her own degree of security. Of course, a political attack may not be gender-based; an insecure person may see anyone else as a potential threat. Women who want to avoid being seen as feminists may inadvertently hold other women to higher standards. Ironically, feminists, too, may bend over backward to seem impartial and preserve their own credibility.

Credibility Points

Like political capital or chits, people build up credibility points with colleagues through their competence, loyalty, and reliability, Burns and Hartsock explain. Because accumulating credibility points takes time and effort, they are hoarded and spent with care. Advocating for another person means spending some points. "A woman who frequently spends her credibility points on any and every other woman may find herself out of credibility," say Burns and Hartsock.

And like it or not, it often may be riskier to spend credibility points on another woman than on a man. A nonsupporter may feel she does not know a woman candidate well enough to risk her own reputation by supporting her. A woman on the way up needs credibility points at her school to accomplish many things on her agenda, Burns and Hartsock note. To spend them on promoting another person just because she's a woman is not always an easy choice. Men feel no such obligation, they point out.

Avoiding the Role of Victim

People who aspire to power often identify with those already in power. Some women, especially if they see men as having the power, identify more with men than women. They may dissociate themselves from those who consider themselves victims. "I'm not a victim. I don't want to be separated into a women's group. I can make it without a victim's crutch!" one college administrator wrote. To some, supporting other women as fellow victims means admitting to a lack of power or control, which may be inaccurate or too painful.

How to Respond

Because each situation is different, look before you leap, advises Maureen Quinn, a consultant in communications and former assistant vice president in the University of Wisconsin system. Ask yourself: Is it really a case of nonsupport or sabotage, or just lousy people skills? Do I fully understand the situation, or is there a hidden agenda? Seek an objective opinion from a confidante, Quinn advises.

Then assess the seriousness of the situation. For insensitive behavior, it may not be worth sticking your neck out. On the other hand, you may have an obligation to confront or report unethical behavior. Next, weigh the risks of action, says Quinn. What do you stand to gain or lose by pressing the issue? If you decide to act, consider the best way to communicate. In person or in writing? Friendly or formal? Should anyone else be involved, such as your supervisor or that of the other person? Finally, decide if the timing is right. For example, if the nonsupporter seems stressed by a major project, wait until it's completed. But if others are coming forward with similar complaints, now may be the best time to act.

Keep It Professional

Above all, says Quinn, stay cool, dignified, and professional. Even if you're upset, don't let your message become emotional, or it may be disregarded. And don't forget diplomacy. You don't need to corner the nonsupporter to get your message across. If she's already feeling threatened, a frontal attack may make matters even worse. If the behavior shows no signs of improving, assess the overall work environment. Are your abilities and contributions appreciated? If not, it may be time to move on, says Quinn. But if you believe you are valued, consider a philosophical view. "Women often have to go to extra lengths to prove that they're capable," Quinn says. "We may not like it or accept it, but we need to recognize it."

Jennifer Hirsch

Language Reinforces Patriarchial Code over Women

December 1996

Ever wonder why it seems so difficult for university leaders to see things from a woman's point of view? Research shows there's historic evidence of a grand scheme to use language to ensure male dominance over women. Just as formal education was once considered for only males, the very word *university* contains the word for man, *ver,* as its root. When our forefathers raised themselves to the status of lords, based on hierarchy and dominance, they deliberately created the language we use today to reinforce their "superiority" by means of a code. It is only by a conscious effort to oppose the patriarchal code that women today can begin to see themselves as anything but inferiors to men.

Louise Goueffic, an independent scholar and executive director of Language Reform International in Toronto, referred to twenty-six thousand words implying male superiority in her presentation at the Organization for the Study of Communication, Language, and Gender in October.

Nonmale Is Nonexistent

The area of language that names and describes speakers excludes the speaker who is not male. In the language of man the not-male person almost always ends up saying what she does not want to say: maleness is superior. In Goueffic's new book *Breaking the Patriarchal Code*, she lists about ten thousand common words reinforcing the code.

The language of "man" is designed to maintain male superiority, she said. To lexicographers, this is not news. But females are so much in the habit of using the words created by men, which are the only words given, that we accept them as true, failing to examine how the words themselves continue to maintain male superiority.

Under a Critical Lens

***The word* man.** In reality, being man entails being male. But we are taught that *man* consists of man and woman. As such, *man* is and is not male. This utter nonsense is glossed over under the rubric of *man* as "generic man." Thus generic man gives us an is-and-is-not principle as basis for our species. This is sheer nonsense.

***The word* (wo)man.** What kind of man is (wo)man, when being man entails only being male? Being not man entails being not male. *(Wo)man* is not male, therefore, she is not a man. As (wo)man, then, she is a man who is not a man. Nonsense begets more nonsense. The word *(fe)male* helps to ease us into the is-and-is-not habit by repetition: (fe)maleness is not (true) maleness. "Wo" does not make *man* mean not-male. Three terms reinforce and repeat the is-and-is-not principle working in these words.

***The word* (hu)man.** It can be said (hu)manity consists of two men, one of whom is not a man, because being man only entails being male. In all four words—*man, woman, human, humanity*—the criterion of *not-male* is used to name the other being in this class. *Manness* is equated with man, and *(wo)man* has a man through the word *man* in her name, again voluntarily granting the superiority of maleness.

***Missing words.** The historical tactic was to rid the language of the words *feme* (sex) and *fem* (being), and discourage use of *sapien* in favor of *(hu)man*. Only about twenty words remain using *fem* as a base. To be consistent, Goueffic uses these premises: the animal who produces estrogens, progesterones, ova, and gestates is *feme,* and the *feme* animal who makes and uses speech to communicate is *fem.* The same consistent premises can be made about *man* and *male.* In all four premises, there is no A that is not an A. *Fem* is *fem (feme)* like *man* is *man* (male).

***Male dominance.** It's the is-and-is-not male that is important in generic *man.* Being not-male is the negative, against which being male is given value. Many words show that maleness, having a penis, testes, and semen, is the positive value, and thus is considered superior: testify, verse.

Vir *and the v-r formula.* *Vir,* L., man. *Verge,* Fr., verpa, L., penis. *Wer,* Old Eng., man. Using vowel variation produces many words with this as the stem: *virtue, universe, university, verb, verity, worship, worthy, world,* and *word.* The word *university* is actually *uni-manity,* as in (hu)manity, because *man* is the universal word for male being. The last sentence repeated versions of *man* seven times, again reinforcing male superiority.

The seed of sign and symbol in semen. *Seme, sema,* and *semi* all mean sign, but they are different signs. One is divine; another is verbal sign (cf. *verpa,* L., penis); and the other is seminal, seeding the issues. Thus, we have *seminal, seminar, seminary, semiotic, semantics,* and *semester,* all again stating the superiority of maleness.

Homogeneous necessity. A society of men is an all-male one. *Homo* is appropriated to mean *man* male, as in homogeneous. *Pareil,* Fr., means same, in which *par* is related to the p-t-r formula for father, and *same* appears to be a vowel variation of the *seme* formula that made *semen,* and probably *semblance,* also found in *assemble, assembly,* and *similar.* The v-r formula indicates "contrary to sameness": *vary, variety, diversity,* and *versatility. Shem* becomes *sem,* which means the fathers of all "mankind," the theological tenet being that semen is the first principle of everything, she notes.

Matriculation and the student. Note that many factors of who and what we are as beings come from the horse-mare and bull-cow metaphors from the stable. Goueffic is always amazed at how few people see the morpheme *stud* in *student.* The stud studies the mare before he mounts and inseminates her. The stud/ent stud/ies "the body" of science (feminine) in order to grasp her and matriculate, *matri,* L., body as mother. That means "he" is mind, and "she" is body.

The one who rules. *Governance, parliament,* and *(hu)manity* are three words telling us who rules. The historical right of male to rule is evident in *duumvirate,* joint office of two men, and *triumvirate.*

Territory and space as male. Consider *parish, empire* (emperor), *par-per* (father); *principality* (prince); *patria; county* (count); *pastor,* from pasture; *dominion,* from *dominus,* lord, etc.; and *verandah, studio, mansion,* and *manse.*

The value of testes. Consider the root of *testify, testament,* and *test.* And the *-ment* at the end of many words such as *parliament, mentula,* L., means the male sexual organs. Now, compare *mentula* and *mental,* . . . but what you don't know won't hurt you.

***The mar in* mar.** Nor were our forefathers content to dominate in a positive way. *Mar* and *mer; mother; margin* (cf. virgin); *to mar; marplot,* a plot to destroy; *martyr; merge; cemetery,* place of the mother. Then there's *meter,* a tool used for measuring, as in "Man is the measure of all things." These negatives also work in favor of the male.

Comparative work. We are told that *per, par,* and *pur* are not related to the p-t-r formula for father-based words because they are morphemes that have a different function, Goueffic notes. "Comparing the words with *mer, mar,* and *mur,* again said to be unrelated to the minor m-t-r formula, shows the paradigm of Father Superior and Mother Inferior is continued," she says. The pattern in the lists below shows a very finite number of morphemes in any language. "It is this finiteness that is used to the best political advantage," she notes. Male root: *pure, on par, to parse, to purge, to permit, peer, patrimony, patron.* Female root: *murder, to mar, to immerse, to marginalize, to merge, mere, matrimony, matron.*

The patriarchal code itself determines that fem cannot speak of herself except in the masculine form. Nor can she speak of the species to which she belongs except in the masculine. Nor can she speak of civilization, social life, finances, and even law and order except in the masculine. But by carefully examining the patriarchal code, one who wants to defy it begins to find solutions.

By far the best solution right now is to use *feme* (sex), *fem* (self), and *sapien* (species), Goueffic says. These three root words stop the roll of is-and-is-nots used as a basis to make the presupposition of male superiority because the basis is "is-and-is-not male." This grants positive value to *femeness* and her *femness* because it names her as existing in the scheme of things. *Feme* and *fem* are rational facts, thus contributing to what is more true and moral. And being *sapien* names the morality of using facts and being rational.

For those of us whose consciousness is just now being raised about the dominance of *man* in our very language, Goueffic's work is an eye-opener about the obvious effort to proclaim the alleged superiority of males.

Mary Dee Wenniger

Sisters in the Academy: Who Will Do the Housework?

June 1997

Faculty women do more than their share of the campus housework. Bosses and students turn to women as nurturers dedicated to service. Being tokens on every committee takes time from their research and teaching. Sisterhood suffers when some women shoulder the burdens, whereas others refuse to be distracted. Sibling rivalry turns painful when administrators who assign the housework reward those who refuse to help out.

The conflict often follows generational lines, according to Lana Hartman Landon of Bethany College, West Virginia, and Brenda A. Wirkus of John Carroll University, Ohio. Women who came of age in the 1960s and 1970s were socialized to service and institutional loyalty. Pleased to get a job, they invested their energy in one school and its students. "The institution is a very unappreciative recipient of that loyalty," Landon says. Without publications, such a woman may find herself stuck like a displaced homemaker.

Those in graduate school in the Reagan years learned to identify with their discipline and career, not with any one school. "They see institutional affiliation as a kind of serial monogamy," Landon says. Portability depends on publications. Too often, they dismiss the previous, service-oriented generation as naive or even stupid, with nothing to offer. "This is very demoralizing to those of us who waited for decades to have more women on the faculty."

The tension between scholars and doers is central to the only New Testament story of women in conflict. Jesus visits the home of Mary and Martha, who live in Bethany with their brother Lazarus. Mary sits at Jesus' feet to listen, while Martha cooks an elaborate meal. When Martha complains that Mary isn't helping, Jesus says Mary has made the better choice (Luke 10:38–42). At the Women in Higher Education conference at Fort Worth, Texas, in January 1997, Landon and Wirkus recast the biblical story in modern terms.

Martha and Mary in the 1990s

Jesus, a prominent scholar, will give a guest lecture at a small rural college. Department chair Lazarus turns to the competent, organized Martha to oversee his visit. Martha is glad to help, but she'll be hard pressed to meet his plane. She decides to ask her colleague Mary for help. When Martha finally reaches her, Mary says she's too busy working on a review article on recent responses to Jesus' work. Martha hangs up, fuming.

"What's wrong with Martha now?" Mary wonders. "Lazarus told me when I was hired that the college wants to improve its national visibility, and that means publish! No one's ever been given tenure for picking somebody up at the airport. Maybe it's too late for Martha to make a name for herself, but it isn't too late for me." Mary turns back to her draft, determined to finish in time to share it with Jesus on his visit. His support could help her move on to a better job, instead of spending her whole career here like Martha. "Sisterhood? Oh, come on. Besides, if she's so busy, why doesn't she just tell Jesus to take a taxi?"

By the end of the lecture, Martha is exhausted. She's been up since 5 A.M. grading papers to make time for driving to and from the airport. At the wine and cheese reception after, she sees Mary, looking fresh and alert, approach Jesus. Mary describes her review article, and Jesus is delighted to see his work discussed even on this remote campus. Martha is too tired for brilliant conversation as she drives Jesus to the airport.

Sisters in Conflict

Both the Marthas and the Marys on campus suffer. The Marthas carry the burden of the housework, unrewarded by their employers and rejected by the younger women they'd hoped to mentor. The Marys are condemned to years of high-pressure, solitary work and geographical moves threatening personal or family relationships. Driven apart, Marthas and Marys lose the benefits of each other's experience and support. Here are the problems.

The two women are acting on different models of excellence. Based on the different graduate school cultures and job markets when they entered their profession, Martha is a nurturer and Mary a scholarly professional. As a result, Mary doesn't see Martha as a role model. Martha, who hoped increased numbers would bring women a larger voice on the faculty, finds that Mary has no time for campus concerns.

Administrators play women off against each other. Both are following directions from Lazarus. Mary will get the greater rewards, as the one the college must compete to keep; Martha, too busy advising students and hosting visitors to publish, won't get offers from other schools. But it's Martha's housework that frees Mary for scholarship. Lazarus needs them both.

Women are weakened as a political voice. In both stories, it's Martha who speaks up, not Mary. An activist committed to one school threatens the power structure more than an isolated scholar who expects to move on. Modern Marys don't care as much about campus policies, and their lack of support neutralizes the influence of the Marthas. Landon fears that "the Mary mind-set will make it much easier for colleges to move away from tenure."

The role of teaching is problematic. Mary bases her teaching on her dedication to knowledge, Martha on her dedication to the school and its mission. Even with identical teaching loads, Martha spends far more hours with students, whom she sees as the central purpose of her job.

How women relate to authority determines how they relate to each other. Their attitudes drive women apart, depriving both Marthas and Marys of companionship and support. They'd gain more by validating the other's approach and joining forces for institutional change.

Housework could be shared more equitably, with tasks rotated through the department. If committee work is important, it deserves recognition in tenure and hiring decisions. If it isn't, not all committees need women. Unimportant housework could be eliminated or assigned to support staff. Unless the sisters solve these problems now, what will happen when the Marthas retire? Will the Marys get stuck with the housework?

Sarah Gibbard Cook

For Crying Out Loud, Support Student Services

May 1997

As schools endure budget cuts and tighten their belts, they show a disturbing trend toward increased support for academics at the expense of student services. Administrators assume that students are on campus to learn facts and that their personal concerns are secondary.

Wrong. Very, very wrong. Sometimes dead wrong.

They've forgotten that their job is to serve the students, often brilliant but immature. Unless students have their personal needs met, their potential to save the world by their future success as scholars, politicians, writers, teachers, businesspeople, inventors, health care professionals, and parents will go unfulfilled.

"We must be very concerned with students' feelings, attitudes, and motivations if we're going to unlock their academic potential," advises Lee Noel, senior executive with the USA Group Noel-Levitz Centers, a leading recruitment and retention consulting firm. "Even high-ability students are dropout-prone if we don't deal with their anxieties in making the transition from a dependent to an independent learning environment," he told *Women in Higher Education*.

Demographics Tell the Story

Today's students are in greater need of social support than ever before. Divorce, drug use, gang warfare, imprisonment, violent crimes, sexual assaults, and other indications of a troubled society are at all-time highs. Students who survive these challenges and manage to go off to college are faced with their own brand of hell. Not only must they use their right brain to adapt to a new environment hundreds or even thousands of miles away, they must use their left brain to succeed at academics. For support, they share an academic adviser with hundreds of others. For nurturing, it's up to those in student services to help them survive the personal challenges so that they can thrive in the academic garden. Lately, the academics have gained the upper hand, and it's time for the pendulum to swing back.

An Example of Misguided Minds

Parents of students at a very competitive women's college recently got a letter from the president, announcing a 4.7 percent rise in the already astronomical fees for next year. Increased support was planned for academic programs and initiatives, faculty development, technological improvements, and classroom innovations. Doubtless, these needs seem very real, but the need for improved student services is far greater. Consider these facts:

- At this same college of twenty-five hundred students, three tried to commit suicide in the week before Thanksgiving and another in March. Last week a student freaked out while doing a paper; her parents took her away.
- There isn't even a student center on campus.
- The RAs are seniors living in the halls, who are paid a pittance to fulfill a crying need for student counseling, while attending to their own education.
- The school's transfer rate has risen to 13 percent as reported in Barron's 1996 *Profile of American Colleges.*
- Half the students flee the campus on weekends; the rest feel trapped there or compelled to study nonstop.
- As a student wrote home, "Yes, I'm here for the academics, but if I'm not happy here, what does that matter? I hate it and I don't fit in."

What Can Schools Do?

An axiom of the Noel-Levitz retention model is that students will stay where they feel comfortable and leave where they do not, especially true for first-year students. Why do schools forget that truth?

"The most powerful trend in retention is offering student success courses, like University 101, an orientation that teaches students how to succeed at that school," Noel explained. "But they also need support later in the term, when they encounter problems and anxieties." They may need help in negotiating the library for a paper, or somebody to ask, "Is it the course or is it me that's weird?"

Quit resting on your laurels, and ask what you've done lately to make a student's life easier. This college's museum has an outstanding collection including works by Picasso, Gauguin, Rodin, Monet, Matisse, Miró, Chagall, and others. Selling just one piece to build a student center would signal a new priority.

Blindly following the male model of encouraging a pressure-cooker academic environment is cruel, especially for a woman's college. Driving half its students crazy or into the arms of a more user-friendly college will affect the bottom line. Its failures will graduate and eventually contribute elsewhere as alumni and parents.

I hope student services professionals like those I met at the NASPA/ACPA convention in March continue to press the need to support the development of the whole student, not just the academic mind. Otherwise, those who call higher education an archaic, irrelevant, and expensive tradition may well have the last laugh.

Mary Dee Wenniger

Fear Factor Challenges Women in Catholic Higher Ed

September 1998

We have all known fear: the clutch in the stomach when an individual in power threatens, intimidates, or imperils our plans. Women in higher education regularly confront fears regarding campus controversies, course topics, and even personal sexual orientation. Yet the fears and the issues differ from institution to institution, from public to private higher education.

People who identify themselves as feminists face a concern about being misunderstood in both public and private institutions, according to Pat McGuire, president of Trinity College in Washington, D.C. There is an element of tension around academic freedom because a college is "a place to challenge and test the conventional wisdom," she said. "It's how we learn and discover truth." Although some specific fears menace women in Catholic higher ed, many of the same issues threaten women in secular schools, in different clothing. Strategies to help women are often similar.

But Catholic colleges often have an added element, McGuire explained. "Our faith through its formal organization has already defined truth that may not be challenged. There is a fine line between what has been defined as truth and cannot be challenged" and issues open to question. "Few on Catholic campuses want to fly in the face of Roman Catholic truths," she said. This situation "poses an inherent tension," according to McGuire. For example, the pope has issued a statement that women's ordination is not permissible. "Good Catholics are now asking: 'How do I know where to stop short and not cross the line?'" she said.

There is the fear of being a stranger in both lands while intending and wanting to be both a good Catholic and a good academic. "It's along that narrow line where most of the private conversations occur" between bishops, college presidents, and other concerned Catholics, McGuire said.

Sometimes people become concerned about issues that really are nonexistent problems, McGuire stated. One Trinity junior faculty member thought using a particular art textbook might not be permitted because it contained work by a controversial artist. "But that is a matter of academic freedom," McGuire said. "We would not have a problem with the text."

Identify True Catholic Issues

"The problems that I see tend to be more garden variety," McGuire continued. "People ask, 'Can I do this?' or 'What would happen to me if I did that?'" These questions are "usually some other kind of issue that comes out of the public climate we deal with that makes people confused about what is and is not acceptable," she said. They are not really Catholic issues. These situations point out the need to communicate "what we're really talking about," McGuire noted.

Margaret Stetz, associate professor of English and women's studies at Georgetown University, agreed that questions sometimes arise close to home: "It's often not a question of going to the bishop, but what kind of flak are you going to get from alumni groups and students connected to outside organizations?" Does that sound familiar to women in secular schools? For example, a small cadre of mostly male Georgetown students produce a publication, *The Academy*, funded by off-campus conservatives. The glossy magazine comes out irregularly, from one to four times a semester, and identifies itself as being in the Catholic tradition. "It has a special interest in targeting faculty seen as feminist," Stetz said. "I'm proud to say that I've had a recent paragraph devoted to telling me to shut up and stop speaking out in student newspapers" and elsewhere. Stetz doesn't have much fear because she has tenure, but the publication could threaten untenured women.

Untenured faculty who teach courses related to sexuality have been mentioned in newspaper and magazine articles, Stetz reported. "The administration tends to be cautious and quiet, so it's not going to send out responses energetically and promptly to defend you and support you. Catholic administrations must consider many audiences that public institutions may not have to consider."

When Stetz's department changed requirements for English majors a few years ago, giving students more choice in their courses, the department received much criticism in the national media. This was "another example of how individual faculty members could feel at risk, even though the administration had supported this change," Stetz said. "It just didn't speak out as energetically as we'd hoped."

Another issue Stetz identified is "the fear factor of wanting to placate alumni and of worrying whether you may become identified as a problem for some donor group." Georgetown is in the midst of a big capital campaign, and the issue is relevant for both faculty members and administrators, according to Stetz. "Faculty don't want to be seen as troublemakers by the administration, and donors may not want to support a radical department."

When the Ride Gets Bumpy, Hang On

To counteract or work around these fears, Stetz reported that she has "coped by waiting it out." When the National Association of Scholars and other conservative groups attacked the department about program changes in the *New York Times, Wall Street Journal,* and other publications, the English faculty fought back, but there was still a period where the only thing to do was just hang in there and hang on.

"We wrote editorials and worked with the office of communication at Georgetown to get our own story out, to get the truth out," Stetz said, "but mostly we just waited for these organizations to pick their next target and move on. If they can't get an immediate victory, they move on to other schools and issues," she explained. "But it took a long time, and it was ugly. We felt very naked and vulnerable. The majority of faculty exposed in this way were women, although sex was not an issue in this case."

Strategize and Pick Your Battles

When confronting issues, "it's very important for women in the Catholic colleges to fight the battles you can win and that are meaningful and relevant, and not to fight every battle," McGuire advised. "Separate out those that may not be real problems," she said. "I hear too much undifferentiated angst about the role and condition of women in . . . all colleges," McGuire said.

"Be more discerning." It's unnecessary "to trash the whole place," she said, advising women to keep "the reaction to issues in perspective." McGuire recommended not pursuing issues that are unimportant, mostly rhetoric or anecdotal. "I don't mean to be unsympathetic, but some of the cases are the worst ones from which to make policy," she observed. Women still definitely face many challenges, and sexism limits women's advancement in administration at all types of colleges. But "we shouldn't feel that we are alone or that our problems are unique or that we can fix them by railing against them," McGuire said.

"Those most likely to be successful are those who think strategically," she recommended. Sometimes that means going around barriers and not trying to move through them. Sometimes winning—and proving yourself in a different way—is the best revenge, McGuire believes. "I also believe in being very honest in the right settings," she said. "You have to engage the discussion with your peers and superiors—your universe—not just with everyone who agrees with you," McGuire pointed out. "It's hard to learn how to say to your chair or bishop: 'We have to agree to disagree.' This requires some diplomatic skills."

Learn from the Founders' Traditions

If women in Catholic colleges face some additional concerns, they also may have additional tools to handle them. Most issues "arise out of traditions of religious orders, and a lot of our faculty don't understand this," McGuire said. "Trying to understand more about the traditions of the founding orders could help in moving around and solving the problems." This can provide "guidance on why we do what we do and how we do it," she continued. Even if it's a men's order, most at their root have an impulse that is deeply spiritual and an education component that is "genderless," McGuire explained. "The best way to argue with the Jesuits is to become one. Rather than rejecting the traditions, use the context to open up the mind," she said.

"My advice to women is always to stay within the system and work with it because there are too many people who want us to be outside the system," McGuire said. "The best way to create institutional change is from within."

Doris Green

Advice to Avoid Burnout from a Campus Change Agent

May 1998

When Martha Kaniston Laurence protested an administration-sanctioned panty raid in 1989, a few years after she joined the social work faculty at Wilfrid Laurier University in Waterloo, Ontario, she wasn't prepared for the outright hostility of campus response. "I've been pilloried, threatened, had everything land on my doorstep. I couldn't understand the hate," she says. From the ashes of her subsequent burnout emerged new approaches that let her enjoy life and become much more effective. She shared her insights at the March 1998 NAWE conference in Baltimore, Maryland.

All women and minorities are change agents simply because they are different. Depression, immobilization, and burnout are occupational hazards of being an agent for change. "I am a deviant; I enjoy being a deviant," she says. White, able-bodied, heterosexual males still make up 80 percent of tenured or tenure-track faculty at Canadian universities and dominate the rest. Women and minorities who don't agree to be dominated are a threat.

The conservative 1950s-style Wilfrid Laurier University hired Laurence in 1989 to meet an accreditation requirement, not to get her input. Accepting with naive confidence, she was shocked and bewildered by the reaction to her panty-raid protest. When she finally took off for sabbatical to New Zealand in 1991, she was so depressed that she dreamed her plane crashed before bringing her back. Instead, she returned refreshed, with new perspectives and strategies to help her survive and thrive.

Centering and Taking Stock

"There's no mileage in getting ourselves shot, beaten, or pounded to pieces," she decided. She created an empowering sense of distance by visualizing the university as her client and framing herself outside it. Thinking in terms of organizational dynamics, she could anticipate resistance and plan how to deal with it. "It's almost like stepping outside and watching myself." Because every action has an equal and opposite reaction, resistance to change is normal and inevitable. It's equally normal for women to feel frustrated, angry, and demoralized in response.

"Pay attention to yourself, and let go of what you can't control anyway," she advises. Women aren't trained or socialized to trust their instincts and observations. "Where you are is okay. It doesn't mean you like it, and it doesn't mean you want to stay there, but it's okay." Similarly, accepting the resistance doesn't mean liking or excusing it but acknowledging it. Because people are the product of their experience, North American men think they're superior to women. Trying to change things that can't be changed is a quick path to burnout. Taking herself and the resistance as given, she learned to choose where to put her energy in each situation:

Vulnerability. How vulnerable do I feel? How vulnerable am I really?

Power to influence. How much power do I have to influence the situation? How much do others think I have?

Women faculty often feel more vulnerable and less powerful than they really are.

Strategies for Change Without Burnout

After returning from New Zealand, she was appointed to the research grants committee, where the old boys funded only traditional quantitative research. The only tenured woman and advocate for nontraditional methodologies, she was assumed to know nothing about research. "I was silenced and fuming. Now what?" She evaluated her vulnerability and power to influence. The men on the committee could be rude and dismissive, but they couldn't fire her. She couldn't change or outvote the men, but she could be "a bloody pain in the butt."

She developed a strategy. When the old boys applied tougher standards to women's research, she pointed out the discrepancies. When a good proposal was in trouble, she moved to table it, buying time to lobby for support. Half of those proposals eventually got funded.

Strategies to Reduce Burnout

Get backup. Serve only on committees with at least one other feminist woman. It reduces harassment and provides a witness for any that occurs.

Attend one-for-two with regrets. Review the agenda, then go to only the meetings where you want to vote. Women need to practice skipping a meeting without a good excuse; men do it all the time.

Expose the secret society. One way the old boys control committees is to make key decisions on the golf course or over a drink. You can "out" the symptoms by questioning how decisions are made or why criteria are applied inconsistently.

Use your invisibility. Because you can't change the fact that men ignore women's voices, make the most of it. Invisibility offers a measure of protection. When Laurence defended proposals by tabling them, the committee chair didn't notice her but thought it odd that so many proposals were tabled for more information that year.

Go with the horses that are running. Spend your time on those you might be able to influence: the well-intentioned, the politically correct, and sensitive New Age guys. Don't waste more energy on blatant or closet misogynists than it takes to neutralize or contain them.

Know your hooks plan your rejoinders. We each have hooks that suck us into pointless arguments. Identify your hooks and plan how to avoid taking the bait.

Find safe places and kindred spirits. Pervasive isolation is a prime cause of burnout. Women and other change agents need to find each other and talk. With Laurence as a mentor, new faculty women have support to keep challenging the system without getting burned out.

Sarah Gibbard Cook

Can Today's Feminist Scholars Reach Ordinary Women?

January 1998

Nostalgic for a simpler era, when you could understand what feminist scholars were talking about? Women's studies in the 1960s and 1970s was simpler and more simplistic, equating white, middle-class U.S. women with womankind and measuring progress by counting female noses. With today's growing recognition of the complexity of women's issues has come a more inclusive language for discussing them. Postmodernism. Deconstruction. Revisionist. Ironically, many women on campus today feel left behind by feminist language and scholarship.

Cynthia Harrison, associate professor of history and women's studies at George Washington University, and Caryn McTighe Musil, of the Association of American Colleges and Universities (AACU), spoke at the AACU women's leadership conference in Washington, D.C., in November 1997. Harrison listed four changes.

1. Women's policy and politics, out of vogue in the 1980s, is back in favor with a broader definition. Political historians no longer study just civil government. Long before women got to vote, they used organizations like labor unions and churches politically to reform the social order.

2. Inclusion in government is no longer just a matter of numbers. With 20 to 25 percent of legislators being women, the focus has shifted to questions of diversity and effectiveness. Who do the women represent, and what do they accomplish? "It's a continuing struggle that changes over time. To our credit, people are not shrinking from it," she said.

3. Objectivity is an old ideal that the new feminist scholars call an illusion. Everyone views the world from a perspective influenced by race, gender, and class. Traditional so-called objective scholarship omits certain voices. It's more honest to acknowledge your perspective than to distort reality by pretending you can be or want to be objective.

4. Globalization of feminist studies has begun to challenge the assumption that North American women represent the world. A broader view is in the anecdotal stage, with U.S. scholars collecting biographies of women in other cultures and marveling at the differences. As U.S. feminists protest glass ceilings, those in some countries are more worried about physical safety or access to education for women and girls. What's the appropriate response to cultural or religious traditions that hurt women, like female genital mutilation? "We can't simply visit our solutions on other countries. If there's a single unifying principle in women's history, it's damned if we do, damned if we don't," Harrison said.

Changes in Perspective Decade by Decade

Caryn Musil also traced changes in women's studies.

Theme. Oppression was the defining preoccupation for women's studies in the 1960s and 1970s. By the 1980s, the focus had shifted from women as victims to women as agents, creators of social networks and service organizations. The focus in the 1990s is on transformation. Scholars look beyond access and entry to ask what it's like for those who get in. "There's still no women's bathroom in the Senate," she said.

Distinctions. The focus of the 1960s and 1970s on differences between women and men gave way in the 1980s to a recognition of diverse ethnic, racial, and economic backgrounds. The 1990s focus is on group intersections and deep commonalities.

Geography. North American women were the subject of women's studies in the United States in the 1960s and 1970s. In the 1980s, American feminists woke up to notice that women's priorities are not the same worldwide. Food and fuel are daily issues for some. The women's conference in Beijing reflected the 1990s search for a global vision. Despite differences, women share a common interest in big issues like armed conflict and violence against women.

Causation. Feminists in the 1960s and 1970s tried to identify a single cause for the world's ills, blaming patriarchy or capitalism or sex or race. Multiple causes and a shifting dynamic became a more widespread model in the 1980s. In the 1990s, scholars see gender as just one piece in a subtle, complex mosaic.

Identification. White, middle-class feminists in the 1960s and 1970s assumed that women think of themselves first and foremost as women. In the 1980s, women of color made the point that gender is only one of many ways a woman identifies herself. Women in the 1990s acknowledge a variety of allegiances, like race, class, gender, religion, and academic discipline. Jewish women are reexamining religious history. Women scientists grapple with their identities as scientists and as women. "At this point, we are more adept at border crossing. We have learned to do it respectfully and wisely," Musil said. From a simplistic image of uniform, downtrodden women, we've advanced to a many-sided image of women in diverse walks of life, from diverse backgrounds, faced with diverse challenges.

Challenging Questions for the Future

To bridge the gap between feminist scholarship and the language and issues of "ordinary" women, Harrison and Musil ask:

- How can we express our scholarly work in language that's meaningful to the most women?
- How can we avoid sounding elitist using the new scholarship to draw women together, not drive them apart?
- How far can identity politics take us? What comes next after a million woman march?
- Have we gone too far toward theorizing about theory instead of studying anything practical?
- If everyone has a voice, should every voice go unchallenged?
- How can we apply our most serious intellects to solving real problems? What can feminist scholarship offer?

Mary Dee Wenniger

The Kingdom of Circles and Triangles: A Fairy Tale for Grown Ups

January 1998
Sarah Gibbard Cook
Independent scholar and historian
Once upon a time, there was a kingdom where everybody was either a circle or a triangle. The ruler of the kingdom was a triangle. Triangles ran all the govern-

ment departments and most of the businesses. They had most of the money and all the best jobs. Circles and triangles both worked very hard.

One day the Kingdom of Circles and Triangles decided to become a democracy. Everybody agreed it would be better to treat everyone equally. The ruler changed the laws to make everyone equal and then resigned.

"Now maybe I can have a good position too," a young circle said to itself. "I'm smart, and I work hard."

"Good," said the triangle in charge. "Everyone is equal now. Why don't you apply?"

The day of the interview, the circle washed its round face and shined its shoes. It put on its best clothes. Soon it took its seat in front of the panel of triangles who would make the decision.

"I'm smart, and I work hard," the circle said. "What else would you like to know about me?"

"How well do you keep your balance?" the head triangle asked. "We learned long ago that it's important to sit solidly on one side and not roll to the right or the left."

"I'm sure I could learn to balance well," the circle replied. "I can also move very fast when necessary by rolling toward my destination."

"Rolling is not a useful skill," the head triangle said. "We learned long ago to manage the kingdom without rolling, and we see no need to begin rolling now."

Another triangle on the panel spoke up. "What interests me most is perspective. We need someone who can see three sides to every issue."

"I can see an infinite number of sides," the circle said. "I can weight them all equally and understand even the most complicated issues in a balanced, even-handed way."

"That sounds worse than useless," the triangle said. "You will never be able to make a decision. No, the important skill is to be able to see three sides."

"I'm sure I can do that, too," the circle said.

After the interview, the panel sent the circle into a nearby room where there was a machine to measure balance and perspective. "To make sure we treat everyone equally, we use a machine that has no way to know whether you are a circle or a triangle."

"That sounds fair," the circle said.

When the circle got home, its friends asked, "How did it go? Did you get the position?"

"No, I'm not good enough at balance and perspective," the circle said. "If I keep working at it, I'm sure I can learn to stand still without rolling to the right or the left. And I know I can learn to see exactly three sides to every issue. I wish I hadn't wasted my school days on learning to roll fast or see an infinite number of sides to everything."

"If we teach our children the skills of stable balance and three-sided perspective, they will grow up to get better positions than ours. What wonders the future holds for them," the circles agreed. "Aren't you glad we finally live in a democracy where everyone gets treated equally?"

CHAPTER SIX

SEX ON THE ROAD

We live in a gendered society, in which a person's sex affects everything from what color blanket covers the newborn in the nursery to what will be the most likely cause of death in the nursing home or geriatric ward. In the intervening years, gender profoundly affects virtually every aspect of our lives, including even how we fit into unisex clothes. (The sleeves are too long for women, reports a communications chair at a SUNY campus.)

Sexual issues virtually always are connected to crimes of power, in which women usually are the victims: rape, sexual assault, harassment, sex discrimination, and on across the continuum. In this section, unlike the *Thelma and Louise* story where sex on the road was brief and pleasurable, we learn that for many women on campus, sex can be a negative condition leading to unpleasurable events.

In a campus environment, issues of academic freedom are often cited as an excuse for behavior that slides down the slippery slope between rudeness and sexual harassment. Despite a court ruling that sexual examples or comments made in class must be directly pertinent to the subject at hand, students continue to complain of harassment in class. What a grad student with a male adviser often has to endure in order to get that degree is yet another issue.

But worst of all is an academic climate that refuses to admit there's a problem, so the issue festers: what starts out as a sore point becomes a full-scale infection, and the whole campus becomes the patient and the loser.

Nor is the issue restricted to the academic side of the house. In student services and athletics, gender counts. Activities that support women, such as women's resource centers and groups for gay, lesbian, bisexual, and transgender students, often come under attack, especially at Catholic and Jesuit schools whose missions of social justice somehow see women as an exception to the rule.

In athletics, sexual harassment is pervasive. Now that men are the majority of head coaches of women's teams in all three NCAA divisions, opportunities for harassment of both athletes and assistant coaches have increased. Homophobia continues to plague female athletes, as society is beginning to accept the concept of strong women but continues to deprecate those assumed to be lesbians or bisexuals.

This chapter considers some of the challenges linked to sexuality on campus.

Anita Hill Won

August 1992

Last fall, as the nation watched the Anita Hill–Clarence Thomas hearings, sexual harassment came out of the closet and can no longer be ignored or taken lightly. If the long-range plan was to lose the battle so they could win the war, those fighting sexual harassment and the mistreatment of women in the workplace couldn't have done a better job. Although she lost the battle to deny Thomas a U.S. Supreme Court seat, Hill won a more important victory: recognition that women have the right to a harassment-free workplace and a national conviction that men ought not be allowed to run everything. Consider some results.

Anita Hill is a hero and a martyr. Although Clarence Thomas won senate confirmation, Anita Hill became a martyr. Her name is a household word, spoken by virtually every leader at the [1992] Democratic convention. Led by outraged Minnesota state legislator Gloria Segal, Hill supporters have raised about $125,000, half the private funds needed to endow a chair in her name at the University of Oklahoma Law School, where she teaches. Although she could have an agent and command big speaking fees, Hill still handles her own appearances.

More women are running for political office. Angered and disgusted by the treatment of Hill by male members of the Senate Judiciary Committee, women have decided to challenge their domination. The hearings galvanized support for women's political bids at all levels. At least seventeen women are running for the Senate, which now has just two women. California could have an all-woman Senate delegation. At least one hundred women seek nominations to the House, which currently has twenty-eight women members.

Highly visible Senate primary victories by women in Illinois, Pennsylvania, and California contribute to the feeling that this just might be the year for successful women candidates. At state, district, and local levels, women are standing up as candidates in record numbers. Contributing to their successes are widespread voter discontent with incumbents, the pro-choice issue, and a hope that women as outsiders can set the country on a more enlightened path.

Sexual harassment complaints are rising. The Equal Employment Opportunity Commission reports that formal charges of sexual harassment filed in the first half of fiscal year 1992 increased by more than 50 percent over those filed a year ago, to 4,754.

Men think twice about what they say and do. At a national trade association headquarters recently, a senior vice president reportedly vacated his office within twenty-four hours after his secretary informed the association president that although she ended their affair, he continued to try to reconcile in an inappropriate way. A male consultant friend lost out on a contract because a woman consultant alleged that he had sexually harassed her. He quietly was not invited to continue consulting for the company.

Secretary of the Navy resigned after failing to investigate sexual harassment charges. Because the U.S. armed forces are not known to welcome women except as support staff who know their place, the resignation of the navy secretary after twenty-six women officers charged navy pilots with sexual abuse and molestation is significant. That the raunchy behavior reported at the Tailhook conference took place is no surprise. But only in a climate of increased sensitivity after Hill's testimony would it cause a scandal and result in the resignation of the Navy's head man. In addition, the Navy's top admiral, Frank Kelso, has ordered every officer and sailor in the entire navy to undergo sensitivity training.

Sensitivity training firms are swamped. Teaching men how to treat women is popular. In higher education, consulting firms report getting calls from the president of a school, rather than someone in the personnel department, indicating that their concern is a priority. Anita Hill lost the battle, but her testimony went a long way toward winning the war for equality between the sexes.

Mary Dee Wenniger

Sexuality Is Today's Flash Point for Academic Freedom

May 1997

Women are united in favor of academic freedom but not when it's an excuse to retain obsolete faculty or harass women and minorities. Then reasonable women differ, according to Ann H. Franke, AAUP senior legal counsel. Keynoting the National Association for Women in Education conference in San Francisco in

February, Franke proposed ways to address women's concerns without sacrificing academic freedom.

Today's issues aren't Marxism and McCarthyism so much as vested economic and cultural interests, Franke said. Businesses feel threatened by research about industrial pollution, logging practices, or the impact of tobacco advertising. A state-run law school clinic in New Jersey sues the state. It takes courage for administrators at cash-strapped schools to stand up to the legislatures or corporations that fund them.

Academic freedom faces assaults everywhere like that at Georgetown University, where curricular changes in the English department recently produced nationwide headlines. America needs safe places for researchers and teachers who question the status quo and administrators who stand by them, she said. Women and minorities, now underrepresented in positions of power, need them most of all.

Speech, Sex, and Harassment

Today's flash point issue for academic freedom is sexuality, Franke said. The state attorney general tried to bar the University of Alabama at Tuscaloosa from hosting a national lesbian, gay, and bisexual conference. A citizen's group filed suit to force Nassau County Community College, New York, to eliminate a course on sexuality. A professor at a religious college in New York lost her job after displaying a "Support Gay Rights" button on her briefcase. Some people tried to keep former Surgeon General Joycelyn Elders from teaching in Arkansas because of her views on teenagers, sexuality, and masturbation.

Divisions surface among women when speech enters the fuzzy territory between freedom and sexual harassment. After a University of New Hampshire professor in his English class compared a belly dancer's movements to Jell-O on a plate with a vibrator beneath it, and a San Bernardino Valley College (California) professor asked his writing students to define pornography, both were disciplined for sexual harassment. Both sued for alleged violation of freedom of speech under the First Amendment.

Colleges and universities need sexual harassment policies that look at how material about sex is used in the classroom, instead of unilaterally banning it altogether, Franke advised. Don't just photocopy EEOC guidelines because business environments are different from academic institutions, whose role is to stimulate new ideas and challenge entrenched ideologies. "To me, a good sexual harassment policy is one that does not mechanically apply the concept of *hostile environment* to the classroom," Franke said. The AAUP says sexual speech becomes harassment if it's "persistent, severe, and not relevant to the subject matter." It's the difference between a math professor opening every class with a dumb-blonde joke and a communications professor mentioning dumb-blonde jokes during a discussion on humor.

Has Tenure Outlived Its Purpose?

Franke called the 1940 Statement of Principles on Academic Freedom and Tenure "the closest thing AAUP has to a sacred text." It details the procedure by which a school must prove good reason to dismiss a tenured faculty member. Good reasons for dismissal are incompetence, neglect of duty, elimination of the program, or severe financial distress that threatens the future of the school. Bad reasons include race, gender, national origin, sexual orientation, or controversial opinions. "At the AAUP, we believe that today tenure is under a more vigorous and sustained attack than we have witnessed in many years," Franke said. Amid calls to treat education as a business, workers threatened by downsizing ask why professors should be immune. State legislators, trustees, regents, and administrators want flexibility to improve productivity by eliminating deadwood.

Tenure may disappear not with a bang but a whimper, Franke predicted, as schools quietly replace tenure-track positions with adjuncts and part-timers. The number of tenured or tenure-track faculty grew from 354,000 in 1975 to 395,000 in 1993, about 12 percent. But full-time nontenure-track faculty exploded from 81,000 to 149,000, a full 84 percent.

Why are women divided over tenure? Some think it protects mediocrity. Franke said schools should stop using tenure as an excuse to avoid hard decisions, like redirecting priorities or firing incompetent professors. Eliminate programs if you must, but first consider the effect on women before you eliminate nursing ahead of pharmacy, or home economics ahead of agricultural economics. Grit your teeth, and start disciplinary proceedings against a professor who doesn't measure up. Don't cop out by substituting faculty-wide posttenure evaluations, a massive waste of resources. If state law mandates posttenure evaluations, use them for faculty development.

Some women dislike tenure because of bias against women in both the criteria and their colleagues' biases in awarding it. Although more women are now earning tenure, men still hold three out of four tenured positions, whereas women predominate among poorly paid, insecure adjunct and part-time faculty. Tenure highlights faculty gender inequities, but eliminating tenure won't end them. Entrenched straight white males will still have the edge.

A better solution is to replace departing associate or full professors with entry-level tenure-track women and minorities, Franke said. In a few years, the new assistant professors may join the ranks of the tenured, free to speak their minds and defend their untenured sisters. "The tenured faculty have a responsibility to protect the academic freedom of their untenured colleagues," Franke said.

Sarah Gibbard Cook

Backlash or Backfire? Sexual Harassment Versus Academic Freedom and Due Process

November 1994

In their zeal to stop sexual harassment, some colleges and universities may be trampling academic freedom and constitutional rights of free speech and due process, say judges, juries, and even a feminist theorist.

A Catch-22 for Schools

Unless they treat accusations of harassment seriously and act to protect victims, schools can be sued for millions by the accusers. But if they act too vigorously against harassers, they risk a lawsuit. Perhaps even worse for academe, schools striving to purge campuses of all harassment also risk hanging the innocent and inhibiting the rigorous exchange of ideas, say some academics.

The Pendulum Swings

To give women a better chance to end sexual harassment, courts now accept convincing testimony and circumstantial evidence. Consider the case last winter, in which two secretaries claimed they saw University of Arkansas President John Mangieri masturbating in his office. The board of trustees fired him on the spot. Trustees gave Mangieri and his lawyer less than a day to prepare for his hearing and did not permit him to question the secretaries, despite the warning from the human resources office that the school was not following its own procedures in the situation.

Mangieri denies the charges and claims they were concocted to destroy his career. His lawsuit accuses the university of denying him due process. "In our country, a person is supposed to be innocent until proved guilty. Yet with charges of sexual misconduct, it seems as though the minute that allegations are made, it is the accused who must prove his innocence. What's more, disciplinary measures are taken against the accused *before* guilt or innocence is established," Mangieri wrote in the *Chronicle of Higher Education* (July 13, 1994). "Why was I required to prove my innocence, rather than my accusers being required to prove my guilt?"

New Precedents Established

Not respecting due process cost the University of Puget Sound (UPS) and Bennington College big bucks. UPS thought it was acting compassionately by letting Professor Harmon Zeigler choose early retirement rather than an investigation of sexual harassment charges filed by three students. Was allowing him to retire unfair to the alleged victims? No, unfair to Zeigler, said a jury, which awarded him $1.5 million for wrongful discharge. UPS erred in not identifying the accusers and giving Zeigler a chance to defend himself and in using "undue influence" to force Zeigler to agree to a retirement settlement, the jury said.

At Bennington, an investigating committee of faculty, staff, and students confirmed charges that Professor Leroy Logan had sexually assaulted a male student before the college fired Logan. Logan sued, and the jury found that the investigating committee had restricted Logan's right to defend himself by not allowing him a lawyer present at the hearing, as specified in the faculty handbook. They awarded Logan $500,000 for breach of contract, which was later reduced to $272,712, under terms of Logan's five-year contract.

Bad Taste Isn't Illegal

What constitutes a hostile environment? To illustrate the term *simile* in his technical writing class, Professor J. Donald Silva said, "Belly dancing is like Jell-O on a plate with a vibrator under the plate." When eight female students complained about this and other remarks, the University of New Hampshire investigated, found Silva had violated its sexual harassment policy by creating a hostile environment, and suspended him without pay unless he agreed to attend counseling.

Silva sued, claiming violation of his rights to free speech. Tasteless? Certainly. But probably not illegal, said the district court judge in a preliminary hearing. He affirmed the First Amendment issue and ordered the school to reinstate Silva pending the trial's outcome.

Protecting Academic Freedom

Feminist Jane Gallop hates sexual harassment but believes that applying the term too broadly compromises academic freedom. The University of Wisconsin–Milwaukee English professor cautions against construing everything sexual as sexist, lest legitimate references to sexuality be threatened. In *Academe* (September–October 1994, p. 21), she notes, "Teachers who include discussion of homosexuality in 'straight' courses might be accused by their homophobic students of creating a hostile environment through 'unnecessary' discussion of sexuality, or feminists who expose the misogyny of pornography might be accused by offended male students of sexual harassment."

How to Define Sexual Harassment?

In the same issue of *Academe,* the AAUP asserts that the academic setting is unique in its commitment to a free exploration of ideas, so the constitutional rights to a nonhostile *working* environment upheld by Title VII do not extend to the *learning* environment. Trying to police the learning environment would be a legal minefield, the AAUP says. "Some students might find themselves alienated, even offended, by 'learning environments' they deem to intrude on personal privacy, while others might be alienated by 'learning environments' they perceive as too indifferent to personal needs."

Instead, the AAUP urges schools to restrict sexual harassment to incidents of targeted harassment, which can be either quid pro quo ("If you date me, I'll give you a good grade or promotion") or else speech or conduct that is personally abusive or humiliating to an individual, or which persists despite the targeted individual's objection. The AAUP's Committee on the Status of Women suggests a broader policy that would not eliminate the concept of a hostile environment but would require that offensive speech or conduct be judged unprofessional, according to AAUP standards, before it can be defined as harassment.

Policy Is Just the Starting Point

As with the Silva case, the AAUP points out that it's not just the policy but how it's carried out: "Many of the problems campuses have experienced stem more from disregarding the mandates of due process than from having inadequate policies."

Should the Personal Be Illegal?

With an unimpeachable record of feminist teaching and organizing, University of Wisconsin–Milwaukee English Professor Jane Gallop was shocked when two female graduate students filed sexual harassment complaints against her. The Affirmative Action Office found her innocent of the complaints, which alleged that she had attempted to seduce the students and retaliated when they refused.

Still, the office "saw fit to chastise me for something of which there had been no complaint: a too intense, too personal, too volatile pedagogical relation" with one student. "This finding suggests an atmosphere in which sexual policy is so widely construed as not only to punish and restrict harassment but also to chill other relations," says Gallop.

Hoist with Her Own Petard

The real irony, Gallop notes, is that feminist teaching stresses the importance and validity of the personal as both a subject and method of learning. Believing that women learn things better by personalizing them, educators have sought to break barriers between the professional and the personal. In fact, sexual harassment itself was ignored and considered a so-called personal problem unworthy of professional attention until women argued that harassment at work is by definition a professional issue.

Sex Isn't the Enemy

Gallop fears that people may forget that sexual harassment is illegal because it is discriminatory, not because it is sexual or personal. "All but forgotten are common nonsexual forms of sexual harassment, like the engineering professor who regularly tells his classes that women can't be engineers" and encourages his male students while making his women students doubt their abilities. That's a hostile environment that discriminates on the basis of sex and fits the legal definition of sexual harassment, even though the professor may have no sexual interest in his women students. "If harassment is a form of sex discrimination, it should be fought within a broad-based campaign whose central target is discrimination"— women's exclusion from opportunities and relegation to second-class status.

Jennifer Hirsch

Campuses Struggle to Define Sexual Harassment

February 1994
Sexual harassment is used to belittle, demean, and control, in short, exert power over a person. They're starting to get it about not touching, but those on campus find verbal and psychological sexual harassment much more difficult to define operationally. Here are examples of the problem.

Harassment or Academic Freedom?

Historically, campus administrators have been reluctant to invade the sanctity of the classroom. Now comes a new concept that changes traditional classroom dynamics: sexual harassment. Faculty may not do whatever they want in their classes if students consider it degrading, offensive, or hostile. At the University of New Hampshire, charges against Professor J. Donald Silva show what happens when professors not only "just don't get it" but use academic freedom as a defense. The Silva controversy began two years ago, when six women students complained that he repeatedly used sexual metaphors to describe writing concepts, and twenty-six of sixty opted to transfer out of his classes.

Although the university receives about a dozen complaints of sexual harassment a year, all but his have been resolved through informal mediation ever since a formal procedure was set up in 1987. After twenty-two hours of hearings before panels of students and professors, the university required Silva to take a one-year leave of absence without pay, seek counseling, and apologize for creating a "hostile and offensive academic environment."

Affirmative Action Director Chris Burns-DiBiasio says the school's panels also considered confidential information as well as public facts. "Sometimes when you look at the facts in isolation," the effect differs from when you "hear how the facts affect the students, their academic pursuits, and their relationships with faculty," she notes. Silva sued the university in November in federal court for restricting his academic freedom. Supporters say the case illustrates how vulnerable faculty is to charges of sexual harassment, whereas the university contends Silva is trivializing the concept of academic freedom. No trial date had been set. Burns-DiBiasio is setting up a spring campus series of educational symposia on reconciling the issues of sexual harassment and academic freedom.

Harasser or Persistent Suitor?

Yet more questions arise when cultures clash and students are accused of harassing each other. At Swarthmore College (Pennsylvania), Ewart Yearwood, a Hispanic from New York City, is accused of harassing Alexis Clinansmith, a white freshman from a Michigan suburb, by lurking outside classes, following her, and repeatedly asking her for dates. "I was perhaps more persistent in trying to date her and strike up a relationship with her than she wanted or than I should have been," the Associated Press quotes Yearwood as explaining (Brin, 1994). Swarthmore's response was to offer him a free spring semester at any school he chose, a deal he accepted until Columbia University rejected him for grades. Hoping the problem, and Yearwood, will go away, Swarthmore is trying to find him a new school.

Manipulative Social Support?

Overt sexual harassment still exists, but there are more subtle ways to control women faculty and administrators, by consciously manipulating their social support, says Lawrence J. Rifkind, dean of arts and sciences at Georgia State University. Calling manipulative social support just another form of sexual harassment, he addressed the January conference of Women in Higher Education.

Social support can be defined as verbal and nonverbal communication that reduces uncertainty about a situation, the self, the other, or the relationship, while enhancing the perception of personal control of one's life. It helps cope with life, especially stressful situations. In a dysfunctional relationship, he explains, "these linkages can be chains" used to manipulate and control one with less power, and he identified four types of manipulative support common on campus.

Support as a commodity. This leads to a bargaining and negotiation process, a quid pro quo form of sexual harassment in which the recipient feels an indebtedness to the benefactor. But the recipient never knows when it will be time to call in the chits. Will the department chair who grants you release time then expect your support for his ideas?

Support as information access. Those in power may pump a new faculty member for information but either fail to provide information in return or deliberately give wrong or distorted information. Women who are unaware of departmental politics and dynamics are particularly vulnerable, he says.

Support as codependency. This leads to the view of higher education as an "addictive system within an organization that self-perpetuates." Because those in power feed off each other, the newcomer is obliged to go along, he says, recalling being asked to reorganize his department's committee structure as a new faculty member. He naively assumed that efficiency should be his guide, unaware that a new structure threatened to disrupt the power held by senior faculty members leading certain committees.

Support as hegemony. This deals with the issue of a subgroup acquiescing to the demands of the dominant group, often resulting in many phone calls, conversations behind closed doors, and a "wait until we get our turn" attitude. In a department historically dominated by males, junior faculty females often must bide their time until they reach a critical mass and influence.

That's the way it works in higher education, Rifkind says. Those unwilling to accept the self-perpetuating system should get out, get mellow, get an organized opposition, or get an outside source of social support to minimize negative effects. That's the good news: women can build their own social support systems and find unconditional encouragement from colleagues, administrators, associations, and informal channels on or off campus.

Mary Dee Wenniger

Hidden Costs of the Campus Sexual Harassment Epidemic

July 1994

Imagine a workforce where a third of the employees feel alienated, disrespected, treated unfairly, and at the mercy of leaders who act in bad faith. Obviously, those who feel disillusioned by their colleagues and betrayed by their institution can't do their best work, and all suffer the loss.

Harassment Widespread, Unreported

A 1989 survey of 449 faculty, staff, and administrators by Goodwin found that 39 percent of women and 19 percent of men reported some type of sexual harassment, defined as behaviors that made them feel uncomfortable. The most common incidents were sexist behaviors, sexual comments, and offensive body language, with 18 percent in the survey reporting unwanted physical advances. A larger, nationally representative survey of 9,402 women faculty at 270 schools examined the effects of sexual harassment. Researchers Eric L. Dey, University of Michigan, and Linda J. Sax and Jessica Korn, UCLA, presented their findings as "Betrayed by the Academy: The Sexual Harassment of Women College Faculty" at the 1994 annual meeting of the American Educational Research Association in New Orleans in April.

Asserting that "The 'epidemic' of sexual harassment on college campuses is even larger than originally conceptualized," they point out that research on it "is limited by the underreporting of harassment incidents," due either to fear of retaliation or not knowing that the behavior is considered harassment.

What Is Harassment?

Part of the problem with sexual harassment is confusion over its definition. Many people label only severe behavior as harassment per se, viewing annoying behavior as a mere nuisance. But "Sexual harassment includes a range of behaviors, from physical assault to verbal innuendos to verbal and physical threats" and "includes some concept of the misuse of power and coercion," say the researchers.

Courts define two types of sexual harassment:

- Hostile environment: sexual jokes, teasing, comments, touching, display of sexual illustrations on walls, lockers, or computer monitors and printouts that denigrate women.
- Quid pro quo: sexual behavior demanded in exchange for a reward or to avoid punishment.

"Sexual harassment creates confusion, blurring the lines between the professional world and the personal world. The harasser introduces and forces the personal element into what should be a sex-neutral situation," the researchers explain. As a practical, hands-on, I-know-it-when-I-see-it definition for administrators in charge of redressing campus sexual harassment, apply the following litmus test: ask yourself, "How would I feel if this incident happened to my daughter, mother, or wife?"

Not Treated with Respect

Among women respondents who had been harassed, 15.1 percent had far more negative views of their colleagues, administration, and campus climate than the nonharassed women. One in five of these women strongly agreed that "People here don't treat each other with enough respect," compared with only one in twenty of the nonharassed women, who were much more likely to strongly disagree with that statement. When asked whether "Women are treated fairly" at their school, harassed women were more than four times as likely to strongly disagree and only half as likely to agree as nonharassed women.

Administrators Don't Act in Good Faith

Perceptions about whether "administrators act in good faith" correlated with harassment experience: harassed women were much less likely to believe that administrators act in good faith. Harassed women reported less overall job satisfaction and more stress related to subtle discrimination, colleagues, and institutional procedures. Asked if they would still choose to be college professors if they could begin again, they were more likely to say no. They were also more likely to consider leaving academe for new jobs.

The harassed women were also less likely to positively evaluate their visibility for faculty jobs at other schools, which may ultimately lead them to feel trapped in an institution with colleagues they no longer respect or enjoy, the researchers say. "These findings clearly suggest that harassment fundamentally alters the way a woman faculty member views the institutional climate. Harassed women are much more likely to hold negative views of institutional norms toward respect for others, fairness toward women, and manner in which the campus administration operates."

Although this relationship is disturbing, it is important to acknowledge. The researchers note that "such differences will likely lead to further negative outcomes as time passes and these negative views influence the way future institutional events are interpreted."

How to Reduce Harassment

Those at schools with more women faculty were less likely to report harassment. The increased presence and visibility of women on campus "may help change the nature of an institution," making it "less likely to accept that sexual harassment has to be part of the academy." Because the definition of sexual harassment remains unclear to many, schools should also work harder to define and communicate appropriate standards of behavior, the researchers advise. Making sure people "get it" will help eliminate incidents resulting from ignorance by the offender, feigned or genuine, of what constitutes harassment.

Harassment Costs Productivity, Employees

The researchers emphasize that their study shows "a broad range of outcomes related to sexual harassment" with generalized effects far more pervasive than specific, due to changes in victims' perceptions and subjective experience. In other words, if workers are less relaxed, less confident, and less trusting, they will be less collegial, less loyal, and less productive, not to mention less happy. These effects come at a substantial cost not only to the employee's career but to the institution as well.

To avoid them, Dey, Sax, and Korn recommend campus administrators take a proactive stance on harassment. "In addition to dealing with the specifics of each sexual harassment episode, members of the campus community need to pay careful attention to issues of campus climate in order to avoid reinforcing the nature—and message—inherent in the initial event."

In a Nutshell

Surveying the largest sample of women faculty ever to be asked about sexual harassment, the Dey, Sax, and Korn study offers the most solid data on faculty sexual harassment available to date, debunking some myths. The researchers used regressions to control for other factors, finding that

- Women faculty most likely to be harassed are in public universities; at highly selective schools; at campuses with few women colleagues; or in fine arts, English, agriculture, or engineering.
- Women faculty least likely to be harassed are at Catholic four-year colleges; at women's colleges; in math, physical sciences, or health fields; or married rather than single.
- Women of color are no more or less likely than their white colleagues to be harassed.

- Rates of harassment complaints may vary with awareness levels. For example, those in women's studies reported more harassment.

Jennifer Hirsch

When the Fox Guards the Chicken House: Campuses Handling Rapes

July 1996

When Christy Brzonkala sued her school after it handed down a punishment of only a one-hour education session to the football player who had raped her, she blew the lid on a campus system that permits select students to get away with murder—or at least rape, arson, and other serious crimes. By not reporting serious crimes like rape to campus or local police, administrations are free to give preferential treatment to athletes and other advantaged students, like those with enough money and chutzpah to sue if they're disciplined.

What's worse, these administrations protect the image of their institutions as secure, low-crime havens, when the truth may be just the opposite. Some administrators may believe they are protecting the confidentiality of the victim and acting in her best interests by not reporting serious incidents to police. But in truth, they are circumventing justice. Parents and future students receive no warning of the sometimes less-than-idyllic campus culture. And student rapists and other felons go free, thinking they can get away with other crimes.

Synopsis of the Virginia Tech Case

Brzonkala accused a football player, Antonio J. Morrison, and his roommate, James L. Crawford, of raping her in their dorm room at Virginia Tech. When the university cleared Crawford and then canceled a one-year suspension of Morrison just before football season began, Brzonkala sued the university and the two students. The amount of her damage claim—$8.3 million—equals the amount Virginia Tech received for competing in the Sugar Bowl last year.

She had sued under both Title IX, which bars discrimination in educational institutions receiving federal dollars, and the 1994 Violence Against Women Act. The discrimination case was dismissed, but Brzonkala has appealed that decision.

Suit Captures National Attention

Because her suit is the first filed under the new 1994 law and the damage claim is so large, it attracted a lot of media attention, most supporting Brzonkala. As a result, she has already succeeded in warning many other students about hidden crime on their campuses.

On the *Women in Higher Education* Web page in April, all comments on the case condemned the campus judicial systems. "I think that sexual assault complaints should be handled outside of school!" e-mailed one woman. "It is so wrong that if you are an athlete or other high profile student, you can do whatever you want!"

The *New York Times* covered the suit extensively, and many readers wrote to complain about the lack of campus justice. One of them was John Silber, president of Boston University, who commented that most campus "disciplinary proceedings don't have the basics required by a fair trial: a professional and independent judiciary, enforceable rules of procedure, effective and fairly applied sanctions." He continued, "Once again, students are receiving special treatment" ("Students," 1996).

That's because most campus systems, he noted, were set up to handle minor infractions of campus classroom and residence hall behavior codes. Silber thinks administrators have an obligation to "refer all criminal cases to the real criminal justice system."

Brzonkala Not an Isolated Case

Another reason for the media outcry is that Brzonkala's case isn't unique.

A University of Nebraska at Lincoln student, Lawrence Phillips, assaulted his former girlfriend, striking her and dragging her down a stairway. The star running back on Nebraska's football team was sentenced to one year's probation, ordered to pay some of the girlfriend's medical bills, and attend psychotherapy sessions as well as classes in preventing domestic violence. But after serving only a six-week suspension, Phillips was reinstated to the football program.

A University of Southern Florida at Tampa man kidnapped and raped a freshman woman who refused to testify for him at a disciplinary hearing. He then shot her brother and killed himself. This occurred after three other women students had complained that the man had stalked or hit them, yet he had never been suspended from the school.

At the University of California at Santa Cruz, several male students committed multiple sexual assaults on freshman women. In a bizarre kind of campus judicial plea bargain, they were all allowed to transfer to other state campuses with clean records.

At Miami University of Ohio, a sophomore woman student dyed and cut her hair and changed her manner of dress after seeing—in her dormitory—the student who had assaulted her the year before. His punishment? "Student conduct probation," meaning that if he were found responsible for any other serious campus violation before graduation, he would be suspended.

Hard to believe? A male student who witnessed the assault on the Miami University woman and testified about it was himself suspended three days after her campus judicial hearing. His crime? Possessing a beer while underage.

Lawmakers Tried in 1990

Lawmakers thought they'd solved the problem in 1990 by passing the Student Right-to-Know and Campus Security Act. It requires colleges to report accurate crime statistics annually.

But many colleges don't comply, and the U.S. Department of Education has done little to punish them, according to advocates of crime victims who addressed a House of Representatives panel last month. Even when institutions do accurately report incidents on the logs of campus police, they routinely overlook cases that were simply handled administratively and ignore cases involving students that took place in off-campus housing only a block away.

In an interview with *Women in Higher Education,* Brzonkala's attorney, Eileen Wagner, cited the example of Virginia Tech, which "reported one rape in an eight-month period [but later, in the course of] bragging about the services of the women's center, mentioned there were twenty rapes in the same period."

Wagner adds, "My assessment of the statistics is that they're only reporting what they have a police report for." And some schools could be calling rape something else. For example, she says Carleton College calls rapes "advances" in sanctions.

Damning Testimony

Among those who testified before the House panel was Christy Brzonkala: "In mid-September 1994, I was raped by two football players in my own dormitory. I had met them for the first time just fifteen minutes before they attacked me. At first all I wanted to do was forget about it. I stopped going to class. I cut my hair. I slept all day and never went out. Things got worse. I attempted suicide the first week of October." Brzonkala talked to the women's center counselor and agreed to file charges under the school's sexual assault policy. She was promised a fair chance to get the football players punished.

But after the initial campus hearing and suspension of Morrison, the sexual assault coordinator and the dean went to her house. They told her that "the school had mistakenly used the wrong policy for the hearing," according to Brzonkala's testimony. "They said the suspended football player was threatening to sue the school. They said the school was not going to court over this."

Brzonkala then endured a seven-hour second hearing and was told: "the accused player was found guilty again, and he was suspended again." But later, she testified, "Without a word to me, Virginia Tech told the sports press . . . that the player's punishment had been 'deferred' until after he graduated."

The nineteen-year-old concluded, "I think Virginia Tech treated me this way because I had the nerve to complain about two of their precious football players. I doubt that Virginia Tech really knows how many of its athletes have criminal histories even before they are recruited. The rest of us come to college believing we are safe. We are anxious to meet new people and make new friends. If I had known there were dozens of sexual assaults at Virginia Tech every year . . . I would have been a lot less trusting with fellow students I had only just met."

House Fails to Act

Despite the testimony from Brzonkala and other involved citizens, the House panel did not lead to effective solutions to the problem of underreporting of campus crime. David Longanecker, assistant secretary for postsecondary education, asserted that most colleges wanted "to comply with the act." He said the goal of the Education Department is to help violators rather than hand out the stiff fines authorized by the 1990 law.

In other words, the lack of backbone and downright subversion of the truth by colleges and universities has been compounded by a wishy-washy federal agency. Who, then, will stand up for fair treatment of women? The answer appears to be: only women themselves, like Christy Brzonkala.

Eileen Wagner has a strategy. "Administrators make all the decisions on the bottom line. Each player is worth $50–75,000 in recruitment, scholarships, and other costs. The athletes are investments. Athletes think they're God's gift to women. But in reality, they are horseflesh, bought and paid for."

Meanwhile, the administrators think they're making a business decision, Wagner said. But even "Businesses have learned it's expensive not to protect women. Now, universities need to learn that if they ignore women, they're going to lose plenty."

[*Editor's note: By a five-to-four decision on May 15, 2000, the U.S. Supreme Court rejected the 1994 Violence Against Women Act, under which Brzonkala had sued the two former Virginia Tech football players. On February 27, 2000, she settled her sex bias suit against the school over the assault for $75,000.*]

Doris Green

Academe's Dirty Little Secret: Women Faculty Are Harassed

December 1996

Hundreds of studies suggest as many as 4.8 million college students may be sexually harassed annually, say Eric Dey, Jessica Korn, and Linda Sax. By comparison, sexual harassment of female faculty members has been ignored, the trio reported in the *Journal of Higher Education,* March/April 1996. They studied data collected in the 1992–1993 survey of nearly thirty thousand full-time faculty at 289 schools done by the UCLA Higher Education Research Institute, where Sax is associate director. Dey is an assistant professor of education at the University of Michigan, and Korn is a doctoral candidate in higher education at UCLA. Harassment blurs the line between the personal and professional world and "forces the personal element into what should be a sex-neutral situation," they say.

Past studies on sexual harassment of faculty found:

- Most often mentioned were sexist behaviors, sexual comments, and offensive body language.
- About one-fifth of the women in one survey reported being harassed by students. But it was "more mild and innocuous than when colleagues were the harasser[s]."
- Women pioneers breaking into traditionally male fields are frequent targets. Married women are less likely to be harassed than those single or divorced.

Dey, Korn, and Sax examined 9,402 responses from women faculty in the 1992–1993 Higher Education Research Faculty Survey to the question "Have you been sexually harassed at this institution?"

One of Seven Report Harassment

Overall, nearly one out of seven (15.1 percent) women faculty in the 1992–1993 survey reported being harassed at their present school. In the 1995–1996 update, it dropped to about 12 percent. Among those teaching women's studies courses, it was more than one out of four (26.1 percent). Among those doing research on women's issues, it was one in five (21.6 percent). Why the difference? The researchers suggest two possibilities: (1) women who are more aware of the definitions and problems of sexual harassment are more likely to report it, and (2) women working in these areas are more likely to be harassed.

Looking at the responses by academic rank, the researchers discovered full professors were much more likely to report being harassed (23.8 percent) at their present schools than were assistant professors (12.6 percent) or instructors (8.8 percent). At first glance, this result appears counter to the theory that harassment is greatest among women perceived to be least powerful, a theory from several previous studies. But the controlling factor is length of time in the position. They observed "a definite trend for harassment to increase with time within rank." But this only partially explains the response: the higher-ranking women faculty were still more likely to report harassment. They suggest several reasons.

First, "women at the lower ranks may be more subject to sexual harassment, but still less likely to report it." Second, higher-ranking women may be more likely to be harassed as a backlash to their power and visibility on campus. And finally, more awareness of harassment may have made the environment safer for junior faculty.

Their initial analysis showed Native American and Latina faculty were more likely to report harassment than were African American or Asian American faculty. But when controlled for length of service and academic rank, the differences virtually disappeared. Compared to white women, only Native American faculty were statistically more likely to report being harassed, with Asian American and African American faculty being less likely and Latinas to be about equally likely to report being harassed. On marital status, they confirmed married women being harassed much less often than divorced or single women.

What's the Effect of School Type?

Unlike previous research, their data found only slightly more sexual harassment among women at public schools compared to private ones. And faculty in four-year colleges were no more likely to report being harassed than those in two-year schools. The only real difference was women teaching in a women's college, who report much less harassment.

How Harassment Affects Faculty Careers

Dey, Korn, and Sax report that women faculty who have been harassed view the institution very differently.

Fully one-fifth (21 percent) of the harassed women agreed strongly with the statement "People here don't treat each other with enough respect." Only 6 percent of nonharassed women and 8 percent of men strongly agreed.

Presented with the statement "Women faculty are treated fairly here," more than one in four (27 percent) of the harassed women strongly disagreed, compared to only 6 percent of nonharassed women and 5 percent of men faculty.

Similarly, to the statement "Administrators here act in good faith," 23 percent of the harassed women strongly disagreed, whereas only 9 percent of the other women and 13 percent of the men strongly disagreed.

These results clearly show that being harassed affects the way women faculty view their own school. What are the specific effects?

Harassed women are more likely to have considered leaving academe. They also reported higher levels of stress, particularly around the issues of "subtle discrimination" and "red tape" in school procedures.

Finally, harassment negatively affects women's perception of their colleagues' professional competence. The researchers suggest that because the harassed women don't tend to "evaluate positively their visibility for jobs at other institutions," they may feel trapped at a school, working with colleagues they don't respect or enjoy.

Their research suggests ways that schools can help improve the climate for women faculty, as detailed above. They recommend that all of the steps happen simultaneously and note that simply increasing the number of women on campus is not enough to effectively change the climate. To do otherwise, they say, is to "betray the basic academic values of fairness and equity."

Update on Legal Trends in Sexual Harassment

Cynthia J. Haston, an employment consultant from Danville, California, and former assistant general counsel for the Maricopa County Community College District, covered the basics of sexual harassment this spring at a conference for community and technical college chairs, deans, and other organizational leaders in Phoenix. She defines sexual harassment as unwelcome sexual advances, requests for sexual favors, and other verbal or physical conduct of a sexual nature.

It is illegal when made a condition of employment or academic advancement, explicitly or implicitly. It's also illegal when submission to, or rejection of, such conduct becomes the basis for employment or academic decisions. Finally, it's illegal when such conduct unreasonably interferes with an individual's work or academic performance, or creates a hostile or offensive working environment.

In her various roles, she's observed some trends in how sexual harassment complaints are handled:

- Increasingly, plaintiffs also sue individual administrators for failing to follow up on complaints.
- In community property states, plaintiffs may also name the administrator's spouse as a defendant.
- Colleges usually provide defense counsel, but only if the administrator strictly followed recommended school policies in handling the complaint.

Her tips for addressing complaints include:
- Treat every complaint seriously.
- Take notes on who, what, when, and where.
- Explain the school's policy, including confidentiality and the prohibition of retaliation.
- Explain that you must inform the proper resource person and that the school must legally address the issue, once an administrator becomes aware of the sexual harassment complaint.
- Take appropriate action where there is evidence of harassment.
- Document every action you take, and keep the file for at least two years.
- Continually monitor your own environment for sexual harassment. Be alert for equal participation, sexual innuendo, comments, jokes, or graphics on posters, software, and screen savers.

How Schools Prevent Harassment

To improve the climate for women faculty:
- Develop a comprehensive definition of sexual harassment that acknowledges the importance of the victim's perceptions.
- Develop a policy statement demonstrating that sexual harassment will not be tolerated.
- Use many different ways to communicate the institution's policies, such as memos, posters, campus newspapers, and course catalogs.
- Educate the entire campus community about the risks of sexual harassment through the curriculum, student life programs, faculty, and staff development efforts.
- Establish an accessible grievance procedure in which the institution proactively protects those who have been harassed and deals with harassers.
- Provide psychological counseling to women who have been harassed.

Doris Green

Sports Culture Encourages Harassing Women Athletes

March 1999

The world of college sports often supports a culture of sexual harassment for women athletes, believes Leslie Heywood, assistant professor of English and cultural studies at SUNY-Binghamton. "A discrepancy exists between the increasing equality and respect for female athletes on the one hand, and on the other, behavior within the athletics culture that shows profound disrespect for female competitors," Heywood told *Women in Higher Education.*

Harassment Fact of Life for Female Athletes

"Sexual harassment and abuse of female athletes are part of the reality of women's sports," Heywood charged. Agreeing is Donna Lopiano, executive director of the Women's Sports Foundation: "Sexual harassment or even sexual assault is a significant problem . . . that often goes unreported." The extent of sexual harassment of female college athletes is unknown; it's an issue most athletic departments prefer to ignore. Heywood told *Women in Higher Education* that she hopes to do the first national survey of harassment of female athletes, "a necessary prerequisite to public awareness that there is a problem."

It's really a question of power. Coaches have ultimate power over who gets to do extra laps and who gets to compete; athletes either fail to notice or fear reprisals for complaining when a coach crosses the line from a teaching role to unacceptable sexual behavior.

Michelle Hite, who ran track at a major Division I university, told Heywood: "One of the reasons I gave up my athletic scholarship was because of the sexual harassment that I felt was as much a part of my athletic routine as practice was."

Reporter Diana Nyad said she was raped by her swim coach.

Mariah Burton Nelson, author *of The Stronger Women Get, the More Men Love Football* (1994), said: "Some of the 'best' male coaches in the country have seduced a succession of female athletes. Like their counterparts in medicine, education, psychotherapy, and the priesthood, coaches are rarely caught or punished."

Although today one in three college women participates in sports, some still assume that "women who excel at sports are really more like men and must therefore be lesbians because they're not conventionally feminine," Heywood said. This myth contributes to discrimination against female athletes in general. Heywood cited other forms of disrespect for female athletes, including coaches mandating weigh-ins and publicly ridiculing them about their weight, diets, and bodies.

Coaches on Power Trips

Anson Dorrance has coached the women's soccer team at the University of North Carolina at Chapel Hill to fifteen national championships. In a 1998 article in *The Nation,* Ruth Conniff applauded him for changing his coaching style to serve women athletes, quoting him: "You basically have to drive men, but you can lead women. I think women bring something incredibly positive to athletics. They are wonderfully coachable and so appreciative of anything you give them." Two

weeks after the article appeared, two former soccer players filed a sexual harassment lawsuit against Dorrance, saying he "intentionally and systematically sub-
jected his players to inappropriate conduct and unwelcome harassment and
thereby created a hostile environment" at the university, Heywood wrote in the
Chronicle of Higher Education (1999). They said he made uninvited sexual advances,
monitored players' whereabouts outside of practice, and sent them harassing e-
mail. Dorrance denied the charges.

"The idea that women are 'wonderfully coachable and so appreciative' has a
sinister ring" in light of the lawsuit, Heywood noted. "The idea that women are
more 'coachable'—that is, open and manipulable—and that they are 'appreciative' of whatever attentions the coach chooses to give them, may lead to unethical behavior." But amid sexual harassment charges, "teams often rally around the
coach and ostracize the accuser," Heywood pointed out. Dorrance noted a "sil-
ver lining" to the lawsuit in that it "unified the team very quickly."

How to Combat Harassment

Although athletics departments claim sensitivity to the issue, most do little about
it. An exception is the University of Arizona, which has established an extensive
education and support system, including seminars for students and coaches on harassment taught by affirmative action officers, providing case studies and real-
life scenarios.

But Heywood sees some problems. First, most originate in affirmative action offices, so it's an outsider preaching to athletics people. Programs should originate in the athletics department "because there is so much more personal contact
and interaction in the world of athletics than in ordinary teacher-student relationships," she believes. Second, "It is hard to convince coaches and athletes
that the problems of female athletes are real and significant. After all, what does
the self-esteem of a few girls matter when we've got to go out and win the big
game? The women themselves . . . view the people who come to talk about harassment as an intrusion or distraction."

Administrators should support education programs that clearly explain coaching behaviors that won't be tolerated, and that inform athletes of their rights
and recourses available to them if they encounter harassment. The programs must
show real support for women who file complaints by providing zero tolerance
for harassment. "The most crucial thing is that we show female athletes that we
respect them, value them, and take them seriously as athletes," Heywood said.
"Greater attention needs to be paid to coaching . . . and how much control coaches
should have over female athletes' lives."

Doris Green

CHAPTER SEVEN

THE DRIVER WITHIN

The woman I was when I started the *Women in Higher Education* newsletter would have shortened this book considerably by not including this chapter at all. I created the newsletter to fill a market niche, to serve a segment of the academic population with XX chromosomes, who had specific problems never mentioned in male-dominated conferences, which most were.

But a woman named Carolyn Desjardins, former executive director of the National Institute for Leadership Development, was an early supporter of the newsletter and me. As sisters sharing the same birthday of June 6, we also shared a love of life, a sense of humor, intolerance of fools and pretenders, passion, and kind hearts. In fact, Carolyn was one of the original leaders of the developing culture of women leaders in higher education who told me to "go for it" when I asked her advice on creating such an animal.

For many years, Carolyn tried to lure me to her Leader's Institute, a one-week program advertised to "change your life," which is held four times each spring in various cities around the United States. In fact, I signed up for one in the Chicago area in 1995, only to be reminded by my daughter Liz that "This is my junior year of high school, the most important part of my life for earning grades to get into college, and you want to leave me home alone for a week?"

The year Liz did go off to Smith College in Massachusetts (just a hair farther away than the one thousand–mile restricted zone), I did place myself irrevocably into Carolyn's clutches by attending a Leader's Institute in Nashville in March of

1997. On the first day, the "sisters" (as the participants in the workshop were called) were asked to list two of their goals for the conference; I selected "becoming more spiritual" and "having a significant other."

It so happened the Leader's Institute program was to meet in a joint session with about two hundred members of the regional AAWCC group, and Carolyn was to address all at the luncheon. Of course, her topic was leadership and spirituality. And seven times during the speech, she interrupted herself to ask aloud: "Are you listening, Mary Dee?" or "This part's for you, Mary Dee."

During that week, I learned that there's much more to being an effective leader than mastering a set of skills; rather, it's the total package that counts, a package that includes the leader's values and ethics being aligned with the goals of the college and its community. Needless to say, all articles in this chapter on inner leadership came from articles published in the newsletter after that life-changing week in March 1997.

Many people go through their entire lives without wondering about what's inside them, "who they be" at the core, ignoring all their fancy titles and job descriptions. Before going through the soul-searching demanded in the program, I had avoided asking myself the question, for two reasons: First, what if there wasn't anything deeper, "the lights were on but nobody was home?" Second, what if the inner driver wasn't someone who could stand the scrutiny of daylight?

The articles in this chapter would be found only in a book on leadership and women because they cannot be described as the linear, logical, empirical, computer-countable attributes that characterized a more traditional, hierarchical type of leadership commonly associated with male leaders. However, the last article is based on a presentation by Sandy Shugart, president of North Harris Community College; he explains why a college president adopts the servant-leader philosophy, as originated by Robert Greenleaf.

In other articles, you'll find the fuzzy, soft words that frequently are associated with women's leadership, words like *collaboration, caring, consensus, teams, fairness,* all of which are based on unmeasurable and nonlinear information such as intuition and gut feelings, ethics and legacy.

Living Your Life on Purpose

December 1997
Emily R. Ward
Doctoral student in higher education at Indiana University, Indiana
Your life is like a train racing at a hundred miles an hour. Although you'd like to make big changes, it's very difficult to slow down enough to make them.

Rather than trying to rebuild your whole life at a hundred miles an hour, consider small changes you can make right now. Start the process by striving to live on purpose. Although we tend to define our purpose in life as how we spend our time, which is usually our profession, it doesn't always indicate whether we're living on purpose. If we're honest, our lifestyle may actually follow the path of least resistance. Society nudges us along a predetermined track: go to school, enter the workforce, establish a home, then move toward exiting the workforce, all in sequence.

Conditioned to keep up an urgent pace that stresses performance and discourages reflection, we organize our daily lives with great precision, never asking whether our activities reinforce our values. We get so caught up with what we have to do, what others expect and need from us, that we don't make our own vision a priority. We've lost sense of what we want, at heart, to be about.

What's Your Personal Mission?

How can we reconnect to those values and reacquaint ourselves with what we want to be about? In this era of strategic planning and statements of vision, mission, and values, how many of us have made the leap to articulating our own personal mission statement? Personal strategic planning can help you discover who you want to be, what you stand for, where you want to go, and how to get there. Most important, it can help you make decisions, in essence reclaiming what you value.

It takes time—very private time—to talk with yourself about your purpose, your core reason for existing, who you want to be, and what you stand for. Although this introspection may produce a self-image different from the one you have now, you'll have created a goal: becoming who you want to be and seeing how close that is to who you are now. This is incredibly important! Every day we're required to make many decisions that tell others who we are and what we value. We're judged by our actions because that's all anyone outside our bodies and minds can interpret. How similar is the image you communicate to the person you want to be?

How to Stay on Track

As we try to survive, it's so easy to lose track of who we want to be. What megaforce sidetracks us from our purpose? Life. In *The Warrior Athlete,* Dan Millman offers four principles from nature to help us function with more purpose.

The principle of nonresistance. There are four ways to deal with the forces of life: surrender to them fatalistically; ignore them and in ignorance make mistakes; resist and create turmoil; or use the forces of life and blend with nature. A nonresister chooses the last one, seeing challenge and opposition as a teacher who reveals her weaknesses and helps her improve.

The principle of accommodation. You decide what you demand of your body, mind, and spirit. Your level of development is proportional to the demand. If your goal is to live reflecting what you value and who you want to be, you challenge yourself to reach outside your comfort zone. If the demand is too sudden, it won't happen. It must be a gradual but persistent effort. Unfortunately, most of us don't trust the law of accommodation. We're always wondering: Can I be any good at this? Will I accomplish my goals? Can I really be who I want to be? These questions weaken our motivation. We should trust the natural law like we trust our own mental noise.

The principle of balance. When we apply balance to how we live, we become immune to impatience and frustration. We recognize that for every up cycle there will be a down cycle. Some days we feel connected to our sense of purpose, and other days we don't. But as we accept and ride these cycles, they actually begin to balance themselves.

The principle of natural order. Ignoring the law of natural order, we're always in a hurry, setting arbitrary time goals we rush to meet. Although goals are important, rigid time goals are unrealistic because we can't foresee the future. We can set the direction of our progress but not the pace because many twists and changes can occur in life.

It's Your Choice

At the core of living on purpose is making the choice to take responsibility for yourself. In every situation, ask, "How did I create that for myself?" When you recognize that you create your own reality, you can start creating what you want, a very powerful realization! At the same time, you create your own value, enjoyment, and fulfillment. For example, you can read this and get no value at all from it, whereas another can gain incredible insights. Whatever is on the page is on the page. What you do with it is your choice! To paraphrase John Steinbeck in *East of Eden: choice* might be the most important word in the world. Choice says the way is open. If we choose to, we can also choose not to. Choice is what makes us great and gives us stature with the gods, for even in our weakness and our worst sin, we still have choice. Life is all about making choices. If we simply accept the responsibility and power of the gift of choice, we can alter our world. "It is not because things are difficult that we do not dare. It is because we do not dare that they are difficult."

Caring for the Soul

February 1999

Imagine an array of glass pebbles just larger than jelly beans. Some are bright, some dull, some smooth, some rough. One is aqua and translucent, another tannish gray and opaque. Take the ones that speak to you and use them to trace significant stepping-stones in your experience.

Not your typical conference workshop? "It's so wonderful to be able to use the S-word—soul or spirit—at an academic conference," Sally Z. Hare said about her preconference session at the Women in Higher Education conference in Charleston, South Carolina, in January. She's a professor of education and director of the Center for Education and Community at Coastal Carolina University, South Carolina.

More and more conferences include sessions on the inner self, spirituality, or similar topics. Some may dismiss it as a fad, but Hare prefers to see it as a "progressive evolution" that's finally gaining recognition. By *spirituality* she means connecting with one's inner wisdom or soul. In her workshop entitled "Care of Our Souls: Women in Leadership," she emphasized the connection between leadership and spirituality. She asked participants a series of trigger questions.

What Makes You Feel Most Alive? What Brings You Energy and Joy?

Here are some of the responses.

"I recall when I was young, everything was new and stress-free. I was free and loved. To reenter myself, I recall that age."

"It's my grandmother's property, on a beach. There's something calming, it's a private beach, separate from the chaos in my life. There's a safety factor there too."

"Having done something that's useful to someone else. Going to my home, it's a garden, a sanctuary."

"I get a rush from my work, my family, my journaling."

"I ride my motorcycle; I also go to my place on the river."

"For me the real rush is about learning. I connect it with my inner teaching."

Hare's workshop created a space to be in touch with those memories and

feelings, an inner journey to help participants remember. "It's not about denying the outer world but bringing the inner into it," she said. It's about healing
the separation between our inner and outer selves. Academic conferences often
heighten the separation by allowing only the outward self to appear, but women
leaders do their most valuable work when they bring their inner and outer selves
together.

What Aspect of the Soul Is Most Fully Housed in Your Work?

Participants mentioned being able to relate to their students and colleagues, working for a greater good, reflecting their value systems, and making a difference.
Hare said that national expert on teaching and learning Parker Palmer has a concept of teacher formation that applies to every form of leadership; we could speak
of leader formation, coach formation, or lawyer formation. "We have to lead by
who we are. Who I am is more important to what I'm teaching than the poem I'm
teaching that day. The more I know who I am, the better I can teach," she said.

What Parts of Your Work or Life Endanger Your Soul?

Hare asked participants to consider what's not working well for them, alerting
them to listen to each other without trying to fix things that are mentioned. We
start life with no separation between the inner and outer selves. Somehow by
our teens they come apart, Parker Palmer says. We grow self-conscious and start
to play to an audience, as though we're living our lives on stage. It can start as
young as age five or six, when a child may develop a phone voice and a camera
face. By the time we're young adults, we may concentrate so hard on the outward
self that our inner wisdom gets temporarily forgotten. We get caught up in the
press of day-to-day demands. When outer life takes over too completely, the soul
or inner wisdom gets wounded in the process. Healing begins when we name,
claim, and frame our lives in the light of our own truth.

Workshop participants took the stones from the center of the circle to reflect on their birthrights and tell about the people or moments or events or questions that shaped their lives. One identified most with a small, irregular brown
stone with rough spots, imperfect like herself. Another made a line of stones starting with several bright clear ones, then growing progressively darker and muddier.
The last one was slightly brighter: "I'm working on getting more light in my life."
Still another chose an opaque stone like "the real me that nobody sees," a shiny
metallic one that reflects back like her work as a writer, two joined together like
her relationship, and three bright clear ones like the bright clear parts of her life
that are going very well right now, representing family, friends, and work.

"I have come more and more to experience care of the soul as learning to live with paradox, to embrace paradox. It's not either-or," Hare said. We can't choose between living as individuals or in a community; we need the community to reflect about ourselves and solitude to reflect on our place in the community. It's not about being a teacher or a learner, an adult or a child, a body or a mind, matter or spirit. You can't have one without the other. Beyond the seeming contradictions lies a deeper unity. She quoted Oliver Wendell Holmes: "I wouldn't give a fig for the simplicity that lies this side of complexity, but for the simplicity that lies the other side of complexity I would give my life."

One of the paradoxes is that throwing ourselves in too deeply separates us from what we're doing. Thomas Merton said a pervasive form of modern violence is activism and overwork. "To allow oneself to be carried away by a multitude of conflicting concerns, to surrender to too many demands, to commit oneself to too many projects, to want to help everyone in everything is to succumb to violence," he wrote.

Women fall into this trap all the harder because we love to say yes. Women are always saying yes to one more thing. How do we encourage growth and not kill the root? "We need to get more skilled at emptying," Hare said. She has drawn a new paradigm from the women's movement. "In the old styles, it was about filling the spaces. Now I see it's about creating spaces."

Everything we need is there in abundance if we make the space to receive it, she said. We need to set the hustle and bustle aside and be present in the moment. Inner wisdom is a shy wild animal, invited by smells and sounds but easily scared away. "The soul is like a deer. I can't go and call it; I need to be as quiet as possible and just be. If I can wait long enough sitting at the base of a tree, I may or may not get a glimpse of it," she said. Waiting for the soul takes silence, reflection, and prayer.

What Would It Be Like to Be Divided No More?

The inner journey of later life is to get back in touch with the inner wisdom of childhood, bringing the ends of the circle together into one continuous whole like a Möbius strip. We begin to name and reclaim who we are, the shadow side as well as what's socially acceptable. Like May Sarton, now we become ourselves. "Believe that it's possible to emerge from this work with more energy, with more openness, with grace, with soft eyes," Hare told those in the workshop. The Balinese look at their children with soft eyes as though they're in love. We started life with birthright gifts; reconnecting with our childhoods helps us remember and reclaim them. Hare keeps a journal of the lives of kids she knows to give them when they're older.

She invited workshop participants to take any three containers of Play-Doh and model what their lives would look like if all the parts were congruent. "I'm an old early childhood teacher, and I believe people have lots of learning styles, so I like to use as many media as possible," she explained. Each new medium offers a new window to the soul. One woman braided three strands of different colors. Another made a ribbon; one showed three vessels carried on a river; and another shaped the figure of a goddess in three colors. The workshop set them off to a good start for inviting their inner wisdom to the rest of the conference.

Guidelines for Workshop Participation

Hare listed these workshop ground rules:

- Be 100 percent there.
- Presume welcome, and extend welcome.
- When it's hard, wonder and question; don't be too hard on yourself.
- Let the beauty we love be what we do.
- Believe you can emerge from this process with more energy and openness.
- Observe deep confidentiality, extending an invitation but never a demand.

Life Skills: A List for Survival in an Age of Information Overload

Hare subtitled the following list, "What I've Learned Upon Reaching Fifty":
- Breathe
- Learn to reframe (for example, see a weed as a wildflower that's growing in the wrong place).
- A thing not worth doing is not worth doing well.
- A thing worth doing is worth doing, even if you can't do it well.
- Laugh often.
- Eat chocolate.
- Be nice.
- Allow thirty extra minutes for *everything.*
- Love yourself.
- Love others, but you don't have to like them or feed them or return their phone calls or sleep with them.
- Breathe.

- Wear only comfortable shoes.
- Each day has twenty-four more hours in which you can try again.
- Nap.
- Eat a really good chocolate chip cookie for breakfast on occasion.
- Listen to a child.
- Listen to yourself.
- Be good to your body.
- Let the beauty you love be what you do. [—Rumi]
- Celebrate more.
- Breathe.
- Be mindful.
- Be gentle.
- Get more skilled at emptying.
- Don't lose heart.

Sarah Gibbard Cook

Let Intuition Guide Your Decision Making on Campus

October 1997
Carolyn S. Westerhof
Research professor, Department of Aging and Mental Health, University of South Florida
In the scramble of decision making, many of the unknown answers really are known. We can reach beyond everyday words and experiences to sense moods of people, assess other people's temperaments, know the outcomes of our actions as well as others', and enhance our own decision-making abilities to sense, feel, hear, taste, and see.

It's called our intuitive self, and training it can strengthen our healing and wellness, as well as creative and decision-making abilities. But reawakening our intuitive inner energies takes responsibility. We need to pay attention to the present moment in time and stop rehashing yesterdays and daydreaming about tomorrows. By staying in the present, we learn how to focus rather than mentally sabotage our thinking. As we become quiet, we start focusing in the present. Ask your questions; listen to your inner voice to get answers.

Before you go into a meeting, find a quiet place and ask yourself the questions you want answered: What is to take place? Who are your opponents? And who is on "your side of the table"? When you're in the meeting, difficulties won't surprise you, and you'll hold disappointments in check so you can concentrate on the positive aspects of the meeting. This will help you to move forward in what you seek to accomplish rather than be sidetracked by an irate question such as "Why?" or "How could they do this?" You'll already know! You'll also know if the solution you want will be achieved or if you're pushing your point of view to no avail.

Doing this will lessen your anxiety about what could have gone wrong, for nothing really goes wrong. It's all learning new lessons and how to handle new situations. This is learning how to build faith in your journey and to let go of expectations. When we seek out our intuition, we learn to recognize that the outcome is not in our hands. It is as it was meant to be, whether or not we like it. If we remember that the origin of our self is within us and we know that our inner and outer systems are woven together, we can open up to the recognition of our intuitive energies and trust and believe in ourselves.

Intuition is one of the best tools that administrators and educators can use. It gives you a true sense of where you are and an awareness of where those with whom you are working, negotiating, and communicating are coming from. Using your intuition reduces your surprises. It's yours, and you can trust it. Intuition is both irrational and nonlinear. It's like a muscle, bringing knowledge from within yourself. Information bubbles up from inside of you through images, words, symbols, feelings, emotions, physical sensations, like tingling in your fingers or arms. Your intuition can guide you to try something new and view your daily routines with new perspectives. It can even facilitate your relationships with others. There are three types of intuition: mental, which embraces visual and sensual; emotional, which is reflected in feeling; and kinesthetic, which expresses itself through physical reactions.

Meditation exercises can help you recognize and welcome your intuitive energies. All you need is a few minutes each day to go into a meditative state. Meditation is based on slow breathing techniques. First, find a quiet place. It doesn't have to be a ritual place but can be in your office, even in your car if you're not driving. Let the only thoughts be the movement of your mind and the concentration on your breathing. If you find your mind wandering, try concentrating on a single word in any language—om, peace, shalom.

Try to hold your concentration for fifteen to twenty minutes. In the beginning or when you feel pushed, it's okay to hold it for only five minutes. There are no hard and fast rules; do whatever works for you. Keep bringing that one word into your mind to hold your focus. When you're ready, slowly open your eyes, and begin to feel new, clear energy. Write down your thoughts: the time of day, your feelings, the scenes you see, the people who walked through your life. The writing is important, for it's part of focusing your mind, so keep a notebook at your fingertips. Let the answers flow from within you. Your ability to concentrate will improve; your mind chatter will be turned off. You'll accomplish much more during the day, for your intuition will have guided you toward a state of calmness and reduced negative energy pressures.

No one's life is in a perpetual state of peace and harmony, but developing and using meditation skills will allow you to stay centered longer and to rise above another person's aura. There is no "if only" when one recognizes the present as a learning lesson and responds to the experiences generated by the new lessons. Your own intuitive energies are your best guide.

We must rediscover and respect the connection linking our inner selves to our wider world. Using your intuition for both your personal and professional selves takes commitment. Know that wherever you go, your intuition is there to guide you, as your very best friend. Einstein, Plato, and Jung spoke of intuition as the most important part of an individual's thinking. Set your sights, follow your vision, but know that the final destiny is not in your control. This path is not without risks. We know that our actions and thoughts have consequences, particularly as we serve, work, teach, and share with others; there are no isolated acts or coincidences. In the process of reaching out professionally or privately, our search begins and ends within ourselves. And that's our gift, as we go forward to make a difference for ourselves and for others through our chosen destinies as educators and servants of the public.

Ethical Decisions Can Prevent Legal Problems on Campus

September 1996

If you're wondering whether to set policies and procedures to meet current legal requirements, or whether to do what you know is right and ethical and fair, it's better to let your values be the judge. "If you are simply in compliance with the law, you're courting disaster," says Marianne M. Jennings, professor of legal and ethical studies and director of the Center for Applied Ethics in the College of Business at Arizona State University (ASU).

Speaking at a conference named "Righting the Standard" in Phoenix in June, Jennings points out that ethics and legal issues are intertwined. "You can't possibly know all the laws," she says. "But you won't make legally incorrect choices if you make ethically correct ones." Using the illustration of a pilot who habitually skims the treetops, she predicts that, eventually, cutting it too close will lead to a crash and burn. "It's safer to operate up here," she demonstrates with a hand held a level higher.

Legal Issues Explode

Observing that education recently has become a "litigation hotbed," Jennings notes that when she began at ASU nineteen years ago, its general counsel worked alone. Now the general counsel has six assistants. A 1995 educator's legal liability survey by Watson Wyatt Worldwide says lawsuits claiming job bias, wrongful termination, and other job issues in higher education more than doubled between 1992 and 1995. Many recent legal issues in education have gone all the way to the U.S. Supreme Court.

Do the Right Thing

Preventing today's ethical dilemmas from becoming legal issues is a key to success. "Those that have the most lawsuits against them are the ones emphasizing just compliance," she notes. Without having the big picture of management and ethics being intertwined, they are just grazing the treetops. Reputation, good or bad, lasts a long time, she said, noting that the University of Michigan's history department was ranked first in the country, even six years after the program ended!

Stanford University's dispute over the use of grant funds for yachts and cedarlined closets resulted in no U.S. government action against the school but caused the public to distrust Stanford. A Stanford spokesperson admitted, "I have come to recognize what we did was legal, but it was not right." Five years later, donations to Stanford are still lagging, as alumni wonder, "If they're doing that with *federal* money, what are they doing with *my* money?"

Emphasizing that those who graze the treetops may look good in "Kodak moments" now, Jennings cautions against taking temporary shortcuts. "You're a marathoner, in for the long run, not a sprinter. When you make a choice that is ethically questionable, the laws of probability do not apply."

Leaders See Around Corners

Predicting future legal issues in higher education is based on "an ability to see around the corners," she says. Take any issue that is now a problem on your campus, and fix it now, before it becomes a legal issue. Otherwise, what is not fixed voluntarily becomes mandatory, and the price is likely to be much higher. For example, ignoring abuses of copyright laws and ethical responsibilities to serve people with disabilities recently resulted in what many consider to be heavy-handed government intervention: the Kinko's case limiting legal copying, and the Americans with Disabilities Act requiring access by disabled folks if there is major remodeling on campuses. Upcoming issues she predicts will result in major legal actions affecting campuses include freedom of speech codes, due process in tenure reviews and student grade appeals, and unionization.

How to Recognize Ethical Dilemmas

Tip-offs to sliding down the slippery slope are:

"Everybody does it" or *"They do it this way at Stanford"* is just a cop-out for refusing to really examine the issue.

"If we don't do it, somebody else will." If there is competition for a project and you're asked to do it without the staff or facilities you know you'll need, take the high road and pass on it. You'll avoid the inevitable hassle down the road.

"That's the way it has always been done." The internal auditor should question who is being protected by this response.

"We'll wait until the lawyers tell us it's wrong." As a lawyer, Jennings says, "It's way too late then. Lawyers operate based on codified law, but they don't put value judgments on it." Citing research that shows pregnant women face risk of fetal harm by spending too much time at computer terminals, she suggests that managers take some precautions now, by limiting time at terminals and giving more breaks. "Even if the research is wrong, what does it cost us, compared to the greater costs in the long run?"

"It really doesn't hurt anyone." When spending someone else's money, the temptation is to let it ride, she says, without examining the larger issues. Ask yourself whether what you're doing is harming someone, even someone who is unlikely to complain or is powerless to respond.

"The system is unfair." If you think that you can fix an unfair system by dishonesty, you're wrong, she says. Better to work to change the system, she suggests.

"I was just following orders." The Oliver North defense has proved not to be legally defensible in court, she says, noting that "Sometimes it is morally wrong to follow orders."

Categories of Ethical Dilemmas

Jennings listed twelve types of transgressions.

1. Taking things that don't belong to you. Most embezzlement starts with a pattern of petty larceny including personal copying, postage, and office supplies. Even the perception that you're stealing is damaging. "When you're in the fishbowl of education, people watch us closely," she reminds, noting that people rationalize their actions, like faculty taking departmental laptops with them to Europe.

2. Saying things that are not true, which she calls "a lovely way of saying *lying.*"

A study of administrators who had survived downsizing—interviews with their bosses and staffs, as well as those who did not survive and their former bosses and staffs—revealed that honesty was the key ingredient. By building trust and credibility, even through brutal honesty, they were able to survive.

3. Giving false impressions. "Honesty and absolute disclosure" are the best solutions, she says. Misrepresentations include classes not being offered every semester, schedules not followed, faculty not teaching classes as listed, average time to get a degree being misrepresented. Terminating an existing program makes schools liable for satisfying students in the program, she reminds us.

4. Engaging in conflicts of interest. Obvious cases of influence peddling may be rare, but even the impression of guilt is equally important, as the public always assumes there's a hidden quid pro quo.

5. Hiding or divulging information. Most people on campus are unaware that every e-mail document ever sent is available on the school's computer backup system. "People put things on e-mail that they would never say face-to-face or put in a memo," she explains, and there is no right of privacy in e-mail. Although retrieved e-mail evidence has been very damaging to administrators in two recent $500,000 cases, most faculty and students don't realize their e-mail is easily available.

6. Taking unfair advantage. When you know the rules and others don't, there is an opportunity to be unethical. For example, cheating policies should be consistent and consistently enforced. One way is by putting the policy in each class syllabus.

7. Committing personal decadence. In the campus workplace, people often have the need and opportunity to do bad things. Sometimes they do.

8. Perpetuating interpersonal abuse. There is a very fine line between sexual harassment and consensual sex, which can be crossed very quickly when a faculty member dates a student. Although it may not be illegal, there's always the question of impropriety. She cites a faculty member who married his grad student, resulting in a tarnished reputation for both even many years later.

9. Permitting organizational abuse. Regular evaluations can help employees improve their performance. But numerical ranking can be devastating, as she notes in an example in which a faculty member committed suicide in his office, leaving on his desk a ranking in which he was dead last.

10. Violating the rules. It's tempting to bend the internal rules to get power, but following your own rules lets you sleep at night.

11. Condoning unethical actions. When a whistle-blower finally gets attention, others will have known of the infraction but remained silent. "If you don't allow people to come forth, you're inviting a culture that allows unethical behavior," she notes.

12. Creating unethical dilemmas. She cites campus women's frequent problems in balancing family and work as an example of an unethical dilemma that an unhealthy climate on campus encourages with too-heavy demands on faculty.

How to Resolve Ethical Dilemmas

Jennings cites research showing far more misconduct in firms that did not have a code of ethics or did not train people in how to apply the code, including examples. Using a school car to make a drive-through bank deposit seems minor, but it's a public, visible example of a transgression.

Once identified, ethical dilemmas can be resolved by answering these questions: How would *you* want to be treated (or how do you think *others* would want to be treated)? Is it legal? Is it balanced (would the other side be OK with it)? How does it make you feel? How would you explain the situation to family, friends, or even to your mother? How would a typical *National Enquirer* sensational headline describe it in the worst light?

Atmosphere of Ethics

To assure an ethical environment, leaders need to communicate clearly and effectively, especially with faculty members who read and hear what they want to. Giving notice in a timely and consistent manner is important, as is being kind and gracious. In addition, it's important to admit and correct mistakes, instead of stonewalling or blaming others.

Lawsuits are less likely to happen when administrators are nice to people, Jennings says. For example, because ASU administrators went out of their way to accommodate her needs to teach nights early in her career and days when she had young children home from school, "There's no way I would bring a legal suit," she says.

Mary Dee Wenniger

Are Women More Ethical? It Depends

July–August 1995

Theorists seeking to empower women by emphasizing distinctively female ways of thinking and calling them female ethics may be creating more problems than they solve. Daryl Koehn, assistant professor of philosophy at DePaul University, Illinois, spoke at the National Conference on Ethics in America at the

University of California–Long Beach in February. She also wondered whether women's distinct way of thinking constitutes an ethic or a code of conduct.

Women Versus Men on Ethics

Theorists point to some distinct differences in how women and men decide on ethical conduct, she said. They say that men rely on a rules-based approach to problem solving, in which they establish rules and rank them hierarchically, deciding which rule "trumps" in order to arrive at an ethical conclusion. Women, on the other hand, are "antirules-" based. They "emphasize a listening approach, in which the standards to be applied evolve through a conversation with the affected parties."

As an example, Koehn refers to a classic Carol Gilligan exercise in which girls and boys are asked what they would do in this scenario: a man whose wife is dying knows the local druggist has the drug needed to save her life. He doesn't have the money to buy the drug. Should he steal it? Gilligan found that boys invariably ask, "What are the rules involved?" and decide which rule trumps. The boys decide that it was unjust to break in and steal another's property, thus allowing the property rule to trump the rule that life is precious. Girls, on the other hand, ask, "What are the options available to the man?" and want to get the parties to talk about them. In this way, "the dialogue reveals the standard by which to act," Koehn asserts.

She says Gilligan also uses this as an example of men's "closed" reasoning process involving a set of established rules, whereas women's "open" process seeks to learn what a dialogue will reveal. Attempting to resort to rules, argues Gilligan, distorts the situation by imposing standards.

The Risk Factor

Another major difference is women's acceptance of the inevitability of risk in any situation and therefore the need for trust, Koehn says. Philosopher Annette Baier says that men believe that risk can be controlled by putting all possibilities into rules and establishing written contracts, so there is no need for trust in the other. In contrast, women believe that an element of trust in the other is always needed, because "you can't control all factors in a situation."

Interpersonal Versus Structure

Koehn says the last major distinction the theorists make is the difference between women and men in reasoning processes: women focus on the interpersonal, whereas men focus on a structure. Women trust the person, not the structure.

But Is It an Ethic?

Koehn presented two scenarios in which participants were asked whether the so-called female ethic helped them come to an ethical solution to a problem. In one, a bank employee is working late with a male coworker, whom she has known for many years. He makes a sexually suggestive comment to her. What should her response be? The theorists would have you "reach out for the other, allowing the other to fill your firmament." Participants said that could put her at risk of assault.

In the second scenario, a salesperson goes to Japan. The Japanese customers know that the salesperson has three days to close a deal. On the last day, they invite the salesperson out for yet another dinner. Should the salesperson feel put out? The female ethics of trust and caring would say no, one should "listen to the other" and "value the relationship." But the ethic of doing whatever it takes to close the deal leads to the same action. In both cases, participants believed the female ethic's focus on trust and caring was insufficient.

Stereotypes Reinforced

In addition to Koehn's concern with whether these distinct ways of thinking constitute an ethic, she points out that they stereotype women and focus on interpersonal relationships, or caring, as an end in itself. The stereotyping is illustrated in the choice of examples used to show how women make decisions. Gilligan uses the issue of abortion: how women decide whether or not to have an abortion, given that they're in a stable, caring relationship.

"Why," asks Koehn, "if you're trying to get at decisions about self and identity issues, is there this focus on mothering issues? Why not look at how women decide on a profession?" Using a model of caring that is focused on the mother and child, she claims, excludes definitions of caring beyond nurturing.

What's the Goal?

She argues that for interpersonal caring to be ethical, it must be "sifted through the lens" of a more concrete goal. For example, the goal of a doctor is not to be nice, warm, and friendly with all of her patients; it's to make them healthy. In business, the idea that a corporation's goal is to "maintain relationships," an argument presented by stakeholder theorists, would sit well with the female ethic of caring. But Koehn argues, isn't there more to a corporation's goal, such as making a good product and a profit?

"What are you caring for?" is the question that must be asked, for context is important. What of the woman who is in a destructive relationship? Female ethics of trust and care would have her stay in the relationship because relationships are highly valued. Rather than get mired in the idea of care for a person, Koehn suggests that one should trust and care "for the argument" or case being presented, as opposed to the structure or the person, and reach for principles while enlisting the cooperation of others.

Dianne Jenkins

Applying Ethics to Everyday Decision Making

April 1995

An ethical decision is one whose consequences do not cause unjust harm and that respect the rights and dignity of all individuals, groups, and other entities. Ethical decision making is a system of making better decisions that universalizes ethics and makes them accessible across the disciplines.

Although each of us has her own built-in values, it takes practice to incorporate them into both professional and personal everyday decisions, according to Veronica Alexander, who presented at the National Conference on Ethics in America at California State University-Long Beach in February. "Instead of constructing elaborate systems for ethical conduct, like a code of ethics or a detailed policy on harassment," it's better to teach a method of decision making that automatically results in socially responsible choices, no matter what the context, she suggests, like the Ten Commandments.

Benefits of ethical decisions she lists are being able to look yourself in the mirror, contributing to making the world a better place, and causing fewer negative reactions from those who are angry at, bitter about, or resentful of what they consider unfair decisions. Here are some methods she suggests "to make the world a better place:"

- "Ethical decisions must include *all* decisions, even those ordinary, everyday ones, instead of thinking of ethics as a separate category."
- "If we use ethical decision making and have it widely available, we can trust others to do so too, resulting in a healthier environment."
- "Responsible people must speak up. We do so much damage because we don't want to step on other people's values. We pussyfoot all the time about things we know are clearly wrong." She cited an experiment in which subjects heard calls of distress. When a "plant" in the audience said, "It's none of our business," others ignored the calls for help, but when the plant suggested helping, everyone stood up to help.
- People must learn a simple method of applying ethics to decision making,

she says, or it will be ignored. It must be easy to learn, too, so that once people know how to use it for big decisions, they can automatically apply it for snap decisions.

Alexander's Steps for Ethical Decision Making

1. Identify the problem clearly, and state the goal. Often you can solve the problem right there, she advises. If the problem is that you hate your job, you need to identify why you do (colleagues, pay, climate, nature of it) and where you want to be.

2. Research the facts. Using information from books and people, get a handle on the situation. Because higher education is a hierarchy that discourages the employee from going over the supervisor's head, even if the supervisor has no information on the issue, this part can be touchy.

3. Identify all those who will be affected by the decision. Asking someone for their advice "doesn't automatically mean putting someone else's opinion over yours," she cautions. Discuss the situation instead of ignoring it; you may even find ways to make it work for both of you.

4. List all alternative solutions. Be creative.

5. Evaluate each alternative. Here's where ethics comes in, considering each of these factors:

- *Practicality.* Is it possible to do it, being flexible, imaginative, and creative?
- *Harm.* To prevent mental or physical damage or injury is the most important aspect, she says. "To protect ourselves from guilt, most people refuse to acknowledge that our actions can cause harm, although most harm others out of fear, ignorance, oversight, or carelessness, or being blinded by the good possibilities of a different alternative. Finding benefits is easier than finding harms," she notes.
- *Emotional factors.* Fear of failure or fear of the unknown can inhibit decision making.
- *Short-term versus long-term effects.* "While it's important not to let immediate gratification blind you to long-term consequences, it's equally important not to put off all the pleasure for a long-term goal that may never be realized," she notes.
- *Objectivity.* Detaching yourself from the problem enables you to see it more objectively. What if a stranger came to you for advice on the problem? Or if the problem belongs to someone on a campus very much like yours, but different?
- *Permanence.* "If you can change your mind, the decision is a whole lot easier," Alexander notes. She recalls being paralyzed by fear over whether

to do research in the Amazon, until someone said, "If you don't like it, you can always come home."

- *Is it fair?* To test fairness in a decision or policy, she suggests considering "the original position," in which you don't know which side you'd be on. For example, in deciding whether to have slavery, you don't know whether you'd be the master or the slave.
- *What if the situation were reversed?* Applying the Golden Rule can clarify issues.
- *What if everybody did it?* For example, what if the National Rifle Association got its way, and all kids, librarians, and postal workers would be armed?
- *What are your responsibilities?* A more dynamic, active view individualizes the problem, asking, "What would you have to do?"
- *Can you live with the decision?* Given your character and values, is your decision morally permissible or impermissible?

6. Set a deadline. Eventually, you have to decide because not to decide is to decide. She notes the important distinction between letting things happen, and taking control of your own life by making things happen. "Every single thing is different," she warns. "People come to me and demand policies and actions," and each case is different. Rather, she teaches them to make quick decisions by asking, "Where's the harm? And why?"

Mary Dee Wenniger

Carolyn Desjardins' Spirit Lives On

August 1997

I expected this to be the final Last Laugh column my soul sister Carolyn Desjardins would read. Told that her cancer would win within several weeks, she welcomed us to her home before the Righting the Standard conference in June. On Tuesday, I started writing this column but gave up after four lines. It just wouldn't come. On Thursday, I worked on the leadership competencies article, trying to reach the National Institute for Leadership Development (NILD) about fifteen times to check a few facts. Their lines were busy all day long.

On Friday, I finally reached the NILD, learning that Carolyn had taken a turn for the worse on Monday, slipped in and out of a coma on Tuesday, and passed away early Thursday morning, July 17. The entire phone grid for Phoenix College was out on Thursday, which an NILD staff member called "an interesting gift."

Having just finished making plans to be cremated and buried in Idaho along-side a daughter who died in childhood, Carolyn finally managed to beat a dead-line: the one her doctor set. I don't imagine being either her surviving daughter Sandy or an NILD staff member was an easy role; those closely associated with special people must bear their foibles as well as enjoy their goddesslike qualities.

Who Was This Special Woman?

Besides sharing the same birthday as me, June 6, Carolyn was an incredible con-nector linking women and leadership on a spiritual rather than skill-driven level. With a counseling background, she could read a person better than a résumé. Her spirit will continue to reside in the more than three thousand Leader Sisters who learned from her at the NILD one-week Leaders' Institutes.

She Came a "Fur Piece"

Raised in the mountains of Idaho, she liked to say she'd come a "fur piece" in her life's journey. An early recollection is her family being too poor to attend church regularly in town. As a special treat one Sunday, the family made the trip. Having found her own brand of spirituality in the Idaho mountains, Carolyn was less than impressed with the church's formal religion, a reaction she expressed to her mother. "See, I told you what living in the mountains without going to a real church would do to her," her mother exclaimed. "Now she thinks she knows more than the church!"

She told of attending Harvard University in the 1980s, where she worked with Carol Gilligan. As she walked across the stage at graduation when she received a Ph.D., she was stopped short by a voice inside her saying, "You just had to do it, didn't you?" The voice implied that she'd learned more in the mountains of Idaho than by earning a Ph.D.

She Made a Special Place for Me

Contemplating starting *Women in Higher Education* in 1991, I contacted several prominent women leaders. Marian Swoboda, then assistant vice president for equal opportunities at the University of Wisconsin, advised me to "Go for it." The former head of an association of women in education said, "I wish you wouldn't" and hung up on me.

Carolyn was friendly, informative, and warm in welcoming me to the cadre of women trying to change the nature of higher education. She told me what to read and whom to contact, and became one of the half-dozen members of the very informal advisory committee that I speak with frequently. Even when I misspelled her name in a very early issue, she laughed it off, more concerned with my personal development than with her own publicity.

She Believed in the Spiritual Side of Leadership

In later years, Carolyn became more involved in the spiritual aspects of leadership. She all but dragged me by the ear to attend a Leader's Institute, which I finally did this March. A practical person, I'd considered anything outside the logical, fact-dominated milieu to be little better than voodoo. Thanks to her, I'm actively opening myself to alternative ways of thinking and making decisions. Perhaps you've noticed a new editorial mix. If she has similarly impacted the lives of the three thousand other Leader Sisters through her program, not to mention dozens of women and men presidents who consider her a goddess, a powerful force now has been unleashed elsewhere in the universe. After all, a power that prevented me from writing this column and shut off the phones at her college on the day she died is nothing to mess with.

Mary Dee Wenniger

Women and Legacy

October 1997
Sarah Gibbard Cook
Independent historian and writer
Most of the time, it's all I can do to plan the week, but occasionally a friend's death, a key birthday, or a brush with serious illness brings the uninvited question of legacy. It came up recently when I was driving to a memorial service for a musician friend dead at fifty-one. People sing her songs who never heard of her. Will anything I do make any difference in the long run?

Ideally, we're well established in our careers by the time reminders of mortality start to nudge. The reality is that midlife often finds women anything but established. Some took time out to raise families and returned to professional life fifteen years older than their male counterparts. Many celebrate fortieth or fiftieth birthdays without tenure. As nontenure-track positions increase in fields where women predominate, some hop between visiting appointments, whereas others stay at schools that offer them little recognition or reward.

Flashes of "I'm getting older and time is running out" can come unbidden. We know Georgia O'Keeffe painted into her nineties, but our larger culture offers few positive images of older women. Those I see on television are usually taking Advil or choosing an investment firm. This doesn't stop at the gates of the university. Those of us who got our graduate degrees long ago too often bog down in institutional service, like the biblical Martha or the organizational wife.

Patterns of Legacy

The content of a legacy is always individual, but the forms fall into patterns.

Legacy of nurture. Parents raise children who grow up to raise their own. Teachers teach students, some of whom become teachers. Administrators and senior faculty mentor younger colleagues who someday mentor others. Personal influence flows down through generations. It requires direct contact with people younger or more junior than oneself. In a legacy of nurture, we pass along a way of being in the world or our profession, more than any specific idea or skill. Our grandchildren may inherit our sense of duty or fun or openness to people who are different from ourselves. Our students may pass on our enthusiasm for scholarship or our habit of questioning assumptions.

Tangible legacy. Write a book or paint a picture, and it carries your message across time and space. Emily Dickinson avoided personal contact, but more than one hundred years after her death a newspaper reported the birds-from-dinosaurs controversy with her line, "'Hope' is the thing with feathers." Publications are the main way that academics convey original scholarship or the synthesis of a lifetime of research.

Institutional legacy. Margaret Hennig and Anne Jardim bolted from Harvard to establish the Simmons College Graduate School of Management in 1974, with curriculum and timetable geared to women's needs. They retired this year after making sure the school was equipped to carry on their mission without them. Whether you start a new institution or change the structure of an existing one (for example, to make the curriculum more responsive to women), institutional legacy requires letting go. Structures must become independent of personalities in order to last.

Legacy of modeling. After First Lady Betty Ford went public with her 1974 mastectomy, breast cancer became for the first time something that Americans could mention without whispering. After Princess Diana removed her gloves to shake hands with AIDS patients, the stigma surrounding AIDS in Britain subsided a notch. Whereas nurture carries diffuse content down through generations, modeling spreads specific behaviors outward like ripples in a pond. Whereas nurture helps the younger or less experienced learn the accepted norms, modeling changes the norms. It violates tradition or goes public with things previously kept under wraps. The legacy of modeling is inherently subversive.

Persistent Subversives

So you're not quite ready to produce your magnum opus? Has the legacy question started to come up for you anyway? Consider generating small legacies as a perpetual subversive. Even if you're insecure in your job, you can still be a gentle thorn in the institution's side. The more hostile your environment, the more your modeling may encourage other women. Never underestimate the significance of helping to build a critical mass.

It can be very empowering to act selectively as if the world were the way you'd like it instead of the way it is.

Some Suggestions

Speak the taboos. Breast cancer has emerged from whispers into ordinary conversation. I've made a point of mentioning menopause to my son and daughter-in-law as well as friends. Silence about our bodies does a disservice to women. Academic culture would have us deny body, spirit, emotion, and any music except classical. To be really subversive, try playing country and western. Each time you break a taboo, you make it a little safer for the next person.

Partner across generations. When older and younger women avoid one another, they both get hurt. Partnerships allow for mentoring. The benefits flow both directions. Younger women can help subvert the devaluing of older women in our culture and on our campuses.

Go public with your personal life. Admitting to a personal life is risky when traditionalists suspect women with outside commitments of being half-hearted or unreliable professionals. On the other hand, it's hard for younger women to plan their lives unless we break the silence about how we juggle the pieces. Once long ago when I was teaching in a very traditional history department, my five-year-old got sick and my backup care systems fell through. I brought the child to my office and rearranged class locations to keep him within earshot. A woman history major thanked me after class. "I've been wondering whether I can go to graduate school and teach college and still have a family. I wouldn't dare raise the question with my other professors," she said.

"Subvert the dominant paradigm" says a favorite bumper sticker. Our subversive examples can multiply until they change the culture. If you think little things don't make a legacy, picture the oldest building on campus, with the donor's name in stone over the door. Now picture the marble stairs worn by thousands of students' feet, as deeply engraved as the stone with the donor's name. If the time isn't ripe for you to write your name over the door, you can still help wear down the stairs.

Why a President Adopts the Servant Leadership Philosophy

August 1997

Most administrators have heard the term *servant leadership* and have a rough idea of what it means. But the concept is deceptive in its simplicity. Really internalizing and applying its truths to colleges and universities can be a challenge for many years. Sanford C. (Sandy) Shugart, president of North Harris College, Texas, shared his experiences in learning to understand and apply the concept at the Righting the Standard conference, held in Phoenix in June.

Servant leadership, a principle popularized by author Robert K. Greenleaf, represents a fundamental reorientation to core values for both leaders and schools, putting people and ethical considerations ahead of short-term gains and personal self-interest. Shugart explained how the servant leader approach can address ingrained institutional problems, and he recalled three epiphanies over his last thirteen years in higher education that pushed him toward it.

His first epiphany occurred at age twenty-six, not long after Shugart was first hired as president of another college, with much of his career journey still ahead of him. A colleague came to his office, explained how Shugart had inadvertently hurt her, and shared her anger with him. "I wasn't being who I am at work," he realized. "Work was changing me. If I didn't shape up pretty soon, it would be too late."

Shugart realized our work has a lot more influence on us than we have on it, and the traditional organizational life is often out of sync with our real personhood. At home, there is acceptance, support, and love, but people don't typically find these qualities at work. "When you leave the house, you leave creativity, risk taking, love, compassion, and wonder at home. You take techniques, rules, and fear to work," he observed. "When you get up to go to work, you leave 20 percent of yourself in bed. You leave another 20 percent at the door. You leave another 20 percent in the car. And you leave another 20 percent at the door of the workplace. When you finally arrive in the office, you function as only 20 percent of your true self."

The second epiphany occurred when Shugart attended a conference cocktail reception with a lot of top male leaders in higher education. Conversing belly-button-to-belly-button, he heard these men bemoan their "poor us" status, damning their faculty and boards for not appreciating the good they do. Listening to their complaints, Shugart realized, "These people once had been bright, creative, and gifted leaders. This is what I'll become unless I make a concerted decision not to become like them."

The third epiphany came a few years later, after he'd accepted the presidency at North Harris and had been working to become a servant leader for about a year. When Shugart arrived on campus, the college operated as a classic authoritarian, controlled patriarchy. "Incompetence was supported over those who challenged the status quo," he noted. The philosophy was one of self-service, and the outgoing president had made out class schedules for the faculty's convenience. There was no public transportation to the college, and the suburban campus attracted almost exclusively suburban students.

A student came to Shugart's office in tears. She had requested but been denied a tuition refund because of a personal tragedy: her fiancé had died five weeks into the semester. Shugart immediately granted the refund but wondered: "Why didn't the first person she asked grant the refund? Why did she have to go to the president?" He realized the answer had to do with "how we structure the institution."

How Servant Leadership Can Help

Shugart thinks the concept of servant leadership can help both the problems that administrators face and the administrators themselves, as they define their own individual leadership roles. Robert K. Greenleaf developed his ideas on servant leadership while at AT&T; although he died in 1990, his ideas are still being published (*On Becoming a Servant Leader,* 1996).

According to Greenleaf: "A new moral principle is emerging which holds that the only authority deserving one's allegiance is that which is freely and knowingly granted by the led to the leader in response to, and in proportion to, the clearly evident servant stature of the leader." Shugart translated: "You may be under the authority of somebody, but you will give allegiance only to those you trust."

Greenleaf said a servant leader exhibits these behaviors: persuasion over coercion, *entheos* or sustaining spirit over ego, foresight over control, listening over directing, acceptance and healing over judgment, and the art of "systematic neglect" over perfectionism.

Shugart called listening over directing the most difficult behavior for him to adopt. "The servant leader asks intelligent, probing questions. In the best meetings, the decision then just happens," he said. Sometimes you can't even tell who made the decision. To determine whether a decision supports servant leadership, Greenleaf suggested asking these questions: "Do those served grow as persons? Do they, while being served, become healthier, wiser, freer, more autonomous, more likely themselves to become servants? What is the effect on the least privileged in society: Will they benefit, or at least not be further deprived?"

The Tricky Part: The Institution as Servant

Although it's possible for many administrators to begin to understand how servant leadership can benefit everyone in the organization—including themselves—the real challenge lies in transforming the organization itself so that it too works as a servant. Many organizations work first to establish and maintain themselves. For example, consider how the IRS and many hospital emergency rooms actually work: filling out their forms often takes precedence over service.

Greenleaf says that what's needed are "regenerative trustees" and that problems occur when the top leaders have "an inadequate concept of trust" and fail "to accept a more demanding role." They need to pick up and use the two-sided coin of trust and responsibility, knowing that increased trust brings an obligation for added liability and personal involvement. Servant institutions modify the hierarchy into teams based on the principle of "first among equals." Shugart gave the example of a group of department chairpersons who wanted him not to replace a retiring dean. Instead, the chairs worked out how to make budget decisions themselves and became generally more assertive and willing to take risks.

Schools operating as servant leaders honor questions and criticisms, and acknowledge and attend to the corrupting influence of power. Shugart suggested the way to do this is to make everything public. "There are no little secrets, so you can be up front about everything," he said. In addition, servant institutions hire by character and not technique, and build trust by performance, rejecting both blind trust and trust based solely on charisma. Shugart pointed out, "Walt Disney created ideas, not George Patton."

One of a president's challenges is balancing the stability of good administration with the creativity of leadership. Shugart said, "I have not been comfortable creating chaos. Our administration is more like air traffic control: we don't control anyone but monitor where they are." A success he noted: "People are creating their own work projects and have a sense of where they fit" within the mission of the organization. And their projects support the organizational mission of servant leadership.

Doris Green

CHAPTER EIGHT

ARE WE THERE YET?

This question comes from a voice from the backseat, yanking us back to the reality that no, of course we aren't there yet. But we're driving down the road, scanning the environment and making progress. Eventually, we'll reach a critical mass and change the value system of higher education, as has already happened on some campuses, especially at community colleges. Sometimes we get so caught up in the ride that it's tough to keep our destination in sight, and they keep changing the road signs on us. As women have found, sometimes the process can consume us and even make the eventual product irrelevant, which is the fate we hope will come to the *Women in Higher Education* newsletter.

Our chance is now, when vast new challenges threaten to shut down higher education as we know it. Consider the challenges resulting from changes in technology, distance learning, partnering with business, student demographics, and globalization. Change is on our side, as desperate leaders are seeing the wisdom of outsiders previously marginalized like women, who just may have the answers, because it's obvious that the current methods are just not working.

Just as the voice from the backseat yanks us back to reality by asking, "Are we there yet?" or "When are we gonna be there?" our inner voices beg for some sort of validation that we are, in fact, on the right road and about to arrive at our destination. And we also want to believe in the tooth fairy and finding our soul mate.

Obviously, we still have a ways to go. If there were true gender equity on campus, both this book and the newsletter *Women in Higher Education* would be superfluous. But there are signs, serious ideas for strategies and tactics that show significant progress toward gender equity on campus. Resistance and advancement go hand in hand.

With committed leaders like those whose words appear on these pages and passionate followers who will respond to the call to action, there's no doubt women on campus will get the last laugh. The future of our children's children's children and the world depend on it.

To Transform a Campus, Bring in Woman Leaders

April 1996

Remember transactional leaders? Their carrot-and-stick management approach means issuing rewards and sometimes punishment to subordinates in exchange for compliance with set norms, policies, and procedures. But that approach can't solve today's problems, says Jacquelyn M. Belcher, president of DeKalb College, Georgia. Belcher was a keynote speaker at a conference sponsored by the National Community College Chair Academy in Phoenix this February.

Currently, difficult issues facing higher education "demand creative, transformational leadership and the development of innovative strategies to meet the challenges created by a changing society," she said. Women seem more ready to learn the skills than do their male colleagues. "Speaking generally, women have had to keep more balls in the air and have learned to deal with many issues at one time," Belcher told *Women in Higher Education* later in an interview. "Complexity is not a barrier to women."

Women have other transferable skills, she explained. "Women have always been expected to mediate and create a sense of community and of family." Some stereotypical women's abilities, like intuition and empathy, which were once "used to look at women askance" are now seen as positive behaviors for this type of leader.

"Transformational leadership feels right to women," Belcher said, because "it's not asking anything that they haven't been doing." These leaders, she said, are "social architects" who must develop a new vision and a set of blueprints for moving the institution toward that vision. They're not building a new structure but rather renovating and rehabilitating an existing organization. Much of it occurs through networks: technical, political, and cultural alliances on campus.

Let Go of the Past

But in order to rebuild, some old networks, structures, and processes must be destroyed. Belcher acknowledged that "the word *destroy* may not feel good to women."

She calls this "a letting go of the past and looking toward the vision for the future, and asking what steps we must take to get there. It's not asking people to forget or condemn the past."

Belcher, who came from Minneapolis Community College last May, established the Agenda for the New Millennium as DeKalb's vision statement. She believes it's easier for an outsider to be a transformational leader because an insider might be blind to existing networks or unaware of their effects on the institution. "You must be conscious that you must reweave the networks," she said.

Coordinate Networks to Manage Transition

A transformational leader, according to Belcher, often works simultaneously with the three types of networks. A speech, for instance, might contain technical, political, and cultural messages. Once a transformational leader has a clear sense of mission and general direction, she can support all the networks through "playful opportunism," Belcher says. A chance encounter can be used to reinforce an important value or to give a political message. Some business practices, such as management by walking around, can help build and maintain networks on campus as well because leaders must interact with faculty and others regularly.

To Improve Your Multinetworking Capability

Use the physical architecture and space as network tools. When designing and renovating new buildings or spaces—and when assigning locations and offices—consider traffic flows and how to increase the probability of meeting people.

Periodically transfer people from membership in one network to another. Just as a multinational corporation uses movement of key executives to build and maintain its global networks, a college can benefit from the alliances that people develop as they work with colleagues in different units.

Create new networks by forming temporary task forces, ad hoc committees, and project teams. Often, Belcher said, "colleges tend to use the same people, who are used to seeing each other and being included. New people bring different values and ideas." Eventually, she added, the old in-group may not be as "in" as previously.

Introduce new management techniques designed to build new networks. For example, the role analysis technique involves people defining their jobs and what they need from others in their "role set." Then they negotiate with everyone in their role set and agree on changes to facilitate everyone's work. The process makes all linkages clear and strengthens the networks.

"A transformational leader," Belcher said, needs to identify others in the organization who are also transformational leaders and reward the behavior that moves the institution forward. The reward should be tailored to the individual. It might be attending a conference or workshop. Their efforts should be noted in their evaluations and acknowledged publicly, she said. "Look to promote these people as positions open up."

Belcher quoted former Chrysler CEO Lee Iacocca on whom to look to for support: "The kind of people I look for to fill top management spots are the eager beavers. These are the [ones] who try to do more than they're expected to. They're always reaching. And reaching out to the people they work with, trying to help them do their jobs better. . . . What makes these managers strong is that they know how to delegate and how to motivate. They know how to look for the pressure points and how to set priorities." In short, they're motivated, focused, disciplined, and positive. They're like Jacquelyn Belcher.

Doris Green

Twelve Ways Academic Women Can Resist

February 2000

Gender is embedded in most organizations, resulting in gendered perceptions, practices, and attitudes. Dr. Pat O'Connor, professor of sociology and social policy at the University of Limerick in Ireland, discussed resistance to gendered issues by academics at the NAWE thirteenth annual International Conference on Women in Higher Education in New Orleans in January.

"Although only a minority of men actively subordinate women, the majority benefit from the patriarchal dividend in terms of honor, prestige, or the right to command," she said, citing statistics on women academics that show a similar pattern worldwide:

- *In Ireland,* women are 28 percent of faculty and 5 percent of professors.
- *In the United Kingdom,* women are 7 to 8 percent of professors.
- *In the United States,* women are 16 percent of full professors but only 8 percent in the Ivy League.
- *In Finland,* widely called women's "promised land," women are only 18 percent of professors.

Based on what she called "inadvertent participant observation" over the last three decades in three Irish universities where she worked, O'Connor identified twelve analytically separate types of resistance, listed in order of their potential for organizational transformation, starting with the least effective.

1. Keep your head down. This is an individual approach involving social, emotional, or physical withdrawal from the organizational structure, to focus on the area where one has the most control, such as one's own desk or lecture hall. At all three universities, doing this became evidence that the women were not promotable. It's the method least likely to cause change in the organization.

2. Create or maintain a separate world. Women collectively create a world where their gender identity is valued. They can share laughter as well as suffering. "Resistance is likely to provoke little negative reaction when the areas involved are seen as trivial," she said, such as in women's studies programs or child care.

3. Challenge the socially created opposition between work and family. Many women remain single and without children, and some with children don't take advantage of their full legal rights to maternity leave.

4. Pass the challenge on to the next generation. The nature of teaching makes it easy to pass on the challenge to students, through content and teaching style. Creating awards to recognize the achievements of young women can encourage them to continue challenging the issue, but it does not address the immediate problem.

5. Tackle the enemy within. The majority of women in the three universities O'Connor observed didn't notice that women were seriously underrepresented in decision making. Universities encourage the illusion that all is fair. References to women or women's interests are usually sexist and attempt to demean women. "A widespread lack of confidence and organizational naïveté appeared common amongst the faculty women," she reported.

6. Name aspects of organizational culture that are not woman friendly. Some look at managerial positions as "man's work," and their ideas on a "woman's place" justify keeping women down. Speaking out about this culture is a method of resistance often seen as an inability to accept authority, leading to the demonization of those who spoke out, reducing their attractiveness as collaborators and labeling them as not being team players. "This is very dangerous," O'Connor said. It is common for organizations to challenge the accuracy of statistics, dismiss concerns as "feminist" and divisive, and claim the bias will change "naturally" in the future.

7. Reveal organizational procedures that are not woman friendly. Organizations met a requirement for gender balance on an interview board by including just one token woman, usually from a lower-level post. Often women lost high profile work to men, making it difficult for them to be seen as candidates for promotion. Men didn't actively oppose women but used the existing structure to promote other men.

8. Expose aspects of gendered career structures. Few men remain at low-level positions, whereas women remain in them for their entire careers. Women have higher teaching loads, especially in strongly female fields, so they can do less of the research necessary for promotion. Senior academics emerge from a narrow channel and get promotions under patriarchal mechanisms, further limiting women at senior levels.

9. Create and mobilize allies. Electronic communication by women has become important for relaying information, such as the admission of bias against women faculty at MIT, and creating a feeling of shared identity and consolidated strength. O'Connor said men in senior positions were better candidates for allies than those in middle management because they are less threatened, more accountable to wider institutional forces and sensitive to their school's performance on a variety of external indicators. To create allies, it helps to refer to the men's own experiences of bias or to discrimination against their wives or daughters. If they can identify across gender, which may be related to their own sexuality, their involvement indirectly legitimizes the resistance.

10. Target key structures. "If women recognize that they are unlikely to be either sacked or promoted," O'Connor said, they are more likely to take action to get on key committees and representational bodies and union structures. One organization decided to introduce quotas, creating an environment where women felt comfortable putting themselves forward and making quotas unnecessary.

11. Blow the whistle. Defining *whistle-blowing* as "the disclosure of illegal, unethical, or harmful practices in the workplace to parties who might take action," O'Connor reported 1994 research by Miethe and Rothchild, noting that "typically whistle-blowers were highly competent employees, although the typical response was to depict them as troublemakers, 'whingers,' or crazy people (if they could neither be gotten rid of nor intimidated into silence). The personal and the financial cost of attempting to raise gender-related issues through whistle-blowing is usually considerable."

Sometimes it does pay to step out of line. In 1998, eight women faculty members at Dublin University went public over the unfair position of women at the university The Office of the Director of Equality Investigations is looking into it, and several of the eight have received promotions.

12. Use negative power. O'Connor quoted Handy's 1993 definition of *negative power* as "the capacity to stop things from happening, to delay them, to distort or disrupt them." She said, "This power is available to everyone regardless of position. It is perhaps worth reflecting that the transformative potential implicit in the use of negative power has only begun to be appreciated by many women.

Does Resistance Have an Effect?

Despite limited changes in the proportion of women at the senior level in the three universities, O'Connor noted these changes at one or more of the schools, which she said might or might not have occurred anyway:

- Formulation of equal opportunity policies and structures to deal with equality issues
- Directives on the composition of interview boards and search procedures
- Formation of a women's network
- Creation of gender-awareness workshops for senior management
- A commitment to identify specific time targets to redress gender balance and ways to deal with an organizational culture that is not woman-friendly

Efforts May Bring Counterresistance

Because resistance seems to generate awareness of gender among both women and men, it can increase backlash and counterresistance, including these tactics:

- Trivialization of gender issues
- Stigmatization of initiatives supporting women
- Demonization of prominent women
- Creation of organizational roadblocks
- Bypassing rules for new ones that favor men

"The process is painfully slow and extremely time-consuming," O'Connor said. "However, the abandonment of the academy to hegemonic masculinity in the third millennium is not an attractive option."

In response to questions, she said often women who are clueless on gender issues are deliberately being appointed managers: "Why on earth would they put in women who would bite the hand that feeds them?" She said a first step to gender equity for faculty should be to reduce the teaching loads for junior faculty. Many female junior faculty say, "I'm only teaching four courses," not realizing that often male junior faculty are teaching fewer courses. But if women do less work, men must do more, O'Connor said, calling it as inevitable as "turkeys bulging for Christmas."

Karina Persson

Leadership Survival Strategies in the Vacuum of Upheaval

February 1995
Adena Williams Loston
Executive Dean, Valle Verde Campus, El Paso Community College, Texas

On every campus, institutions are confronting the challenge of change. It may be driven by economic conditions, accrediting agencies, unfunded mandates, reduced funding from legislatures, or more accountability pressure to develop sound academic programs and increase graduate placement rates. Or it could be an expectation that institutions assume increasingly more shared responsibility for the economic growth and development of the surrounding communities.

Both internal and external forces can stress the institution, and responses by governing boards to "streamline the organizational structure" can generate employee doubt, fear, anxiety, concern, and frustration. During restructuring, leadership can become even more challenging, due to an ambiguity in roles and responsibilities, a lack of directional leadership and cross-supervision of certain areas—especially while decentralizing the institution. For the manager, it feels like operating in a vacuum.

That's when your leadership skills as a female are even more important. Amid the constantly changing environment, you must demonstrate more flexibility—organizationally and administratively—to both survive and position yourself as a significant contributor to the institution in the future.

Administrative Survival Skills

Demonstrating solid, appropriate administrative skills is the key to your survival.

Establish your credibility. In addition to demonstrating superior skills, competencies, and a solid knowledge base, a leader must be believed by team members, subordinates, and supporters. When there is credibility at the helm, a leader can weather any storm.

Provide a stated vision. All institutions need a clear vision, which gives direction and provides a framework for your response to various situations. A leader who is focused on the horizon will not be blown by crosswinds and lost in uncertainty, doubt, or confusion about the next course of action.

Show confidence in yourself. Leaders must exhibit a strong, bold belief in themselves and their capabilities. Others are reluctant to follow a leader who lacks confidence.

Display courage. Courage distinguishes the manager from the leader. Even when surrounded by confusion and doubt, a leader should express strong convictions and demonstrate the courage to act on them in day-to-day activities.

Empower others. Especially during change and restructuring, there are plenty of chances to give others an opportunity to demonstrate their skills and ideas—or lack thereof—to identify alternative approaches to solve problems.

Personify integrity. A leader must be perceived as stable, honest, trustworthy, and straightforward, especially in a state of organizational flux. Although subordinates may not always agree with your decisions, they will trust that you are being honest and have weighed all aspects of the situation if you have integrity.

Do the right thing. When confronted with situations, questionable acts, and decisions that leaders have the authority to rectify, they must take action. Subordinates may not remember how the situation developed, but they will forever remember their leader's failure to act. It's more important to do the right thing than to do things the right way.

Organizational Survival Strategies

With the organization in a state of confusion, these strategies will help assure your survival:

Link organizational vision to units. Having developed an institutional vision, you need to assure that each title knows its role as a stakeholder in helping to shape the vision and attain the goal.

Clarify each unit's purpose. When there is a matrix form of administration or functional approach to administration, units and reporting channels can get blurred, adding to confusion, frustration, and resistance. It's your job to make sure each unit knows its role.

Respond proactively to impending chaos. A leader needs a true sense of potential threats to the institution, a clear assessment for its strengths and weaknesses, and an accurate gauge of the institution's capabilities for rebounding when confronted by adversaries. From them, you can plan and build a strategy for responding to impending chaos.

Maintain open communication. By assuring that all have an opportunity to express their opinions, ideas, observations, and varying points of view, leaders can get an accurate read of what's happening both in and out of the institution. Feedback keeps you from operating within a vacuum—and being blindsided.

A leader with a stated vision, integrity, credibility, demonstrated skills, and the courage to take a stance and act on her convictions during periods of uncertainty is assured of surviving institutional upheaval.

Women Scarce as Trustees, But Bringing a New Priority

April 1994

Considering the trustees' key role in making policy, setting priorities, and determining the future of the academy, women are being shortchanged. Although women now are in the majority of students and make up about 40 percent of faculty in higher education, the composition of college governing boards has not kept pace. In 1992, women were only 23 percent of trustees.

Governing boards still draw heavily on middle-aged white businessmen, a profile that has changed little since 1923, when Upton Sinclair wrote, "You could not tell a chart of the Columbia trustees from a chart of the New York Central Railroad." Other social historians have criticized college governing boards, especially nonelected trustees, as being unaccountable to and unrepresentative of the institutions they control.

The Trustees' Decade

Governing boards will be the key agents of change for higher education in the 1990s, predicts Clark Kerr, president of the University of California system from 1958 to 1967, in *The Guardians: Boards of Trustees of American Colleges and Universities* (1989). Kerr calls the 1960s the decade of students, the 1970s the decade of faculty, and the 1980s the decade of administrators, and predicts that the 1990s will be the decade of trustees. His reason is that government rules and court decisions will spotlight the authority and liability of education's governing boards.

Women Present But Not Accounted For

In the first in-depth study of women trustees in 1971, researcher Helen Godfrey found no obligation of governing boards to reflect their constituencies. By 1978, this had changed. Women trustees reported that their male counterparts expected them to have a better understanding of women's educational needs. Yet "if women are the experts with reference to women's education, then why do their numbers on trustee boards not reflect female populations?" asked researcher Mona Generett.

In the 1980s, the closing of some religious colleges and entry of men into former women's colleges meant a further drop in women trustees, as men took over slots formerly reserved for women. Today, the importance of women in the faculty and administration is broadly recognized, even federally mandated at public schools, but it does not yet extend to governing boards.

Give, Get, or Get Off

From her survey of 305 trustees at eighteen private Pennsylvania liberal arts colleges, Kathleen Rex Anderson, director of development at Chestnut Hill College, Pennsylvania, notes problems for women in joining and staying on governing boards.

Money. Trustees are expected to "give, get, or get off." Women often can't or won't match the fiscal resources or fund-raising clout of men.

Experience. Trustees and academic leaders view business issues such as strategic planning and marketing as primary board responsibilities and feel that women lack experience and confidence in them.

Inhibition. Many women trustees lack the confidence or desire to be influential, controversial, or to really seek or exert power. In full board meetings or finance committee meetings, women trustees "seem to just go along," said one male respondent in Anderson's survey.

Residual bias. The old boys unconsciously relegate women's opinions and concerns to second place and fail to include women in informal and behind-the-scenes decision making.

Contrasting Perspectives

Men respondents also claim difficulty in finding women qualified to be trustees. Female candidates are "too busy, too young, unable to make financial commitments, family obligations, etc.," one wrote. But a woman respondent said the problem was "one of perception: male trustees perceive that women are either incapable, or a possible threat to their 'old boy' network. In either case, women are shut out from active involvement and participation."

Yet Anderson notes that many critical comments concerning women trustees came from women, who cautioned about being perceived as soft or identifying too narrowly on certain issues. Most striking was that men and women view the board's priorities differently, Anderson found. For men, financial planning and related budget issues (fund-raising, cost control, development) were the number one concerns, with quality of education second. Women trustees listed quality of education as the top priority, followed by long-range planning and financial security.

Among both men and women trustees, the executive and finance committees rated first and second as "most influential" committee. Yet most women chose to serve on committees for academic affairs, student affairs, and strategic planning. Asked whether board composition adequately reflected the college population, 75 percent of the men said yes, compared to only 46 percent of the women.

Start with the Nominating Committee

To create a board more representative of and responsive to constituents, Anderson advises trustee-nominating committees to assess their decision-making process on the following points: Does it create a diverse pool of nominees? Does it include a proactive effort to identify qualified women? Does the committee itself include women and minorities?

Anderson suggests publicizing case studies that document success stories to dispel myths about women's ability to raise funds or chair committees. "I know there are competent and capable women trustees. However, the research still indicates that the relative importance of women in the role of institutional stewards is pathetically uneven."

Mary Dee Wenniger

Case History: A Chair Becomes a Transformational Leader

June 1996

When Marilyn Sheerer was elected to chair the twenty-eight-person department of elementary education at Edinboro University of Pennsylvania, she received no training. "Usually, the history of the place is your guide," she observed. "Here it was the male old boys' network model: you didn't question the system. If you went too far, you got isolated."

As a new administrator, Sheerer notes, your own orientation toward change is your guide. "You either improve the situation you're in or you buy into the static model." With her strong interest in leadership issues, she wasn't about to back the old way. She decided the entire teacher education curriculum needed reconceptualization. "I didn't want to just tinker with a class here or there, I wanted to change the how and why of what we were doing."

Thus began her three-year journey to create a model of transformational leadership in a setting long accustomed to a traditional, hierarchical model. As the first female chair of a department on campus, she had much to do. Her journal documents the learning process for all involved. Sheerer was scheduled to present at the National Association of Women in Education conference in Chicago in March but literally lost her voice and was unable to do so. Reached by phone, she discussed her experiences with *Women in Higher Education*.

What Is Transformational Leadership?

Transformational leadership is a style that enables a mission to be redefined and helps members of the organization to renew their commitment and to restructure systems to accomplish goals. Its primary tools are collaboration and relationship building. "I had three goals: to help staff develop and maintain a collaborative, professional school culture, to foster teacher development, and to help them solve problems together," Sheerer recalled.

In the process, she learned a lot about how men and women approach leadership and change. "I found that women, with their heavy emphasis on relationships, move easily into this model," whereas men, for the most part, are much more comfortable with the hierarchical, top-down power model. Transformational leadership, she asserts, is feminist leadership.

Barriers to Change

Here are some barriers to change she learned as chair that reflect how women and men in her department differed in their views of leadership.

Men believe if you're in charge you're right. She found that the men in her department were "not accustomed to the inclusion of customers' perspectives." In accordance with the power model, they believe the person in charge is right. Why change an entire program when it's doing okay from your perspective as a tenured faculty member? Yet Sheerer and others knew there were models of teacher education that might better serve the needs of the public school community.

Women deal with change better than men. Quoting feminist historian Gerda Lerner, Sheerer says the process of change requires an awareness that something is wrong, the development of a sense of community around the issue, and the definition of goals and strategies for change.

Out of this process emerge alternative visions for the future. "Change causes upheaval," Sheerer notes, "and women are more willing to deal with it." The women in her department were more likely to think about what was required to do a good job and to help the faculty develop. The men, on the other hand, were threatened by the possibility of admitting fault in the program as it currently existed. Most had the attitude of "We're not getting complaints, so why change anything?"

Men are not accustomed to a cooperative collaborative model. In fact, it makes them uncomfortable, and they're not always sure why. For example, Sheerer recalls a male faculty member coming to her office after a department meeting in which she discussed an integrated curriculum that would be "not my agenda, [but] our agenda." She had noticed that he and a few others seemed uncomfortable throughout the discussion.

"They seemed to be against what I was saying but not willing to articulate what they didn't like." Later, the faculty member said he wasn't used to working with others and liked the "personal academic freedom" of working independently.

"Basically, he was telling me that he preferred the authoritarian model of 'You tell me what I have to do, and I'll do it.'" She likened his view of collaboration to "opening your underwear drawer: you have to come clean with how you do everything." He didn't like the idea, asserting that he "should have the freedom not to have to do that."

Men don't trust that the female leader is seeking anything but power. "They think there must be a hidden agenda," she notes, no matter what's being discussed. Sheerer recalls that when she was considering running for another term as department chair, one of the male members of the department was deciding whether to run against her.

Close to election time, she held a departmental meeting about some changes she wanted to make. Her opponent, who was opposed to what she was doing, commented, "I see you're lining up the women to support you." "He figured I was thinking it would be a feather in my cap," Sheerer said, "if I had these changes in place before I ran again, and that was why I was doing all this. It was a power game!"

Meanwhile, she thought the collaborative process spoke for itself in terms of her style and approach to leadership. She learned that those accustomed to a hierarchical model couldn't imagine that anyone would approach it otherwise, despite evidence to the contrary. Further, she notes that many have told her, "You're male in the way you lead." Although she interprets this comment as meaning she's willing to be assertive, she also thinks what they mean is that "I'm about power."

Again, it's the men who perceive her this way. "It's hard for them to believe I'm not just being manipulative. But did they think I'd change the whole curriculum just so I can get votes to be chair?"

It's difficult to change from a star system to a collaborative model. Dealing with tenured faculty offered some unique experiences in implementing an equalizing model. Sheerer recalls having to make summer teaching assignments early in her role as chair. Under the former chair, full professors had a history of being given more summer hours than junior faculty. It was considered a big perk because more hours meant more money and more credits toward their pension.

She approached the issue from a different point of view: what students needed and what faculty expertise was available. She then divided summer hours equally among all the faculty, including herself. After the assignments were announced, two full professors came to her, angry that they didn't get as many hours as they had previously. They believed it was a perk to which they were entitled. Sheerer's response was to go public with the formula she had used to allocate hours, which a department chair had never done before. By openly presenting how she calculated the distribution, she prevented questions about its fairness.

Those who view leadership differently will try to force you into their model. Sheerer notes that those who view the leader as the "answer person, sitting atop the pyramid, all knowing and all wise" will try to force your hand. For example, they will let you know that producing a plan is your job, not theirs.

"It's a myth that the leader is all knowing," Sheerer asserts. But when she encouraged others to give their opinions on issues, the men essentially told her it was her job to make things work. Their attitude was that she wasn't doing her job if she didn't act according to the authoritarian model. "You're the leader," they'd say, "What are you doing?" Of course, leadership has its responsibilities. "I see my role as one of facilitator, moving the discussion forward. But I also believe that together we can figure it out," she said.

Transformational leadership isn't easy. "It's a real challenge to nourish the dynamic nature of relational leadership, as opposed to this static idea of the leader as all powerful" and to figure out how to encourage others to participate. "My bias is that women are more likely to be transformational leaders because they're comfortable in other than hierarchical structures. Women are socialized into a collaborative-relational style that's more amenable to transformational leadership than men's hierarchical style." For example, Sheerer cites an Ohio State study conducted in 1991 that asked women leaders how others would describe their leadership style. The descriptors used most often included "creative problem solvers," "developers of vision and ideas," "demanding of self and others," "models integrity," and "involves others."

She guesses that the list generated by asking men the same question would be quite different. "None of this empowering, participatory stuff" would make it, she said. "They'd be more task-oriented, not relational. They get things done, they're organized. Harmonious? Ha!"

Sheerer's story had a happy ending. Her department did reorganize its teacher's education model, and she was reelected chair.

Addendum: Roles of a Department Chair

Consensus builder, diplomat, business manager, faculty recruiter, mentor, strategic planner, advocate, visionary, politician, counselor, mediator, communicator, assessor-evaluator, negotiator. Women tend to emphasize roles of visionary, planner–consensus builder, and counselor. Men tend to emphasize roles of politician, mediator, and negotiator.

Dianne Jenkins

Female CFO Redefines Financial Leadership Focus

December 1998
Mary Soroko
Director of Institutional Research, St. Cloud State University, Minnesota
The world of financial management has been shaped largely without ideas or input from women. Likewise, financial management in higher education has been largely dominated by male principles and values. Rockefeller, Carnegie, and other industrial barons who strongly influenced the development of college and university financial principles introduced the notion of "controlling" costs. They also assumed that an adversarial relationship necessarily exists between management, who are concerned with the bottom line, and labor, who are concerned with improving their quality of life and reducing their workload. Translated into the academy, this means administrators are always at odds with faculty and each other over fiscal matters.

Much has been written based directly or indirectly on their notions. In a zero-sum game, there can be only winners and losers: to the victors alone go the spoils. Only within the past twenty years, as women have entered the workforce in increasing numbers, have they begun to assume financial leadership positions and impact the financial management of colleges and universities.

Women's View of Management

Feminist leadership theorists argue that women approach leadership with a different paradigm: it's more complex, holistic, and ecological in its concern for the greater good. For my dissertation, I chose a case study analysis of a fifty-two-year-old female finance officer, to see if she approached her duties and responsibilities differently, despite a history of professional enculturation in traditional financial dogma.

I was also curious to see if the philosophy and principles espoused by the financial leader affected the culture of their organization. I conducted my research on a female chief financial officer at a small, private college in the Midwest. My goal was to expand financial leadership theory by doing an in-depth examination of a single subject. I relied primarily on qualitative research techniques, interviewing her for twenty-five hours and conducting one-and-a-half-hour interviews with twenty-five people who worked for or with her, which were transcribed and then reviewed with the person interviewed. I analyzed the findings in a manner consistent with qualitative research methods.

8

I found that my subject did approach her responsibilities in a different, more complex manner. Instead of focusing solely on dollars, she seemed more concerned with creating an environment in which personnel could be maximally productive. Rather than focusing on controls, she introduced flexibility into work schedules and ideas from outside the organization so that staff could learn from the ideas and mistakes of others.

She introduced in-service training, expanded communication networks, promoted teamwork to reduce individual stress, and helped to clarify roles and expectations so that staff knew what was most important in order to make the best use of their time. Whereas her male predecessor expected staff to be "front and center" during regular business hours and controlled resources to avoid "waste," my subject focused on results and gave her staff the freedom to decide how to achieve them, using whatever methods or styles they chose.

Effective Financial Leader Counters Negativity

Energy Drains	*Countered by*
Confusion	Clarification of expectations
	Focus
	Joint goal setting
Stress	Teamwork
	Sharing the load
	Networking to learn and develop confidence and support
Anxiety	Open communication
Discomfort	Nonjudgmental attitude
Uncertainty	Serving as a thinking partner
Politics	Honesty, directness
Distrust	Openness
Fear	Encouragement

Optimism Promotes Change

Unlike the male CFOs I interviewed, who reported that needs always exceed available resources, the subject of my study held a much more optimistic viewpoint. Her sense of optimism in the organization tended to promote change, whereas a sense of pessimism tends to promote the status quo. Pessimism seems to bring out a fear of making mistakes; optimism tends to bring out confidence and a willingness to try new and different things.

The hurdle to overcome was not insufficient resources but rather finding ways to work together. Her staff described her as "a breath of fresh air" because she seemed to have faith in their abilities to get their work done and was not overly concerned with how they went about accomplishing their duties. She embraced a much broader definition of *resource* to include goodwill, optimism, and other intangibles that are frequently overlooked by traditional finance theory. In her opinion, these resources were important and needed to be managed just as much as traditionally defined resources are.

Because anxiety, uncertainty, and negative attitudes all diminish staff focus, increase individual stress, and thus reduce productivity, the subject did all that she could to counter each of the organizational energy drains.

In addition, my subject defined her role as a financial leader even more broadly by serving on several boards of nonprofit organizations in her community and higher ed professional societies. Participating in activities outside of academia helped her to maintain balance and perspective in both her personal and professional lives.

Financial Officer Has Broad Impact

This study shows that how an organization is managed and led has a significant impact on its culture and thus the productivity of its staff. Because the finance officer has control over organizational resources, her impact on organizational culture is even greater than that of other leaders.

The subject of my study developed a leadership style whose focus was on creating an environment that was tolerant and supportive rather than stifling and controlling. It was important that the president of her school was very supportive of her feminine style of leadership. In many other schools, only a few styles of leadership are valued.

As a result, there is more pressure to conform rather than permission to be your own person. The CFO's freedom obviously promoted her effectiveness and allowed her to do the same with her staff. Permitting a diversity of styles encouraged personal effectiveness and productivity.

Interestingly, many of those interviewed did not perceive the subject as being a leader per se but rather someone who was just very effective at what she does. This suggests that old paradigms have been so ingrained in how we view and assess leadership that we seem to be blind to new types of leadership even when they are clearly visible.

New Financial Leadership Versus Traditional Model

Subject's Emphasis	Traditional Model Emphasis
People, outcomes	Money, allocations, inputs
Environmental focus	Financial focus
Optimism—There's enough to go around if we work as a community	Pessimism—Wants and needs always exceed available resources
Cooperative model: work together to get the best use of resources	Political model: allocate resources according to competing priorities
Finance officer as partner	Finance officer as adversary, protecting the purse
Value	Cost
Share resources, be a resource	Control resources
The ultimate goal: engage everyone to improve institutional performance	The ultimate goal: protect the bottom line, balance the budget, increase financial performance strength
Create a productive environment	Create an efficient organization
Resource defined broadly	Resource is money
Money is not an end in itself, but is a means to accomplish.	Money represents power to influence.
Collective leadership: "How should we manage our resources?"	Paternalistic leadership: "I know best how to manage resources."

Humor as a Management Tool Helps Women Lighten Up

August 1998

Men tell jokes; women listen to jokes. Some women get tired of pretending to be amused and decide humor doesn't belong at work, but they're missing out on an important management tool.

Just because women don't tell as many jokes as men doesn't mean they lack a sense of humor. Although most jokes are at another's expense, the humor more typical of women grows out of real-life situations. "The world is basically absurd," Suzanna McCorkle said. When you acknowledge the absurdity of a situation, you can draw on it to ease tensions, pull a group together, alter perspectives, build consensus, and promote organizational change.

She and Jane Ollenburger, respectively associate dean and dean of the College of Social Science and Public Affairs at Boise State University, Idaho, led a workshop on humor at the NAWE conference in Baltimore in March 1998. Mc-

Corkle finds humor a valuable tool for conflict management in her second role as director of the university's Office of Conflict Management Services, which consults with business and industry in the area.

Good Humor, Bad Humor

Humor is tied up in the dynamics of power. When the boss tells a joke, everyone laughs. That's not a reason for leaders to avoid humor but rather to use it differently. Humor can dominate or equalize, silence or empower. McCorkle described a continuum of uses.

Controlling humor. "We're most familiar with humor as an instrument of control that hurts and silences people," she said. Good old boys' jokes and ethnic jokes degrade and make people uncomfortable.

There are always losers. People who use humor for control say things that would be outrageous if they didn't masquerade as wit. "Can't you take a joke?" or "Just joking," they say, labeling objectors as spoilsports.

One reason women are sometimes stereotyped as humorless is that many have gotten up the courage to protest offensive jokes. Speaking up without a smile can sometimes communicate effectively; in other cases, your message may get past people's defenses when you speak both clearly and with humor.

Social humor. Humor can be valuable in diffusing a difficult situation. When a meeting gets tense, a shared laugh can pull the group back together and help it get on with business. Social humor breaks the tension and builds solidarity. For an individual or a small informal group, it's a great relief to laugh about a rough day at the office with sympathetic friends.

Empowering humor. More than easing the moment, it brings positive growth, helping groups bond and communicating difficult truths without hurting anyone. With a light touch, you can:

- Make people feel good about where they are and what they do
- Move the group from hierarchical interactions to a more collaborative style
- Suggest a new perspective or a different way of looking at things

A job candidate faced a room of white male interviewers, all the same age, wearing identical suits. "Where did you hide all the women?" she laughed. Breaking the tension, she made her point without attacking or appearing defensive, showing she could see the situation and work within it.

Opportunistic humor. This type makes the best of a tense situation. "If we're in a meeting and something goes wrong, something will happen to fill that gap. If someone spills a cup of coffee, it's an opportunity to step in with humor to relieve the tension," she said.

One day a student was sobbing in McCorkle's office about not being allowed to drop a course. Suddenly, one of McCorkle's earrings popped off and flew across the room. With opportunistic humor, she was able to turn the mishap into an asset. "The situation gave us a common experience. It had an equalizing effect. We were able to talk more freely after that."

The ability to seize and lighten the moment can be used to control, break tension, or empower. If we don't develop skills to use spontaneous humor wisely, someone else's wisecrack could reassure part of the group at the expense of the rest.

Learning Humor as a Leadership Skill

Humor is a skill to be learned through study and practice. Research suggests it's well worth learning. Amid the hassles and stresses of everyday life, lack of humor is associated with high levels of burnout and low self-esteem. With the self-confidence to use humor effectively, you can reduce the risk of burnout for yourself and those around you.

It's important to be able to laugh at yourself. Low self-esteem may cause some women to put themselves down by inviting others to laugh at them. But with high self-esteem, you can use your own foibles to build solidarity.

McCorkle recently gave a budget presentation when she was coming down with pneumonia. The meeting ran late, and the audience was half asleep. Instead of apologizing for her conspicuous sniffles and scratchy voice, she told the drowsers, "I want you to know that sniffling and coughing are postmodern signs of enthusiasm!" They awoke with a laugh and listened more attentively than if she'd asked for sympathy.

There are pitfalls. You need to know the context and be aware of the power dynamic in the situation. If you joke without cultural sensitivity to the listener, your humor may fail to bring the group together, despite your good intentions. And your humor must be sincere; a fake smile can destroy it.

If you're not comfortable using humor, find safe places to practice. Work to expand your repertoire across the continuum: from social humor to humor that empowers, from humor in predictable settings to impromptu humor in contexts you can't foresee. Humor is a powerful and positive addition to your management toolbox.

Sarah Gibbard Cook

More Voices Mean More Voice for Today's Campus Women

March 1999

Women have made huge progress in higher education since the early 1970s, but there's work yet to do. That's what ninety-eight women at colleges and universities across North America told Eugenia Proctor Gerdes, dean of arts and sciences at Bucknell University in Pennsylvania.

Laws, policies, and climate changed significantly between 1976 and 1995, as women increased from 25 percent to 36 percent of full-time faculty and from 26 percent to 44 percent of full-time administrators, Gerdes said at the twelfth annual Women in Higher Education conference. She wondered if women whose careers spanned the gradual changes were aware of them: "They say the fish doesn't know the water's wet."

Keen awareness surfaced when she put open-ended questions about change to eleven presidents and chancellors, forty-nine other administrators, and thirty-eight faculty. Almost all received their top degree or began their academic career in the late 1960s or early 1970s. Gerdes wanted to interview the pioneers before they retired: "They think about it a lot; it wasn't just because I asked that they noticed." A characteristic response: "The changes for women have been significant. Affirmative action in the academy has had an effect. A more open and democratic process of evaluation and review also has changed things significantly. Having more women in professional positions has halted the 'token women' issues at least in the arts and sciences. There seems to be more support and understanding for family issues."

Some called the changes significant, dramatic, or massive, whereas others said things had improved only marginally.

Numbers Do Matter

More than half mentioned an increase in the number of women in academe, especially in senior administration and the faculty, the doctoral candidate pool, professional organization leadership, and traditionally male fields.

Some saw more mentors and role models, networks and informal support groups, and chances to gain senior positions. A president wrote, "More and more women are being tapped for significant administrative roles. I am very pleased to see these changes and believe they will only enhance opportunity for women at all levels."

Gerdes cautioned against overestimating progress. "Because there's been a lot of growth, the numbers go up faster than the percentages, and that sort of fools us." But larger numbers do create a critical mass, even if percentages stay the same. It's better to be one of three faculty women in a department of nine than the only woman in a department of three.

"As more women have assumed leadership positions and been successful, the overall situation for women was bound to be affected," one wrote. In the words of another, more voices mean more voice. A science department chair said: "There are more women colleagues. For whatever reason (it might just be that you end up talking in the bathroom), women tend to interact in groups just as men have traditionally done. Also in meetings men are more apt to use sexist language and behavior if you are the only woman in the room than if there are more women present. Thus by having more women colleagues, men are at least superficially more respectful."

Blatant discrimination or sexism has virtually disappeared. "The sheer numbers have changed things for the better. It is not acceptable in most circles to discriminate openly, and it is even difficult for hard-line woman haters to find excuses to keep women out," one wrote. No longer does a man return from an interview and report that the committee told him they'd never hire a woman.

They mentioned changes in hiring procedures, affirmative action, equal opportunity, legal protection, and gender-equity initiatives. Women today receive more nearly equal pay, recognition, and assignments. Policies are more family friendly. Two said there's less sexual harassment, and women are more willing to complain when it happens.

Changes Not Observed

Changes the women didn't note are as revealing as those they mentioned. Gerdes was surprised that only eight mentioned ways that women's interests affected scholarship, such as women's studies, women's history, research on gender issues. They apparently don't jump to mind as readily as numbers, policies, and norms.

Also conspicuously missing is connection to students. Only three observed an increase in women students in traditionally male fields, two an increase in women in grad school, and one an increase in respect for women students and their aspirations. Only two mentioned a change in student attitudes, saying students today are more willing to value women professors.

One wrote that when she started twenty-five years ago, "I had no female mentors because there were none. Now, I try to help younger women, and in most fields young women can find good female mentors and role models." One who wouldn't have considered having a child as an assistant professor now helps younger women combine family and career.

Things Are Better, But . . .

"It was very hard for people to talk about what was good without adding qualifications," Gerdes said. The subtler climate has not changed as much as laws and policies. They noted large but inadequate improvement in awareness of gender issues, appreciation of diversity, respect for feminist scholarship, treatment of women as colleagues, respect for women students, respect for women leaders, awareness of sexual harassment, less condoning of discrimination, less stereotyping, and less of a male standard for success.

The women said that, compared with the early 1970s, they feel more at home in their professions and schools, and less isolated, vulnerable, and different from the norm. Yet the old boys' network remains, and progress is slower in prestigious institutions and in traditionally male fields. Several said being women had not hurt their careers but recognized problems for those who aren't white, heterosexual, and middle class.

More than 90 percent said bias remained, but it was more subtle. They cited dramatic increases in female administrators in two-year colleges and as part-time faculty but noted that women still faced strong bias in research universities. The more prestigious the school and the higher the position, the fewer women were there.

"Gender bias became more subtle, though it did not disappear. I think it is becoming more overt again," one wrote. Backsliding is a real fear. A dean said, "I am troubled at how fast and to what extent society's support for affirmative action has shifted—and what this may mean in terms of few opportunities for women and minorities."

Despite lingering problems, it's important to realize how far we've come. The way universities treated women in the 1960s is hard to believe today, Gerdes said. "Back then, I couldn't complain to my department chair about colleagues showing X-rated movies at 3 P.M. while I sat in my office working because he was there too," she recalled.

"The biggest thing for younger women to remember is that it hasn't always been this way," Gerdes said. We need to recognize and value our gains if we're to keep them from slipping away.

Sarah Gibbard Cook

New Southern Polytech President Values Scientific Background

July 1998

On August 1, Lisa A. Rossbacher will join an elite group. She'll become president of Southern Polytechnic State University in Georgia, one of few women nationwide to head a public engineering university and the first in Georgia. That shouldn't shock her old friends. When Rossbacher was working on master's and doctorate degrees in geology at Princeton University in the early 1980s, friends liked to kid her, asking: "So when are you going to do some fieldwork?"

That was a little difficult because she was researching data that NASA had brought back from the 1976 Viking mission to Mars. But she was undaunted. "I applied as a candidate with the NASA shuttle program, just to shut them up," she says. Assuming her chances were nil, she was brutally honest and admitted to wearing glasses and getting carsick. She finished her doctorate, took a teaching job at Whittier College in California, and was a visiting researcher in Sweden when NASA tracked her down and said, "We need you to get some eye tests and fingerprints."

That shocking call launched Rossbacher, a forty-five-year-old dean of the college at Dickinson College, Pennsylvania, on one of her greatest adventures. She was one of 128 candidates that NASA selected to interview from more than five thousand applicants for the astronaut program. In spring 1984, she was poked and prodded by medics, underwent intense neurological evaluation, endured motion sickness tests, and toured the space center. She passed the medical tests easily. But NASA told her she should take flying lessons, and she'd have to give up science to become an astronaut. Her phone rang again fifteen minutes later. This time it was the geological sciences department at California State Polytechnic University in Pomona, offering a tenure-track job as associate professor. She accepted.

Crossing That Line

Rossbacher moved from academia to administration early in her career; she'd been at Pomona less than a year when the president asked her to head a long-range planning study. Frustrated because the only people she'd met were in her department or on her floor, she accepted. "It was a chance to see that broader perspective," she recalls. A year later she became associate vice president for academic affairs.

Although she didn't follow her own advice, the new president cautions women offered administrative jobs: don't cross over from faculty too early in your career. Rossbacher suggests that those with administrative aspirations get a regular faculty position and "earn tenure the old-fashioned way." Why? If you do your job well as an administrator, you have to break some eggs. "I'd advise someone to carefully examine her soul as to why she wants to go into administration," Rossbacher warns. "It's hard to go back to being a colleague with people when you have made decisions on their budgets. People should not think of it as something to try for a little while."

Science Background Helps Women Leaders

Rossbacher firmly believes that being a scientist has helped her in academic affairs. She's able to relate to faculty and feels better prepared to evaluate and hire professors, and can understand the difficulties of the research process. For example, one faculty member recently under review was having a terrible time accessing information in an unstable foreign country. Rossbacher recalled the difficulties a geologist has when the weather is poor or a property owner won't grant access. "It helps me in the evaluation process, and it gives me important credibility with the people I'm evaluating," she says.

She thinks geology, in particular, may be the best scientific background, due to its interdisciplinary nature. To graduate, a geologist must take math, chemistry, and biology. "There's writing, critical thinking, and problem solving. All of those things students should learn in education are all parts of geology." Asked why women scientists often are tapped as presidents and key administrators, she offers several theories.

Scientists are more often trained in problem solving using the scientific method. "Scientists came to the point a long time ago of realizing that no one does things alone," she says. "You have to do research and figure out how other things connect. It's useful in administration when you have to pull people and information together and understand that sometimes you have to reach a conclusion when you don't have all the data you want. That's really true in geology, when you can't go back two hundred thousand years to see what's really going on."

Scientists achieve credibility based on their own work and what they accomplish. She points to English as an example of a field that is "notoriously mired in academic politics." For example, if someone chooses to study an author who's not held in wide regard, it can hold back her career. The same can happen in sociology if someone studies a certain movement or social theory; others who disagree with it may dismiss that person. "I would argue that things in the sciences are often verifiably true, and that leaves less room for the politics."

Being a female scientist in fields where women are underrepresented makes a woman more visible. Although in many of the sciences women are catching up in numbers, there's still a perception that women are unusual. Rossbacher never intended to become a scientist. She started as an English major at Dickinson College, Pennsylvania, hoping to write the great American novel. But after registering for geology, the only science lab class still open, she fell in love. It wasn't hard in a city nestled between the Blue Ridge Mountains and the Appalachians. "I love to be able to walk around outdoors and understand how things work," she says wistfully, "to pick up a rock and just think about the amount of time it represents."

A Rock-Head at Heart

Although she's about to become a college president, Rossbacher has no intention of giving up geology. She writes a column every other month for *Geotimes,* has written science scripts for National Public Radio, and continues to publish articles, abstracts, and textbooks. And she and her husband, also a geology professor, are working with a team of scientists to study a dry lake along the San Andreas fault in California, seeking insight on recent climatic changes.

"I've put myself in a position where I'm forced to stay caught up in my field," she says. "Because I write the column every other month, I have to think about geology. I go to professional meetings and stay in touch with people. It's a matter of not embarrassing myself in front of my other professional colleagues."

Gender Not a Factor to Her

Although Rossbacher will be the first woman in Georgia to lead a public engineering school, she doesn't put much emphasis on her gender. If she's been discriminated against in her career, she isn't willing to say it's because of her sex. "Can I say it's because I'm a woman? Or is it because I was born in Virginia or went to an Ivy League college or because I have brown eyes? There can be a hundred reasons, and I don't automatically assume gender is the problem."

She says the most difficult point in her career was when she took a job as vice president of academic affairs at Whittier College. Her husband was on the faculty, so she knew many of the faculty socially. "People looked at me as somebody's wife or spouse," she recalls. "Our previous social connections sometimes got in the way of being effective." Some assumed she'd act on the job just like she did at dinner parties. Others assumed she held the same opinions as her spouse, which was not always the case. "It's a problem of being married to someone else in education and maintaining a separation between professional and social life," she says.

Now, Rossbacher is looking forward to reuniting with her husband after a three-year bicoastal marriage, when he becomes department chair of geology and geography at Georgia Southern in Statesboro. And she's excited about developing a higher profile for her new school, by emphasizing its assets and adding new academic programs over the next five years. "I want to fuse the technology-based education with skills of liberal arts: teamwork, collaboration, problem solving, and communication," says Rossbacher. "I want to combine those skills to give students the ability to learn, evolve, and adapt so they'll be prepared for their last job as well as their first job."

Meanwhile, Rossbacher will probably continue to take tap dancing lessons, paint with watercolors when she's doing fieldwork, and spend New Year's Eves at the Grand Canyon with her husband. Although she may never be an astronaut, she hasn't given up her dream of writing that great American novel.

Melanie Conklin

EPILOGUE, OR THE LAST LAUGH

There you have it, an assortment of words of wisdom from some very extraordinary women leaders in higher education in the United States and elsewhere and from some ordinary women who have thought long and hard on their specific subjects.

As I write this in November of the year 2000, I can't help but notice the many changes affecting women on campus that have occurred since these articles were first published; overwhelmingly they are steps forward, with a few regressions. Each year, women are earning a larger and larger percentage of the undergraduate and graduate degrees, teaching awards, research grants, senior administrative posts, and even presidencies, with the latest ACE data showing that women occupy 19.3 percent of the CEO chairs on U.S. campuses.

When will we reach true equity? As many astute female leaders on campus have observed, it will occur when an average or even inept woman has as much opportunity to hold a position as an average or inept man. That's when we'll all get the last laugh.

Mary Dee Wenniger
Editor, Women in Higher Education

If you have enjoyed this collection and would like a continuing, monthly source of words that "enlighten, encourage, empower, and enrage" women on campus, please contact the Wenniger Company for a free sample issue of *Women in Higher Education*®.

Women in Higher Education®
1934 Monroe Street
Madison, WI 53711-2027
Phone: (608) 251-3232
Fax: (608) 284-0601
Web: www.wihe.com

REFERENCES

Acosta, R. V., and Carpenter, L. J. *Women in Intercollegiate Sport.* 2000.

Ambler, M. "Women Leaders in Indian Education." *Tribal College: Journal of American Higher Education,* 1992, *4,* 20–23.

American Association of University Professors (AAUP). "Academic Freedom and Sexual Harassment: Report from the 80th Annual Meeting." *Academe,* Sept.-Oct. 1994, *80*(5), 64–72.

Baier, A. C. *Moral Prejudices: Essays on Ethics.* Cambridge, Mass.: Harvard University Press, 1994.

Barron's Educational Series. *Barron's Profiles of American Colleges.* Hauppauge, N.Y.: Barron's Educational Series, 1996.

Bartlett, J. "Samuel Johnson, 1709–1784." In *Familiar Quotations* (10th ed.). Boston: Little Brown, 1919.

Belenky, M. F., Clinchy, B., Goldberger, N., and Tarule, J. *Women's Ways of Knowing.* New York: Basic Books, 1986.

Bellah, R. N., et al. *Habits of the Heart.* New York: HarperCollins, 1986.

Brin, D. W. "The Harassment Case Nobody Wants." *Wisconsin State Journal,* Jan. 22, 1994.

Coniff, R. "The Joy of Women's Sports." *The Nation,* Aug. 10, 1998, pp. 26–30.

Darder, A. *Culture and Power in the Classroom.* New York: Bergin and Garvey, 1991.

Frye, M. *Willful Virgin.* Freedom, Calif.: Crossing Press, 1992.

Fulghum, R. *All I Really Need to Know I Learned in Kindergarten.* New York: Ivy Books, 1989.

Gallop, J. "Sex and Sexism: Feminism and Harassment Policy." *Academe,* Sept.-Oct. 1994, *80*(5), 16–23.

Gilligan, C. *In a Different Voice.* Cambridge, Mass.: Harvard University Press, 1982.

Goodwin, M. P. "Sexual Harassment: Experiences of University Employees." *Initiatives,* 1989, *52*(3), 25–33.

Goueffic, L. *Breaking the Patriarchal Code*. Manchester, Conn.: Knowledge, Ideas, and Trends, 1996.

Granna, J. *Images of Women in Transition*. Winona, Minn.: Saint Mary's Press, 1976.

Greenleaf, R. K., Spears, L. C., and Frick, D. T. *On Becoming a Servant Leader*. San Francisco: Jossey-Bass, 1996.

Haber, S. (ed.). *Guide to the Universe of Women in Higher Education*. Madison, Wis.: Wenniger Company, 1994.

Handy, C. B. *Understanding Organizations*. New York: Oxford, 1993.

Harragan, B. L. *Games Mother Never Taught You*. New York: Rawson Associates, 1977.

Hennig, M., and Jardim, A. *The Managerial Woman*. New York: Anchor Books, 1977.

Heywood, L. "Despite the Positive Rhetoric About Women's Sports, Female Athletes Face a Culture of Sexual Harassment." *Chronicle of Higher Education*, Jan. 8, 1999, p. B4.

Josefowitz, N. *Paths to Power*. Reading, Mass.: Addison-Wesley, 1980.

Kerr, C. *The Guardians: Boards of Trustees of American Colleges and Universities*. Washington, D.C.: Association of Governing Boards of Universities and Colleges, 1989.

Kouzes, J., and Posner, B. *The Leadership Challenge*. San Francisco: Jossey-Bass, 1987.

McBroom, P. *The Third Sex: The New Professional Woman*. New York: Random House, 1992.

McCauley, C. D. *Job Challenge Profile*. San Francisco: Jossey-Bass, 1999.

Miethe, T. D., and Rothschild, J. "Whistleblowing and the Control of Organizational Misconduct." *Sociological Inquiry*, 1994, *64*(3), 322–347.

Millman, D. *The Warrior Athlete*. Walpoole, N.H.: Stillpoint Publishing, 1985.

National Institute of Business Management. *Black Book of Executive Politics*. New York: National Institute of Business Management, n.d.

Nelson, M. B. *The Stronger Women Get, the More Men Love Football*. Orlando, Fla.: Harcourt Brace, 1994.

O'Leary, D. *The Gender Agenda: Redefining Equality*. New York: Vital Issues Press, 1997.

Peterson's Guides. *Peterson's Register of Higher Education*. Princeton, N.J.: Peterson's Guides, 1997.

Ross, M., and Green, M. F. *The American College President*. Washington, D.C.: American Council on Education, 2000.

Rothschild, J., and Miethe, T. D. "Whistleblowing as Resistance in Modern Work Organizations." In J. M. Jerimier, D. Knights, and W. R. Nord (eds.), *Resistance and Power in Organizations*. London: Routledge, 1994.

"Students Should Not Be Above the Law." *New York Times*, May 9, 1996, p. A19 (op-ed).

Tannen, D. *You Just Don't Understand*. New York: Morrow, 1990.

"The Three Levels of the Glass Ceiling: Sorcerer's Apprentice Through the Looking Glass." *Dataline*, Sept. 1991.

Tracy, L. *The Secret Between Us: Competition Among Women*. Boston: Little, Brown, 1991.

Wilson, R., and Melendez, S. E. "Strategies for Developing Minority Leadership." In M. F. Green (ed.), *Leaders for a New Era*. New York: Macmillan, 1988.

Index